Fabrics and Pattern Cutting

Fabrics and Pattern Cutting

Fabric, Form and Flat Pattern Cutting – an updated and simplified 3rd edition

Winifred Aldrich

Book design, photography and computer graphics by James Aldrich

WILEY

A John Wiley & Sons, Ltd., Publication

This edition first published 2013
© 2013 Winifred Aldrich

Registered office
John Wiley & Sons Ltd, The Atrium, Southern Gate, Chichester, West Sussex, PO19
8SQ, United Kingdom

Editorial office
John Wiley & Sons Ltd, The Atrium, Southern Gate, Chichester, West Sussex, PO19
8SQ, United Kingdom

For details of our global editorial offices, for customer services and for information
about how to apply for permission to reuse the copyright material in this book
please see our website at www.wiley.com.

The right of Winifred Aldrich to be identified as the author of this work has been
asserted in accordance with the UK Copyright, Designs and Patents Act 1988.

Wiley also publishes its books in a variety of electronic formats and by print-on-
demand. Some content that appears in standard print versions of this book may
not be available in other formats. For more information about Wiley products, visit
us at www.wiley.com.

Designations used by companies to distinguish their products are often claimed as
trademarks. All brand names and product names used in this book are trade
names, service marks, trademarks or registered trademarks of their respective
owners. The publisher is not associated with any product or vendor mentioned in
this book. This publication is designed to provide accurate and authoritative
information in regard to the subject matter covered. It is sold on the understanding
that the publisher is not engaged in rendering professional services. If professional
advice or other expert assistance is required, the services of a competent
professional should be sought.

Library of Congress Cataloging-in-Publication Data

ISBN: **978-1-119-96717-0** (pbk), ISBN: 978-1-118-54814-1 (ebk), ISBN: 978-1-118-54812-7
(ebk), ISBN: 978-1-118-54813-4 (ebk), ISBN: 978-1-118-54815-8 (ebk)

A catalogue record for this book is available from the British Library.

Set in 9/10 pt Palatino by Toppan Best-set Premedia Limited

Contents

Acknowledgements

We would like to thank the following people who have made the production of this book possible: Hiroko Aldrich, for her help with the text, research and collation of the book;
David Bell of Assyst Bullmer Ltd, for the images of 3D fabric simulation in Chapter 2;
Bill Skidmore of Huddersfield Textile Society and Helen Rose of Manchester Metropolitan University, for their advice on new fibres;
From John Wiley & Sons Ltd: Hannah Clement, the production editor, for the book's production; and particularly Andrew Kennerley, who has supported and monitored every stage of this edition.

Acknowledgements for the material used in this and earlier editions

We had a great deal of practical help from people and organisations during the production of the earlier editions of the book, but their realisation would not have been possible without the inspiration and support of the following people:
Mark Cooper, who made up nearly all the designs photographed in this book and helped us to construct the fabric boards and throughout the project.
Dina Furtado, the model for the photographs and the drawings.
Professor Newton of the Nottingham Trent University, who gave me time from other duties to work on this book.
Gillian Bunce of the Nottingham Trent University, Christine Smith, Brian Stanley of the Nottingham Fashion Centre, for their assistance and the extensive use of its Fabric Resource Library.
Richard Prescott, for his professional advice, high quality photographic printing of the garments and the electronic reproduction of the fabric boards.
Steve Maddox of Colourbase Ltd, for his lighting and technical assistance during the photography of the garment designs.
A group of students attending a course at the Nottingham Fashion Centre who participated in the testing and the revision of my theories.
Alec Aldrich who constructed the testing equipment for the first edition of this book (see Appendix 1). The equipment was used to register the fabric codes associated with the sample garment designs.
Richard Miles of Blackwell Publishing, for his great support of my book.

Other people and companies who provided equipment, information and advice:
David Bell of Assyst Bullmer
Stephen Chalkey of Concept II Research
Len Boxall of Kennet and Lindsell Ltd
Brian Smith of the Nottingham Trent University
Sue Pike of the Nottingham Trent University
Emma Nixey of Nix-E Design
Terry Parkin of TEZ
The fibre manufacturers and associations who provided technical information, and the many fabric companies who supplied samples and sample lengths for the book.

Introduction

The aim of this book is to help fashion and textile students understand the vital part that fabrics play in creating the shape of a design. The excessive information in the earlier edition of this book may have deterred many students, yet it is vital that they gain this skill early in their studies. Therefore this book has simplified, re-organised and updated information from the previous editions.

New developments have taken place in the use of generic (basic chemical source) fibres and also in the technical engineering of the structure of existing fibres. This has produced many new fabrics that have a very different appearance and handle. Designers need to gain a 'fabric sense' and an ability to use it creatively.

There is no substitute for working directly on the dress stand for analysing how fabric works with a human body form. Working in this way offers more opportunity for creating new dimensions of cut. However, most designers working in mass production have the difficult task of translating 3D mental images into 2D pattern shapes. It can take years of experiencing success and failure to do this effectively, and the appearance of new fabrics continually challenges the designer's skill. Knowledge of how fabrics will behave is essential in the speculative cutting of new garment shapes.

Fabric technology is not covered in depth in this book, but it offers an introduction to the technology and an overview of fabric sources and ranges. It also directs students to where further information can be found. Tests are used in industry for fabric properties, comparisons between similar fabrics, or their performance in specific conditions. However, this book isolates five major characteristics that determine a garment's shape. These are:

weight   thickness   drape   shear   stretch

This book shows how they determine the shape of a garment from the simplest wrap to a complex tailored suit.

This book is arranged so that students can use basic principles to work from simple shapes to complex cutting. The flat pattern cutting techniques include direct measurements, working on flat grid drafts and the adaptation of both 'flat' blocks and 'form' body shaped blocks.

Specific information

Although this book can be used alone, where specific detailed methods are needed, cross references to *Metric Pattern Cutting* can be made. This book describes how different types of blocks have been developed from simple flat geometric shapes. All the designs are shown on one model, size 10, 175 cm (5ft 9 in) height. The same fashion model was used for the photographic figure images and for the drawings. In order to ensure consistency, a size 10 stand was constructed with the extended back neck to waist measurement of the model. Chapter 13 provides basic images of the model poses and the stand for students to use as templates for technical illustrations.

The pattern diagrams in the book are the actual patterns used to create the garments. They were adapted from the basic size 10 block, with the extended back neck to waist measurements of the model. The blocks given in Chapter 14 have the standard back neck to waist measurement.

The designs were all made up as unfinished garment toiles working directly in the original fabric. Colour and printed textile design have been deliberately ignored in order to see the garment form clearly. It has been a tradition in workrooms to work on initial shapes in cream, white or beige fabrics; it reduces the distractions, and the style lines or modification lines become more apparent. This book will illustrate some forms in black and some in white or beige; this is to provide a reference for students for comparing shapes in opposing tones.

The depth of research into fabric characteristics that has formed the basis for this book is described in Appendix 1.

Creating the blocks manually, using CAD and the Internet

Most colleges now have access to CAD programs and different size printers. Three methods of obtaining full size blocks from the diagrams shown in the book are explained fully in Chapter 14.

Method 1 A block can be scaled up by copying the shape onto 5 cm squared paper and using the squares as reference points.

Method 2 A block page can be scanned into a CAD program (e.g. photoshop), then scaled up and printed to an A0 printer (or to an A4 or A3 printer in sections).

Method 3 The full size blocks can be accessed as a PDF file from the publisher's Website. This file can be loaded into a software program or taken directly to an A0 printer in a college or CAD bureau.

Garment design and the selection of fabrics

Design and shape

Designers can select the mood, the colours and the technical fitness of a fabric, but to complete the image of the range they have also to design and construct the garment shape. The intuitive understanding of the concepts of the 'handle' and 'drape' of a fabric, and the shape that it will create, is crucial in the creation of a range. This book is an attempt to help students to develop this skill at an early stage in their pattern cutting studies.

Selecting fabrics

Designers select fabrics for their ranges as much as twelve months before the garments reach the stores, although this time length is reducing. The fibre and fabric producers aiming at the fashion market have to take note of the prediction companies who try to capture the future mood of the customer. A designer's initial fabric selection is usually influenced by fashion and fabric magazines, prediction companies and fabric fairs. Two major fabric fairs, *Premier Vision* and *Interstoff*, show spring and autumn collections. Some years ago, designers were restricted to buying their fabrics from producers' existing ranges; but today, particularly where large orders are at stake, designers often work with the fabric producers to develop fabric ranges, particularly print design. The fabric shows are a vital point of contact between designers and producers; producers gain knowledge of the performance of their previous products and of future requirements.

Buying from fabric swatches is difficult. Small sample lengths may be available, but many producers no longer hold large fabric stocks, but produce to order and require orders of 500–1000 metres. This is a problem for small companies producing limited ranges. The basic information usually given on a fabric swatch is:

Quality or Design number .... **Width** ....
Composition .... **Weight** ....

Information such as the finish or other qualities such as thermal, windproof and organic, may also be listed. Further technical information, for example dimensional stability during wear or laundering conditions, can be gained from the large fabric suppliers who will supply care labels on the purchase of the fabric. Getting information from smaller suppliers can be difficult or time consuming.

Designers working in particular product areas will usually select their fabrics from specific manufacturers, but fashion fairs are a means of seeing the latest fabrics. As fabrics become more scientifically based and yarn structures more complex, designers can find themselves overwhelmed by the mass of technical information.

Technology and fashion

Flexibility and high profile marketing has a greater significance today. Response to new trends and customer needs is now essential; fibre producers now have sophisticated promotions of their products, and the speed of communication through the Internet accelerates the demand for a quick response. The problem facing the fibre and fabric manufacturers is the balance between the infinite opportunities that fibre engineering offers and the ability to produce them commercially. Other pressures include the timing of fashion and consumer demands and the growing concerns around ecology.

Competition from man-made fibre development has led to new efforts to 'improve' the qualities of natural fibres, by fibre engineering, fabric finishing and blending with other natural or man-made fibres. The greatest change that has taken place in the textile industry is the reduction in woven fabric production and the increase in knitted fabric production. The competitive pricing and the stretch characteristics of knitting structures make these fabrics very attractive to the middle to low cost retailing area. The finishes that are available to the cloth manufacturer can produce fabrics whose appearance has little relationship to the loom state. Some finishes are applied to garments after they are made up. The changes of shape that occur have to be taken into account when the garment patterns are constructed.

Cloth manufacturers strive to produce novel fabrics to tempt customers; some fabrics are released before they are fully tested, or they may fail in unforeseen conditions. Designers need to be assured that the fabric will perform in specific conditions and need to be aware of any technical limitations.

The technical information that is available is often not useful or not presented in a way that can be easily understood by a designer/pattern cutter. Technical testing is aimed at 'fit for purpose' comparisons of fabrics; it is often done within narrow limits for quality control purposes or for staged improvements of a fabric. Successful cooperation between technologists and designers does occur and long term directions do proceed alongside the turbulent fashion switches of mood that many technologists find perplexing. Many fabrics take years of development, and the process is often an act of faith by research teams as they struggle with the difficulties of production.

The world of laboratories and technologists is a great distance away from the world of fashion prediction books and the show business environment of trade fabric fairs. The prediction companies do not see many of these activities as a part of their remit, leaving a gap in the middle ground. Designers in smaller companies outside the large manufacturing groups and without immediate access to technical assistance have to operate in this middle ground. The environment at trade fairs is frenetic; building a fashion range requires a speed of fashion reaction that can involve switches of 'fancy' and changes of focus. Bombarded with new fabrics, the designer has to work with intuition and knowledge. The 'technically correct' fabric is not a commercial choice unless it responds to the current mood or reflects the aesthetic style of the range.

PART ONE: FABRIC CHARACTERISTICS AND BODY SHAPE

Chapter 1 Fabric characteristics and garment shapes

Fabric characteristics and garment shapes
FABRIC CHARACTERISTICS

The background

This book has been revised to help students and designers make intuitive decisions when handling and comparing fabric ranges. Its aim is to help them identify the fabric characteristics that effect the final shape of a garment. It explains how they can determine the cut of the garment pattern.

This does not mean that technology is not important. Chapter 12 offers a basic overview of the main processes used in producing fabric. It is essential that all clothing design students understand a fabric's fibre, structure, finish and technical performance, and also how to access the necessary technical information. However, this is not a book on textile technology, it is about the relationship of fabric to pattern cutting.

The visual appearance of any garment is directly affected by the characteristics of the fabric in which it is made. Selecting the correct fabric for a design is difficult when working with the infinite variety of fabrics used in the textile industry. Some computer programs are used to realise three dimensional (3D) models of fabric on virtual models (see page 22). However, the selection of a fabric by a designer usually comes at a much earlier stage in the creation of a range. Computer programs at this stage are more useful for decisions such as colour and pattern. Determining the suitability of a fabric for the *shape* of a design at the concept stage still relies on human discrimination.

Flat pattern cutting is successful when a designer's intuitive knowledge can generate a 3D mental image that is a *visual sense* of the shape that will be created when a flat pattern is cut in a particular fabric. To illustrate this point, the photographs opposite show a circle of two different fabrics:

> **viscose jersey** cut at two different lengths
> **cotton twill** cut at two different lengths

They illustrate two important points:
1. When the circle of the same fabric is cut at a different length, it will produce a different shape.
2. Different fabrics produce different shapes.

Working in small scale Some courses use small scale models for pattern development, but the photographs show the false images of garment shapes created by working in quarter- or half-scale.

Pattern cutting – five fabric characteristics

As it is obvious that different fabrics will produce different shapes, a way to assess them is required. The pattern cutting method or block chosen for creating a style should start with an analysis of the fabric. When the ranges of fabrics were limited, methods of cut were predictable; however, a new approach is required to assess the very different fabrics available today.

The five crucial characteristics that should be considered before deciding the method of pattern cutting or the choice of pattern block are:

weight   thickness   drape   shear   stretch

Simple examples in this book illustrate the changes that a fabric can make to the same pattern shape. More complex examples show how the fabric has a great influence on the choice of cut and sometimes the underlying structures that are required to hold a shape.

The five characteristics are listed in this book on a characteristic scale.

The fabric characteristic scale

Weight	light	medium	heavy
Thickness (visual)	thin	medium	thick
Drape (visual)	high	medium	low
Shear	high	medium	low
Stretch	high	medium	low

Each fabric illustrated in the book is described in these terms. Throughout the book, there are no rules that dictate which fabrics should be used for particular blocks or pattern shapes, but visual examples are given which show what is likely to happen when they are cut in fabrics with different characteristics. This approach to pattern cutting does not dismiss aesthetic qualities (for example, colour or texture) but these, and practical decisions of product type and 'fit for purpose', are different parts of the design process.

Testing fabric characteristics

Chapter 2 describes simple testing methods for fabric characteristics. It is designed so that students can develop a sense of a fabric's character and how it will behave. If students begin to assess fabrics in this way, they should be able intuitively to code a fabric for comparison quite quickly. This helps the process of visualising a fabric's capability to produce certain shapes when selecting fabrics.

Notes on the term 'characteristic'
The term 'characteristic' is used because it is a descriptive term that is useful when making design decisions about a garment's shape. The term 'property' should be used when it refers to a fundamental chemical or biological property.

There are enormous problems in defining and measuring some fabric characteristics. Tests and standards have been devised (see Appendix 2) but they have to be carried out in laboratory conditions. The choice of characteristics, and the methods of testing and measuring them (see Chapter 2), were created to be used solely for the purpose of pattern cutting, in order to identify how a fabric will determine a garment's shape.

Viscose jersey　　　　*Cotton twill*

Full-scale model stands

Viscose jersey　　　　*Cotton twill*

Half-scale model stands

Viscose jersey　　　　*Cotton twill*

Quarter-scale model stands

1

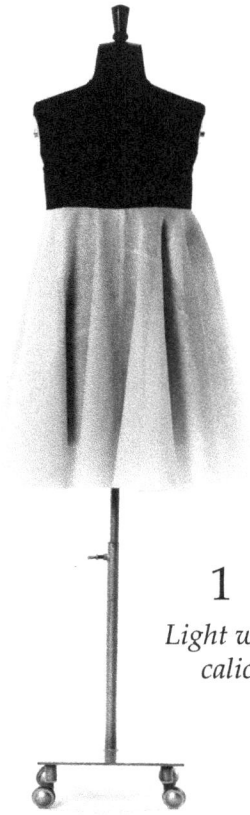

*Light weight
calico*

2

*Medium weight
calico*

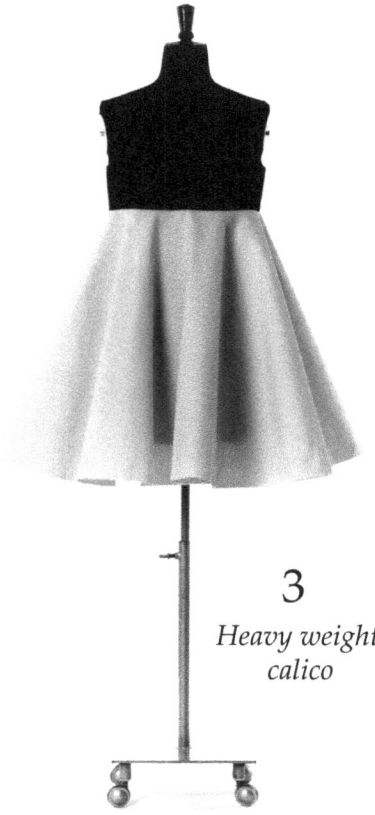

3

*Heavy weight
calico*

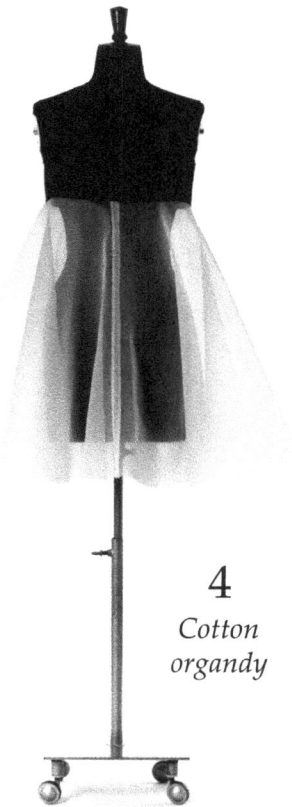

4

*Cotton
organdy*

5

Wool

6

*Polyamide
(warp knit)*

FABRIC CHARACTERISTICS AND GARMENT TOILES

Fabric characteristics

The images on page 9 show that when a circle is cut at the same length in different fabrics (viscose jersey and cotton twill), quite apparent differences in shape will occur. This is because the characteristics of the fabrics are quite different.

Toile fabrics

Most students use calico, mainly of medium weight, for creating garment toiles. Calico is relatively cheap and the fabric structure is fairly stable. The shapes that are produced are predicable (images 1–3 opposite page).

Because unbleached calico is usually unfinished, its drape or stretch qualities are low (see the table below). Therefore, its relationship to many fabrics with drape or stretch characteristics is tenuous.

The images 4–6 (opposite page) show that if the drape or stretch of the fabric selected for a garment is very different from calico, very different shapes will be made. In this case, alternative cheap fabrics with similar drape or stretch qualities should be sought. Calico should never be used to represent knitted fabrics.

Images 1–3: Three circles of the same length cut in calico. The lightweight calico is a different weight and thickness, but the characteristics of drape and stretch are the same. The shapes are predictable.

	weight	thickness	drape	shear	stretch
1. lightweight calico	light	thin	low	med.	low
2. medium weight calico	med.	med.	low	med.	low
3. heavyweight calico	med.	med.	low	low	low

Images 4–6: Three circles of the same length, cut in different fabrics. They illustrate how fabric characteristics, particularly drape, can change the shape of a garment pattern quite dramatically.

	weight	thickness	drape	shear	stretch
4. cotton organdy	light	thin	low	med.	low
5. wool	med.	med.	med.	med.	low
6. polyamide (warp knit)	light	thin	high	low	med.

Constructing a circle for a skirt

(Cut in 4 quarter sections).
Take the waist measurement.
To calculate the radius for a circle: divide the waist measurement by 6.28; example: 62 cm (waistline measurement) divided by 6.28 = 9.87 (round up to 9.9 cm).

To create a quarter circle section:
Square both ways from 1.
1–2 the radius (e.g. 9.9 cm).
1–3 the radius.
Draw a quarter circle from 2–3.
2–4 the length of the skirt (e.g. 60 cm).
3–5 the length of the skirt.
Using a tape measure or a metre stick, mark out the lower edge of the skirt 60 cm from the drawn waistline.

The circle, multi-circles or sections of a circle can be attached to a simple body shape.
The circle, can be attached to a band or yoke to form a skirt.
Circles or parts of circles can be integrated into a pattern shape, in sections or in layers.

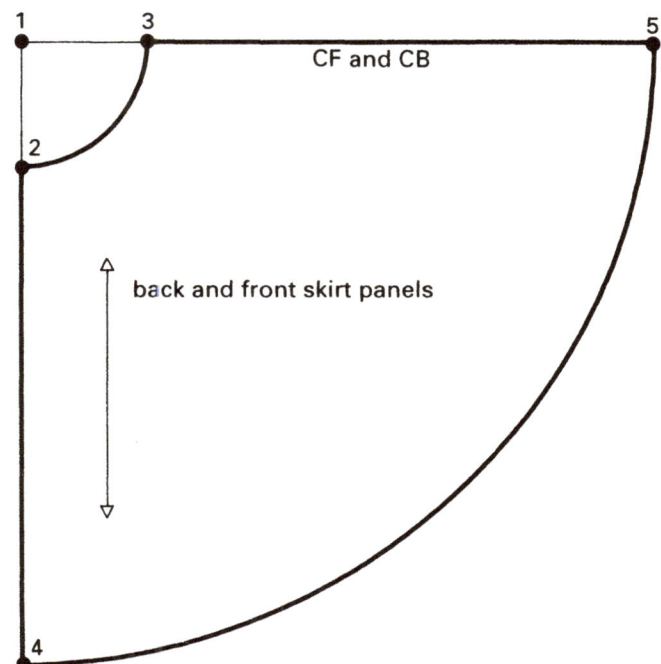

CF and CB

back and front skirt panels

FABRIC CHARACTERISTICS AND BODY SHAPES

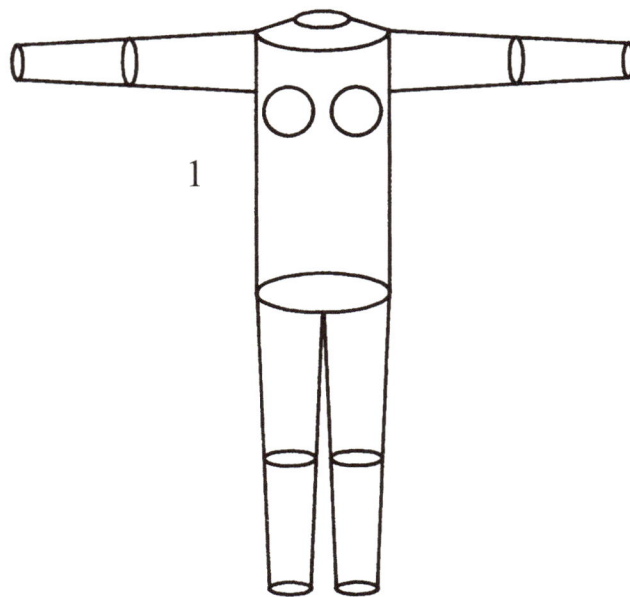

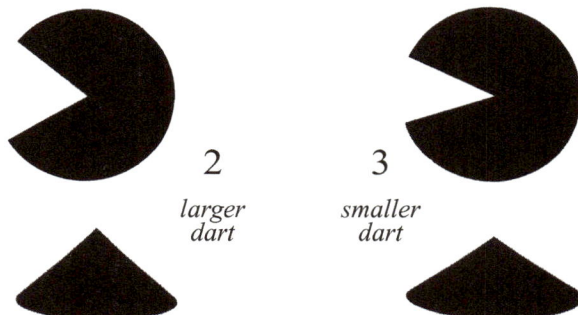

The Close Fitting Dress Block

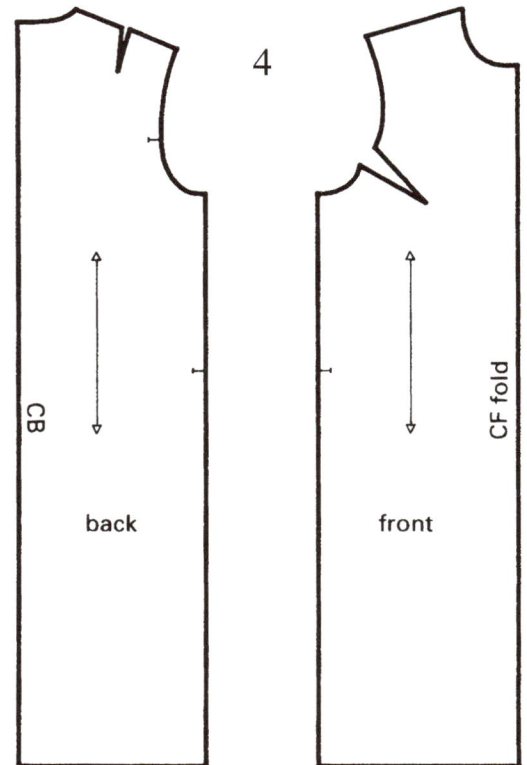

Look at the human body shape in a simple way. Diag. 1 shows a basic cylinder (the trunk) with other cylinders (limbs) attached. Historically, simple but effective garments were cut based on these basic shapes. But, as you move closer to fit the body shape, it becomes more complicated. The body shapes of women, men and children are all different; curves and eruptions occur in different places and on a different scale. Because the bust is the most extreme example, a female dress stand is used for illustrating fabrics and body shapes.

Blocks are simple cylindrical basic body shapes, developed by pattern cutters for different parts of the body; they can be used as initial shapes for creating designs. Fabric characteristics play a crucial part when selecting a block. The fabrics on the dress stands (opposite page) are of light or medium weight, but have differences in drape and stretch.

Fabrics with high drape or stretch

Image 1 (opposite page)
If a fabric has high drape or stretch characteristics, a close fitting block without darting can be used.
The fabric stretches over the bust and shoulder curves, and then hangs as a vertical cylinder.

Fabrics with low drape and stretch

Image 2 (opposite page)
Fabrics with low drape or stretch cannot accommodate an eruption such as the bust. Drag lines will be created that will pull the side seam forward. Therefore, a bust dart is required.

Darting
If a section of a circle is cut out (diag. 2), and the lines are joined, the centre of the circle will rise.
The smaller the section cut out (diag. 3), the lower the rise will be.
A dart in a body block has the same effect.
The closer the fit, the larger the dart has to be.
A dart is required in a close fitting garment made up in a fabric with little drape or stretch.

Image 3 (opposite page)
The close fitting bodice (dress) block with a bust dart was selected (ref. page 208).
The bust dart was transferred to the armhole (diag. 4).
The garment now has a perfect 'hang' and a vertical side seam.

1   *Acrylic (weft knit)*

Low shear, high drape and stretch

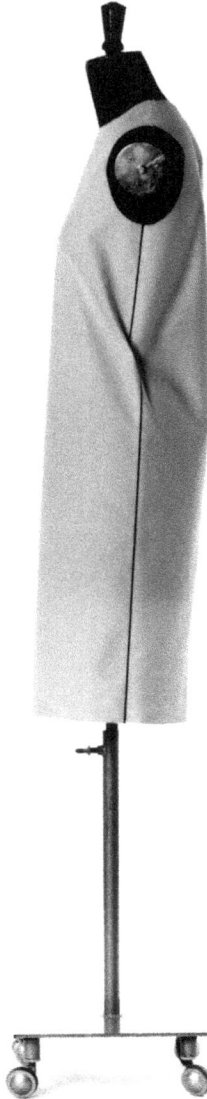

2   *Polyester (woven)*   **3**

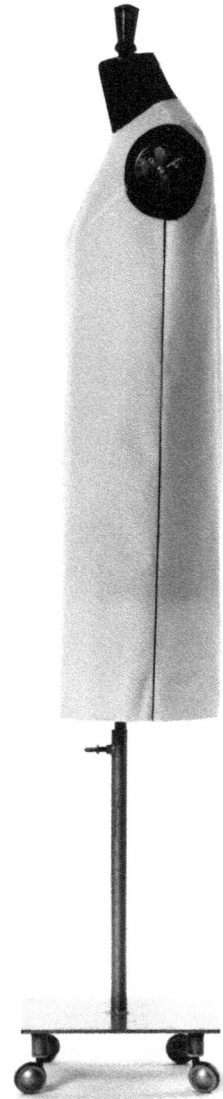

Low shear, drape and stretch

Fabrics with high shear and drape

If a fabric with high shear and drape is made up into a close fitting garment, it will create a good balanced shape. But if the fabric has no natural recovery, it will become distorted during wear. This means that this type of fabric is usually cut in easy fitting shapes where the strain on the fabric will be less.

However, if a fabric has high recovery, it will allow the narrow shape to have resilience and recover during wear. For example, fabrics made from micro-fibres have this quality and are widely used in lingerie.

PART ONE: FABRIC CHARACTERISTICS AND BODY SHAPE

Chapter 2 Fabric testing

Fabric testing
TESTING METHODS AND FABRIC CHARACTERISTICS

The simple testing methods

The characteristics recorded throughout this book were taken using specially devised equipment (see Appendix 1). They were measured to a high accuracy level and numerically coded. Previous editions have recorded these codes. However, a similar result has been achieved by simplifying the tests and converting the codes to descriptions.

This has been done to help students at the beginning of their studies. If they assess fabrics in this simple way, in quite a short time they should be able to make intuitive fabric comparisons quite quickly. This helps the process of visualising a fabric's capability to produce certain shapes. I hope that it may also be useful for designers, particularly when dealing with stretch fabrics.

Special note: This new approach to assessing fabric behaviour is not designed to replace technical testing. It is restricted to solving the problems that arise when a designer selects a fabric to produce the shape of a design.

Fabric characteristics

In Chapter 1 it was explained how the five crucial fabric characteristics below could assist a designer when deciding on the method of pattern cutting or the choice of pattern block:

weight   thickness   drape   shear   stretch

The five-point fabric characteristic scale
The five characteristics can be assessed by a scale that divides them into three categories using the opposite ends of each characteristic:

Weight	light	med.	heavy
Thickness (visual)	thin	med.	thick
Drape (visual)	high	med.	low
Shear	high	med.	low
Stretch	high	med.	low

Note: The term 'visual' is explained on pages 18 and 21.

THE SIMPLE TESTING METHODS

The only fabric sample that is usually available to a designer when beginning to construct a range is a fabric swatch piece of approximately A4 size. Therefore, the tests are based on using a 20 cm square of fabric that could be cut from a fabric swatch.

Preparing the test piece
1.   The 20 cm sample piece of woven fabric should be cut accurately along the warp and weft threads, and along the wales of knitted fabrics.

2.   The fabric piece should be checked to determine that it is perfectly square before the tests are carried out.

3.   If only one 20 cm square fabric sample is available, less distortion to the fabric will occur, if the drape test is carried out first, before the shear and stretch tests.

FABRIC WEIGHT

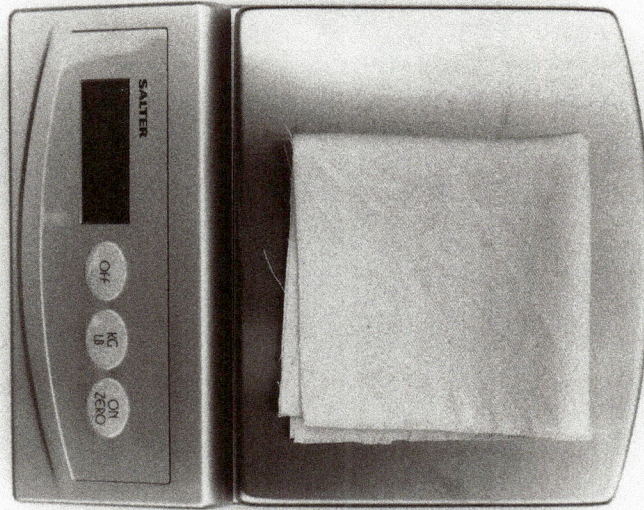

Figure 1 Measuring weight   A 20 cm square of fabric measured on a domestic scale that records at 1.00 gm intervals.

Fabric weights

Weight in a fabric will help to make graceful vertical folds and will 'swing' dramatically. Many wool fabrics are of a heavier weight. However, there has been a general movement to lighter weight cloths and towards lighter wool fabrics; but as they are usually made from higher-grade fibres or yarns they can be expensive.

Light fabrics with low-drape and low-shear (example: cotton organdy), often give sharp crisp outlines but often crumple in use. This feature has been overcome to some extent by the crinkle finishes now available. Light fabrics with high levels of drape and stretch give wonderful body fitting and drape lines; for example, single jersey. Compact, closely woven medium weight fabrics with high drape are excellent for crossway cutting; for example, crepes or some micro-fibre fabrics.

Fabric weight measurements

Weight information is usually recorded by the square metre, and to the nearest gram. It should be listed on a fabric swatch or be available from the manufacturer.

A number of European manufacturers may list the weight per running metre. To convert grams per metre length, to grams per metre square: divide the weight by the fabric width and multiply by 100.

Some UK manufacturers may still show the weight in ounces. To convert oz. weight to gm. weight: multiply the oz weight by 33.91.

Measuring fabric weight

A domestic scale that records in 1 gm intervals (see the photograph in Figure 1) is adequate for this simple calculation based on a 20 cm square of cloth. More accurate scales are available for more rigorous tests.

Fold and weigh the 20 cm square of fabric as shown above.
Multiply the result by 20 to calculate the weight per square metre of fabric.

The weight categorisation scale shown below was re-calculated from the old scale to give three simpler categories.

The weight scale in grams per square metre

light	medium	heavy
0–129.9	130–374.9	375+

FABRIC THICKNESS

Figure 2 Measuring thickness A 20 cm square of fabric placed between blocks, and measured with a linen tester (a magnifying glass marked with mm).

Fabric thickness

Fabric thickness is so variable that each fabric has to be judged individually. Fabrics that appear thick can be highly compressible; other fabrics have uneven thickness that may be unevenly distributed.

Most thick garments are adapted from the easy fitting blocks. Closer fitting garments will require extra ease allowances, unless the fabric has stretch and recovery qualities. Where there is gathered or pleated fullness, particular pattern cutting techniques have to be used to reduce the bulk. Thick fabrics with low drape and low shear characteristics can give exaggerated and stable geometric outlines.

Thin fabrics are generally used in quantity. Most designs include gathers, tucks, pleats or layers. Some thin fabrics, particularly those with high shear, will require an under-body structure to hold the shape.

Fabric thickness measurements

Fabric thickness is extremely difficult to measure. Technical laboratories measure it under pressure; it is recorded with a 'load' reference which flattens the fabric. This is useful for the making up of fabrics, but is of little use for pattern cutting. A *visual* measurement that does not distort the fabric is more useful.

When comparing fabrics that are very textured, or are unevenly woven or knitted, a measurement can record the thinnest and thickest points, and take an average measurement.

Measuring fabric thickness

Place the edge of 20 cm square of fabric between two blocks as shown in Figure 2.
Use a linen tester to measure the thickness. This is a magnifying glass marked in millimetres, and used in thread counting.

The thickness categorisation scale shown below was re-calculated from the old scale to give three simpler categories.

The thickness scale recorded in mm.

thin	medium	thick
0–0.6	0.7–3.4	3.5+

FABRIC DRAPE

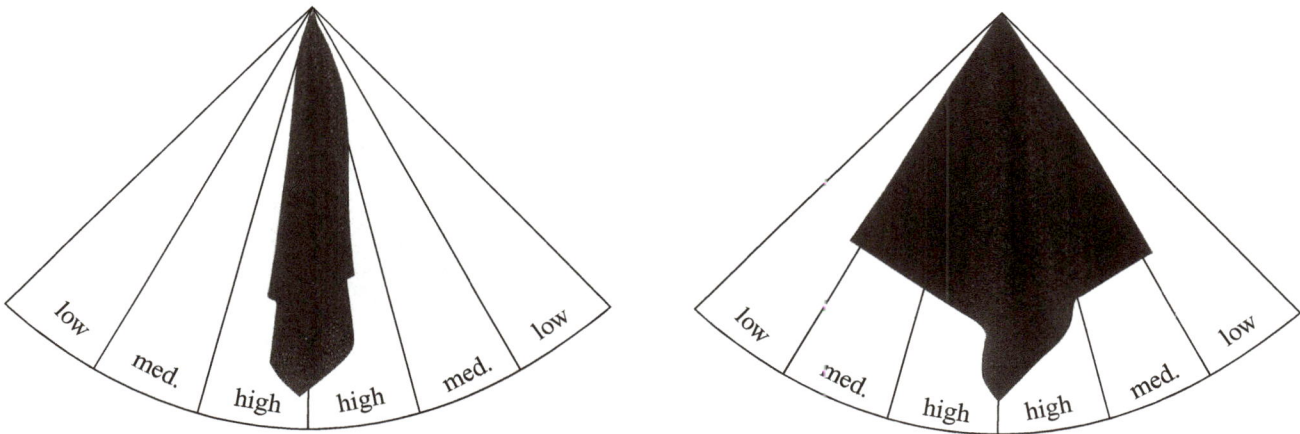

Figure 3 Measuring drape Two different fabrics measured on a card scale. The fabric on the left shows a high drape, the one on the right a low drape.

Fabric drape

Drape is the ability of a fabric to hang in soft folds and to fit around a figure, particularly in movement, without creating distorted creases. Good draping is required when cutting flared shapes.

Drape is a characteristic valued in many fabrics; it is only a part of an elusive quality called 'hand' or 'handle'. It combines many qualities that differ in different fabrics, and is almost impossible to measure (see Appendix 2). However, the simple drape test shown in Figure 3 is a good guide to how a fabric is likely to drape.

When crossway cutting a fabric with high drape, the weight of the fabric increases the vertical drop, and narrows across the fabric. This has to be taken into account when pattern cutting. The difficulty of assessing fabric behaviour in crossway cutting is discussed fully in Chapter 7.

Creating a scale for measuring drape

On a piece of thick white card mark a centre point near the top and draw a centre line 40 cm long. Draw two lines 40 cm long, at 45° each side of the line. Mark out points 40 cm from the centre point between the outer lines. Draw a curve through the points in order to complete a quarter circle. Divide each half into three sections. Mark each section high, med. and low as shown in Figure 3.

Measuring fabric drape

Hang the corner of a 20 cm square of fabric on the top centre point with a large drawing pin. The drape amount can then be recorded by the position of the fabric square on the board. This is shown in the illustrations in Figure 3.

FABRIC SHEAR

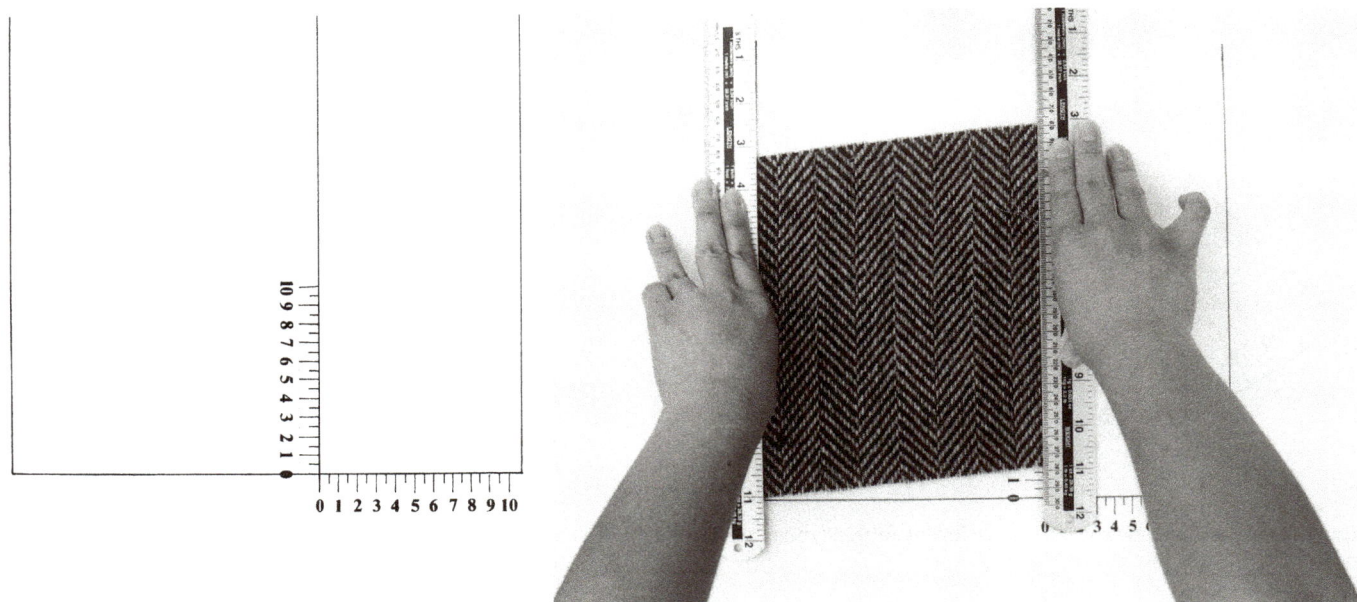

Figure 4 Measuring shear A 20 cm square of fabric taped to two rulers (right), with the amount of shear measured on a card scale (left).

Fabric shear

The amount that a fabric shears (distorts in the warp and weft; see diagram below) can be measured. Shear can be an advantage or disadvantage and the amount is important. The amount of recovery after strain is very important.

Closely woven fabrics with a high shear characteristic (for example, micro-fibre silk-like fabrics or some crepe weave fabrics) are very stable when used in crossway cutting.

Open-weave high shear fabrics distort if under strain. Many complicated luxury fabrics, particularly fabrics in linen, silk and viscose have high shear.

Fabrics will tailor more satisfactorily if there is some shear quality – it allows the tailor to shape the garment; however, too much shear becomes a problem.

Fabric shear

Creating a scale for measuring shear and stretch

Draw a horizontal line at the bottom of the card.
Draw two lines at right angles to this line 16 cm apart.
Mark the right vertical line and horizontal line in 0.5 cm intervals for 10 cm, as shown in Figure 4.
Draw a third vertical line at the end of the scale.

Measuring fabric shear

Tape the 20 cm square of fabric onto the underside of two rulers placing 2 cm of cloth on each ruler.
Place the first ruler firmly at the left-hand start of the scale.
Move the second ruler under tension in a vertical (shear) direction along the marked scale.
The shear measurement is the amount that the fabric shears before ripples appear on the surface of the cloth. The amount of recovery can also be measured.

The shear categorisation scale shown below was re-calculated from the old scale to give three simpler categories.

The shear scale recorded in cm

high shear	medium shear	low shear
+3.2 cm	3.2–1 cm	0–1 cm

FABRIC STRETCH

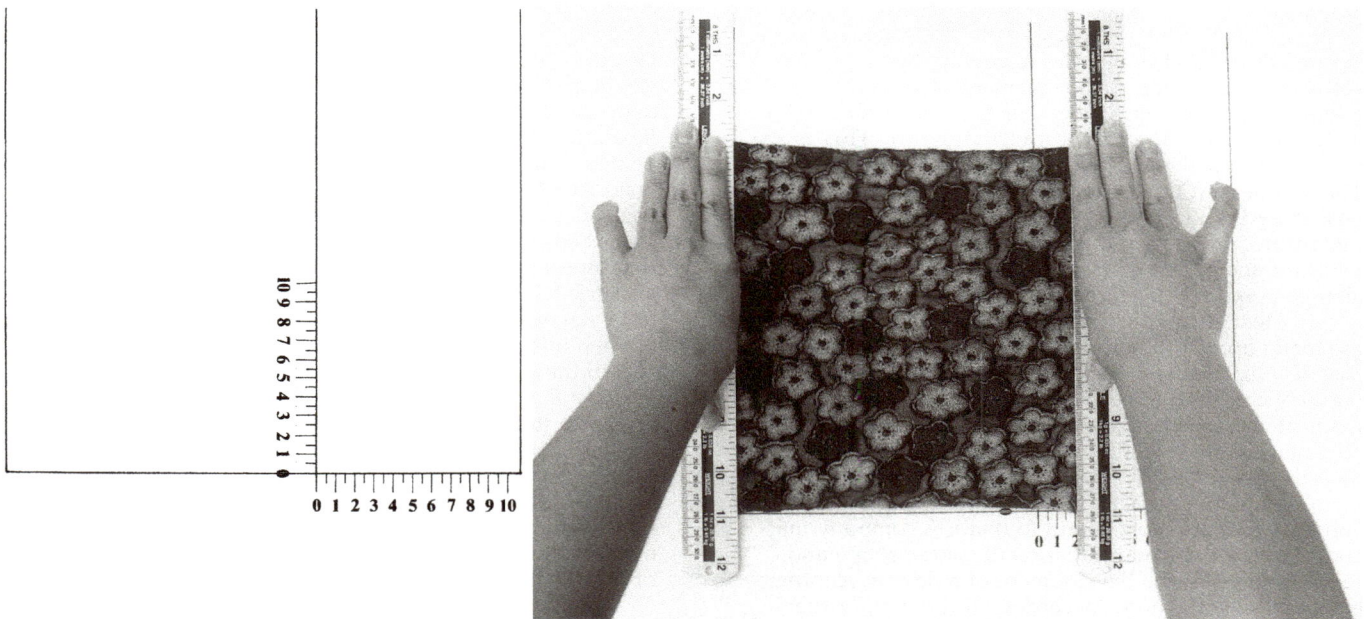

Figure 5 Measuring stretch A 20 cm square of fabric taped to two rulers (right), with the amount of stretch measured on a card scale (left).

Fabric stretch

Stretch characteristics in fabrics offer a means of cutting close to the body without complex shaping of the pattern. Simple shapes will fit closely to the body. Knitted fabrics may stretch, but their recovery can be weak. The introduction of a small amount of elastane can make a remarkable difference to its stability. The introduction of elastane into woven and knitted fabrics has now penetrated a large sector of the market.

Visual stretch The amount a fabric will stretch can be measured. Instruments can measure precisely the maximum stretch horizontally, followed by the stretch vertically. However, these practical amounts are of little use if the fabric appears visually unpleasant at very high stretch or near the stretch limits of the fabric. The basic pattern cutting shape has to be based on a basic **visual stretch** measurement. On body fitting garments or other garments, the designer has to decide the amount of stretch that is visually acceptable and then has to cut the garment pattern accordingly. This is the **visual stretch** that is recorded in this book.

Measuring fabric stretch

Use the card scale created for measuring shear and stretch (see the instructions on page 20).
Tape the 20 cm square of fabric onto the underside of two rulers using 2 cm of cloth on each ruler.
Place the first ruler firmly at the left-hand start of the scale (as shown in Figure 5).
Move the second ruler under tension in a horizontal direction along the marked horizontal scale.
The **visual stretch** measurement in the weft direction is the amount that the fabric stretches before it begins

to distort unpleasantly. The amount can be measured on the horizontal line of the scale.
The amount that the fabric does not recover to its original size after stretching is important. A fabric with low **recovery** has to be put under less strain.

The stretch categorisation scale shown below was re-calculated from the old scale to give three simpler categories.

The visual stretch scale recorded in cm

high stretch	medium stretch	low stretch
+3.2 cm	3.2–1 cm	0–1 cm
20%+	20%–6%	0–6%

Percentage stretch
The percentage stretch can be calculated by the following equation:

$$\frac{\text{amount stretched}}{\text{original length}} \times 100 \quad \text{e.g.} \quad \frac{2\text{cm}}{16\text{cm}} \times 100 = 12.5\%$$

Other measurements
Other measurements can be taken on the scale when cutting close fitting body garments in stretch fabrics, for example:
1. The decrease in measurement of the fabric vertically when the fabric is stretched horizontally.
2. The vertical (warp) stretch of bi-stretch fabrics.

FABRICS AND 3D CAD IMAGES

CAD in the clothing industry

A number of CAD companies have developed software that creates virtual garments. Garment pattern pieces are joined together to create a 3D CAD image of a garment worn by a virtual figure. This visualises how the garment will look on a person. The mannequin's skin, face and hair can be customised. The figure's shape and size can be determined by the input of manual or body-scanned measurements. These virtual figures can revolve, change poses and perform many human movements.

In most companies, many garment samples of designs are made up, but then discarded. CAD suppliers claim that 3D CAD realisation could reduce this apparent waste of time and materials because decisions could be made at an earlier stage in the design cycle. A further advantage is that the fit and stress of the garment can be measured technically.

Garment manufacturers select the functions from the software that are most useful to them. A company may concentrate on the manipulation of colour, shape and textile pattern in the development of a design. Another company may be more concerned with the fit, or the garment stress of body movements in sportswear. However, the common feature in all the programs is the realisation of the image, which enables the company to see how different types of plain or patterned fabrics will hang and drape around the figure.

Realising the fabric image through CAD

Figure 7's images are of *Vidya 2011* (marketed in the UK by Assyst Bullmer Ltd). It displays drape realistically, depending on measurements such as rigidity and flexibility. This requires the inputting of measurements related to mechanical properties of the fabric. The majority of program developers are using *The Kawabata Evaluation Systems for Fabrics* (KES-F TEST); this is described in Appendix 2. It is usually large companies that invest in these CAD systems and they have access to fabric testing laboratories that conduct these types of tests. An example of the fabric properties required can be seen in Figure 6.

In the *Vidya* software images shown, the human being or body shape and volume are integrated by means of automata (taken from *Size by Human Solutions*). The images opposite show the garment shape changing when different property values are input into the system. Some systems allow designers to use the sliders interactively. Exact visualisation creates a common ground for discussion between designers and pattern makers; errors or measurable effects can be quickly addressed.

Students of CAD will find that an intuitive knowledge of fabric characteristics and behaviour, so necessary for their manual pattern cutting, will also be invaluable if they use this type of software in a company.

Figure 6 The fabric property data required by the software, to realise the garments on the virtual models in Figure 7. Screen images shown by permission of Assyst Bullmer Ltd ©.

Figure 7 Realising fabrics on the virtual model from the fabric property data in Figure 6. Screen images shown by permission of Assyst Bullmer Ltd ©.

Selecting fabrics

It is always difficult for the designer to select the ideal fabric to realise the shape of the finished garment. The sample fabrics in this chapter were collected to help students understand how the handle of a fabric is largely determined by its fibre content, fabric structure and finish. The chapter illustrates a varied selection of woven and knitted fabrics and it is organised by the fibre groups that are shown on garment labels.

All the fabric samples were measured for *weight – thickness – drape – shear – stretch* on the scale explained in Chapter 2. These characteristics are noted, and how they are likely to influence pattern cutting methods is briefly explained.

Further technical information is covered in Chapter 12, *Basic textile technology*.

Selecting fabrics

Fabrics and fibres

Fabric qualities

The important fabric characteristics (*weight, thickness, drape, shear, stretch*) are largely determined by the fibre and construction of the fabric. The following pages offer very basic information about a selection of illustrated fabric samples which describes these qualities, along with comments of the fabric's use in garment design. More detailed technical information about fibres, fabric construction, fabric finishes and new developments can be found in Chapter 12.

Methods of fabric construction

Most fibres are spun into yarns. Yarns and fibres are woven, knitted, interlaced or pressed into fabric form. The designer reacts to the finished fabric when selecting the fabric range for a collection. It is the combination of fibre, yarn and construction that determines the fabric characteristics. Methods of fabric construction are shown in Figure 8.

Fabric labels

Most garment fabrics are made from textile fibres. Since 1986, all piece fabric or clothing made in new fabrics sold in the European Community has had to be labelled with the percentage fibre content. The generic (chemical group) rather than the trade name has to be used to prevent confusion. Fabric swatches and garment labels list the fibres and their percentage: for example, 50% cotton 50% polyester. Students should know the names of the basic fibre groups that have to appear on labels and understand the range of fabrics available in each fibre group. It is also useful for students to look at interesting garment shapes in the stores and investigate the fibre of the garment's fabric as shown on the label.

Fibre groups

The fabric samples in this chapter are separated into individual fibre groups; there are also pages where blends and mixtures are shown. Fibres are divided into two main groups: natural fibres and man-made fibres.
Natural fibres: Natural fibres come directly from a cellulose–vegetable source (e.g. cotton comes from a seed boll of a plant) or a protein–animal source (e.g. wool comes from the fleece of a sheep).
Man-made fibres: Man-made fibres are produced chemically. Regenerated fibres originate from natural sources, e.g. vegetable or animal, that are broken down to a chemical liquid and then re-spun (e.g. viscose is produced from waste cotton linters). Synthetic fibres have a chemical base (e.g. polyester is produced from oil).

Some chemical processes, using vegetable sources, are producing new fibres that are difficult to classify (see Chapter 12).

Two simplified fibre classifications are illustrated in Figures 9 and 10; they are divided into the natural and man-made fibre groups. They show the fibres most used on clothing labels and can be used for quick references. A more extensive technical classification of fibres is given in Chapter 12, *Basic textile technology*, page 173.

Methods of fabric construction

Major methods			Minor methods		
WEAVING	**KNITTING**	**INTERLACING**	**embroidered**	**braiding**	**non-woven**
	weft knit	lace	lace	braid	film
	warp knit	crochet	Broderie Anglaise	macramé	felt
		tatting			interlinings

Figure 8 Basic fabric structures. The major methods are shown in RED CAPITAL LETTERS.

Natural fibres

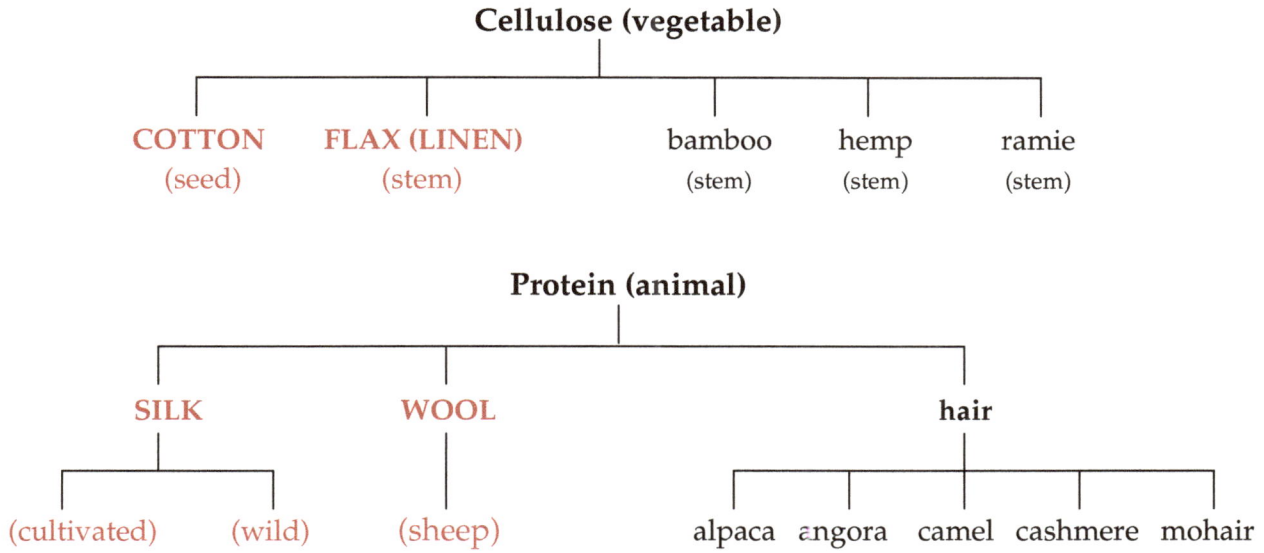

Cellulose (vegetable)

COTTON   FLAX (LINEN)   bamboo   hemp   ramie

(seed)   (stem)   (stem)   (stem)   (stem)

Protein (animal)

SILK   WOOL   hair

(cultivated)   (wild)   (sheep)   alpaca angora camel cashmere mohair

Figure 9 This very simplified classification of natural fibres lists the names of fibres most used on garment labels. The major fibres are shown in RED CAPITAL LETTERS. A more complete classification is in Chapter 12.

Man-made fibres

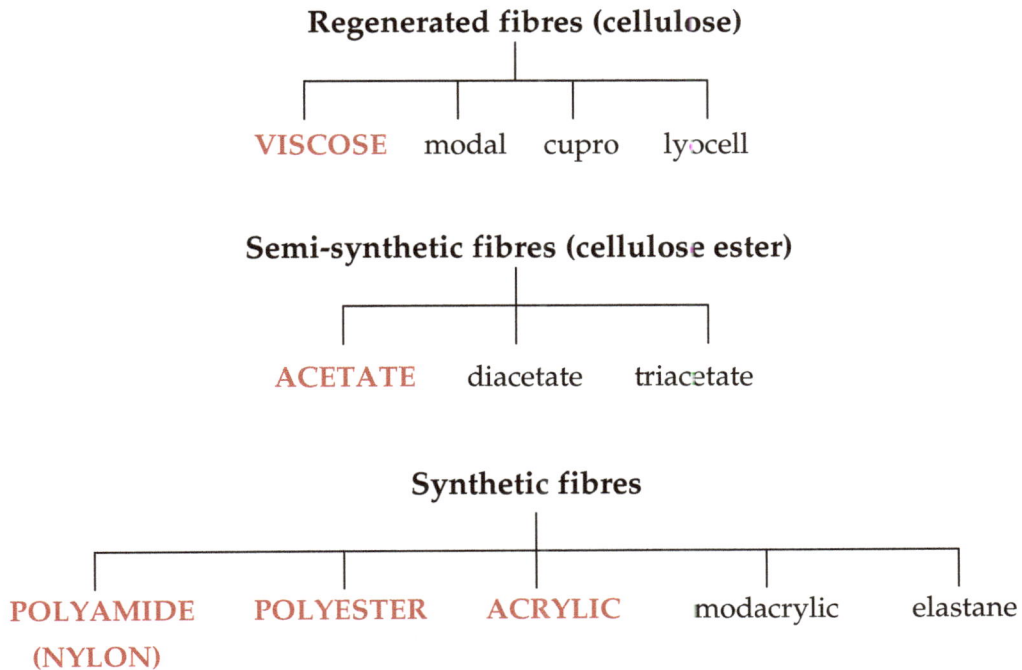

Regenerated fibres (cellulose)

VISCOSE   modal   cupro   lyocell

Semi-synthetic fibres (cellulose ester)

ACETATE   diacetate   triacetate

Synthetic fibres

POLYAMIDE   POLYESTER   ACRYLIC   modacrylic   elastane

(NYLON)

Figure 10 This very simplified classification of man-made fibres lists the names of fibres most used on garment labels. The major fibres are shown in RED CAPITAL LETTERS. A more complete classification is in Chapter 12.

Natural fibres and fabrics

Fibre source and fabric production

Cotton grows inside the seed pod of plants from the *Gossypium* family. The seed pod or boll can contain up to 150,000 fibres. The fibre is flat, twisted and ribbon-like, and can be up to 65 mm in length. The finest comes from the West Indies (*Sea Island Cotton*) and Egypt. America, the largest cotton exporter, produces strong fibres, which are continuing to increase in length and strength (*PIMA-7* is the longest and strongest), and India produces short coarse fibres. The main properties of the fibre are its strength and absorbency and competition from man-made fibres has driven new finishing developments in natural fibres.

One of the earliest fibres used by man, cotton had the largest production total of any fibre until 2003–04 when it was just overtaken by polyester fibre production. However, its price and the continuing popularity of denim has helped it to retain its importance in the market. Part of the fluctuation in fabric production is related to fashion trends; however, moves towards sustainability may increase its future growth.

Fabric ranges

The fabric ranges produced in cotton are enormous, they offer: feather-light cotton voiles, silky poplins, fine embroidered fabrics and laces; soft fluid jerseys to heavy knits; medium cloths from piques to denims; heavy-ribbed and canvas workwear cloths; thick, soft brushed and pile fabrics such as, flannel, corduroy, velveteen, moleskin, terrycloth and fleece.

Illustrated cotton fabrics

A selection of fabric samples that can be found within a cotton fabric range.

Light and thin fabrics

Lawn
Medium drape and shear, but low stretch.
It is a stable fabric usually cut with gathered fullness, pleats or tucks.
Main uses: underwear – nightwear – skirts – blouses – printed dresses – scarves.

Single jersey (weft knit)
High drape, medium shear and stretch.
It is a stable popular jersey fabric used for all types of garments.
Main uses: underwear – nightwear – sportswear – tops – dresses – trousers.

Medium fabrics

Denim/twill
Low drape, shear and stretch.
Its great stability makes it a popular fabric, easy to cut in structured or classic shapes.
Main uses: skirts – jeans – casual wear – dresses – jackets – accessories.

Patterned (weft knit)
Medium drape, shear and stretch.
This type of patterned knitwear has the pattern piece shaped by fully fashioned knitting machines.
Main uses: sweaters – knitted jackets – scarves.

Heavy and thick fabrics

Block weave
Low drape, shear and stretch.
A very structured fabric; any body fit has to be cut by pattern shaping, but the fabric will hold shapes cut away from the body.
Main uses: overgarments – tailored garments.

Guipure lace
Low drape, high shear and medium stretch.
Dresses and jackets often have an inner structure to hold distortions from the high shear.
Main uses: evening wear – tops – dresses – jackets – bridal wear – decorative trimmings.

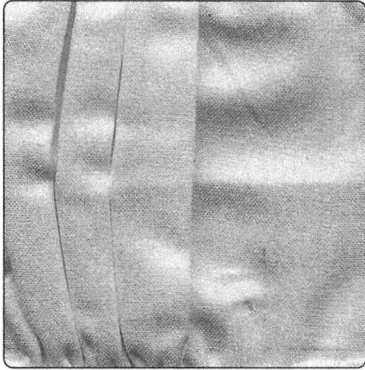
Lawn

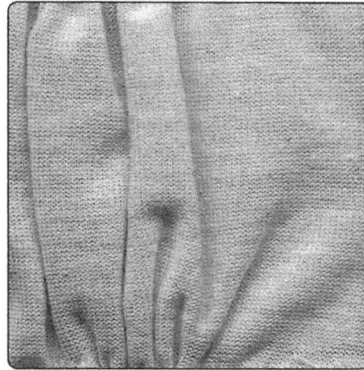
Single jersey (weft knit)

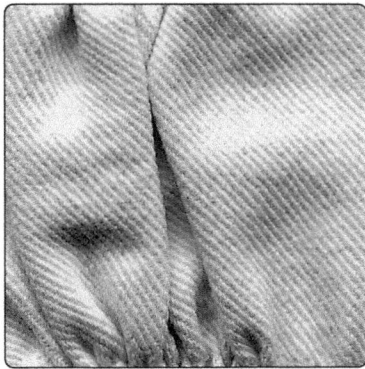
Denim/twill

Patterned (weft knit)

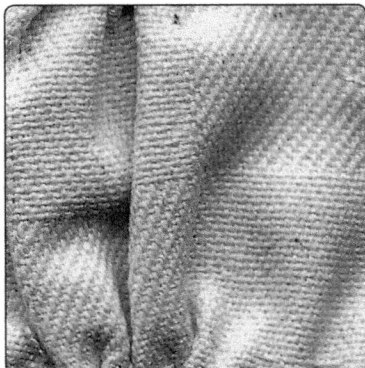
Block weave

Guipure lace

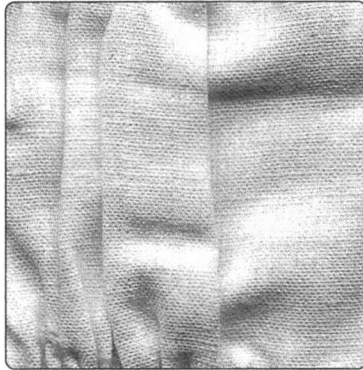

Slub

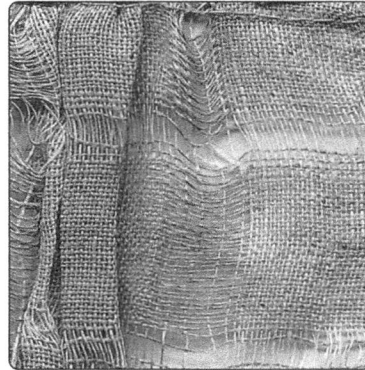

Spaced weft

Distorted weft crinkled finish

Twill suiting

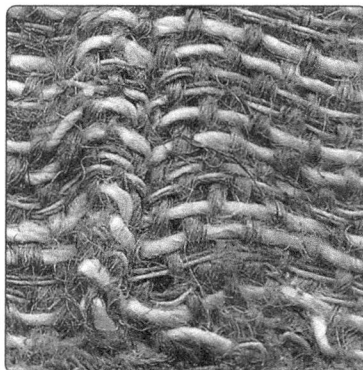

Contrast yarns

Patterned (weft knit)

Flax (linen) bamboo hemp ramie   Natural fibres

Fibre source and fabric production

Flax is a bast fibre produced in the stem of the flax plant and is largely pure cellulose fibre; other coarser bast fibres (hemp, jute and ramie) are mainly used in blends and mixtures for 'natural' fashion appeal. Flax is the strongest and least elastic of the natural fibres; the fibres vary from 6–60cm in length and are highly absorbent. The fibres are cylindrical in shape with swellings at intervals. Hemp, ramie and bamboo fibres are mainly used in blends and mixtures.

Flax is believed to be the earliest fibre used by man. Its production, although small compared with cotton, is rising. Grown mainly in Russia, Ireland and the Low Countries, heavy investment has taken place in the industry and 'fashion attitudes' to linen have changed. Seen as a rather boring classic, then as an expensive fashion statement, it then became hot 'ecology' High Street fashion with a variety of finishes imposed on it. The contrast of its rough texture yet lustrous appearance is very appealing, and linen has gained a perverse affinity due to its natural creasing qualities. Knitted structures and blends and mixtures with other fibres add qualities that enhance its rough textured appearance yet give it subtle stretch and drape dimensions that the fibre lacks in its natural state. Its outstanding qualities have yet to be explored fully by designers.

Fabric ranges

The fabric ranges produced in linen are extending, they offer: light open weaves and fine embroidered fabrics; classic linens in all weights; fashion fabrics in a wide variety of weaves, knits and finishes; linen tweeds. Up-market alternatives to cotton are being produced, waxed linen for weatherwear, and linen denims, twills and chambrays for casual wear. Gossamer fine voiles and muslins have also been produced.

Illustrated linen fabrics

A selection of fabric samples that can be found within a linen fabric range.

Light and thin fabrics

Slub
Low drape, shear and stretch.
The slub yarn and weave gives it texture and its lightness. The low sheer makes it an easy fabric to create a range of pattern shapes.
Main uses: lightweight shirts – blouses – dresses.

Spaced weft
Low drape, very high shear, low stretch.
The very high shear makes it a difficult fabric to handle. It has to be cut with fullness and requires some under structure to hold the shape.
Main uses: evening wear – luxury tops – skirts.

Medium fabrics

Distorted weft crinkled finish
Low drape, very high shear, low stretch.
A difficult fabric to handle and it also requires some under structure to hold the shape.
Main uses: tops – evening wear – creative design.

Twill suiting
Low drape, medium shear, low stretch.
A stable fabric where the shear can be manipulated to create tailored shapes.
Main uses: skirts – trousers – dresses – suit – jackets.

Heavy and thick fabrics

Contrast yarns
Low drape, very high shear, low stretch.
The novelty yarns will require easy fitting simple shapes and some under structure.
Main uses: overgarments.

Patterned (weft knit)
Medium drape, shear and stretch.
This type of patterned knitwear has the pattern piece shape fully fashioned by knitting machinery.
Main uses: sweaters – jackets.

Fibre source and fabric production

Filament silk is unwound from the cocoon of the silkworm, *Bombyx Mori*. The unwound silk strands consist of two filaments held together by a gum. Tussah or wild silk is produced from a number of different but similar species of silkworm and the silk is coarser and more irregular. Large quantities of waste silk are produced during the reeling process; this is combed and spun to produce spun silk for use in pile, knitted and many textured woven fabrics.

Most silk is lustrous, strong, absorbent and has excellent draping qualities. However, silk can be damaged or distorted by heat and water. China is the largest producer of raw silk. Silk is often sold at below its production price in order to obtain hard currency. India has become a major producer of raw silk and of finished fabrics at competitive prices. High quality silk fabric production still takes place in traditional areas of Italy and France. Silk fashion promotions and the availability of inexpensive silk have helped to make silk a High Street fashion fabric.

Fabric ranges

Classic silk fabrics associated with particular names (e.g. habutae, dupion, shantung) are listed in the Glossary (page 56). The wide fabric ranges currently presented have extended beyond the luxury and classic markets to produce: decorative sheer fabrics and laces; lightweight shirtings and dress fabrics; crepes, rich textured silks and brocades; soft fluid jerseys to textured knits; silk tweeds and rich pile fabrics.

Illustrated silk fabrics

A selection of fabric samples that can be found within a silk fabric range.

Light and thin fabrics

Georgette
High drape, low shear and stretch.
Silk georgette is a luxury fabric often cut in layers for evening wear.
Main uses: lingerie – evening wear – scarves.

Sandwashed satin
High drape, low shear and stretch.
The filament yarn gives high sheen. Satin is available in heavier weights (Duchesse satin).
Main uses: lingerie – evening wear – scarves.

Medium fabrics

Slub spun bourette
Medium drape, high shear, low stretch.
The high shear offers tailoring qualities. The spun, slubbed yarn gives texture to the fabric.
Main uses: tops – skirts – dresses.

Snarl single jersey (weft knit)
High drape, low shear, medium stretch.
Produced with a spun textured yarn, filament yarn gives more fluidity and sheen.
Main uses: skirts – dresses – tailored garments.

Heavy and thick fabrics

Coarse slub stripe
Medium drape, high shear, medium stretch.
Complex textures can create design possibilities but they can also create problems.
Main uses: outerwear – soft tailored garments.

Tweed
Low drape, high shear, low stretch.
The high shear and the loose weave of the fabric can restrict pattern shaping.
Main uses: outerwear – soft tailored garments.

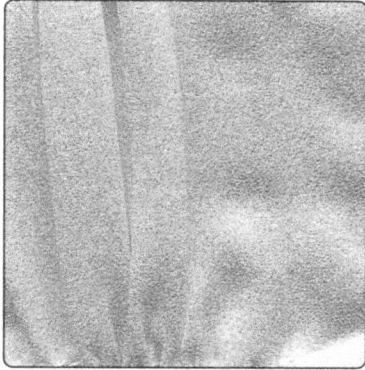

Georgette

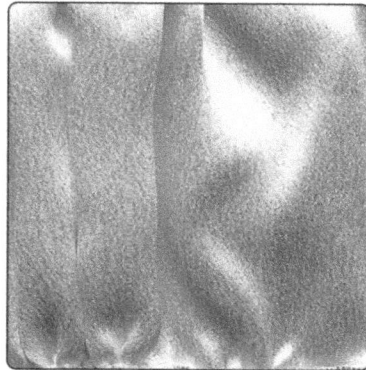

Sandwashed satin

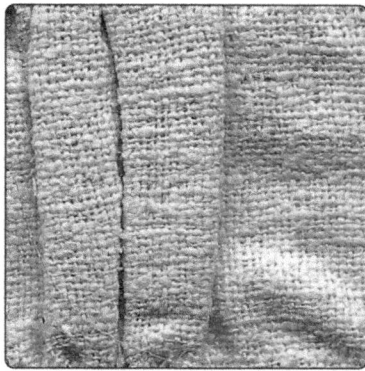

Slub spun bourette

Snarl single jersey (weft knit)

Coarse slub stripe

Tweed

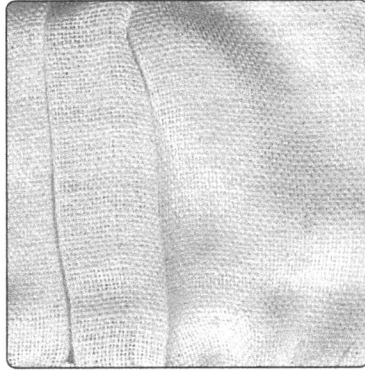

Gauze

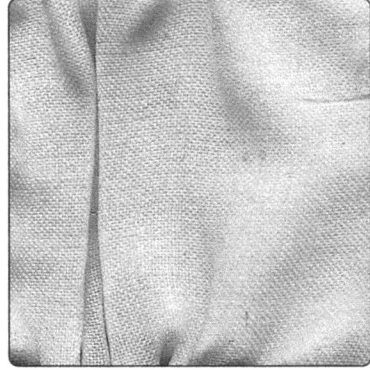

Fine worsted

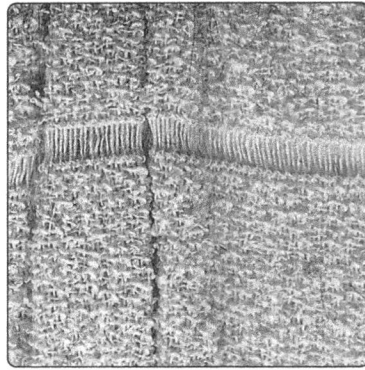

Boucle

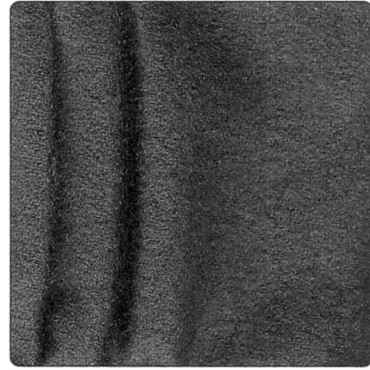

Wool/cashmere

Patterned (weft knit)

Herringbone tweed

Wool: hair alpaca angora camel cashmere mohair   Natural fibres

Fibre source and fabric production

Although wool and hair have the same chemical structure (keratin), they differ in their physical properties. Shorter coarse wool fibres, less than 32 mm, are spun in a random form for woollen yarn; longer finer fibres are laid parallel and spun with a high twist to produce worsted yarns. The fibre is cylindrical, with a scaly surface, a high crimp and a fibrous internal structure. This gives it the unique natural qualities of warmth, elasticity, drape, and the contradictory qualities of being water repellant yet absorbent. Its notoriety for shrinkage has been the focus of much research and development.

Hair fibres, longer and finer than wool (e.g. cashmere, vicuna, alpaca, mohair), are usually blended with other fibres in high quality textiles.

Wool and hair fibres are only a small proportion of world production, but they are unique fibres with characteristics that defy mimicry.

90% of animal fibres produced are wool. Australia is the largest producer; New Zealand, South Africa and Russia are also significant. Wool has to fight the price competition of man-made fibres and their increasing versatility. The International Wool Secretariat promotes wool by research and development and establishing quality trade marks, for example the Woolmark symbol.

Fabric ranges

The fabric ranges are extensive, they include: light-weight georgettes and laces; fine soft draping woven woollen cloths; soft fluid jerseys to heavy knits; rustic cloths and jacquard weaves, hard wearing worsted suitings and gaberdines; heavy woollen coatings and tweeds of immense range and character; brushed and pile fabrics with interesting surface textures.

Illustrated wool fabrics

A selection of fabric samples that can be found within a wool fabric range.

Light and thin fabrics

Gauze
Medium drape, high shear, low stretch.
A light, thin fabric used in all kinds of large pattern shapes. It also has great dye affinity.
Main uses: printed blouses and dresses – evening wear – scarves.

Fine worsted
Medium drape, high shear, low stretch.
The high shear means that the fabric is ideal for lightweight tailored garments.
Main uses: tailored dresses – suits – trousers.

Medium fabrics

Boucle
High drape, shear and stretch.
A highly textured fabric, but its high shear means that it usually requires some inner structure to hold the shape.
Main uses: suits – coats – overgarments.

Wool/cashmere
Medium drape, shear and stretch.
A stable fabric, with enough shear to make it an ideal fabric for all types of tailored and shaped (usually expensive) garments.
Main uses: tailored coats – overgarments.

Heavy and thick fabrics

Patterned (weft knit)
Medium drape, high shear and stretch.
This type of patterned knit usually has its garment pieces fashioned by fully fashioned knitting machines.
Main uses: sweaters – jackets – overgarments – scarves.

Herringbone tweed
Low drape, medium shear, low stretch.
A stable fabric, with enough shear to tailor well, but its bulk and weight can limit the pattern cutting possibilities.
Main uses: tailored coats – overgarments.

Fibre source and fabric production

Fabrics are available that may contain three or even four natural fibres. The use of ramie, hemp and jute can give 'character' to many cotton knits. Elastane (largest producer LYCRA) yarns are described on page 48, but many natural fabrics now have added elastane. Otherwise, the tendency of natural fabrics to distort (high shear) has to be compensated for by high-twist yarns or firm weave or knitted structures.

Examples of mixed fibre fabrics, with cotton warps and woollen wefts, have been found in ancient Peruvian textiles, and the Egyptians in the first century used linen warps and wool wefts. Nowadays, woven and knitted fabric manufacturers produce many fabric blends and mixtures. A fibre lacking a property could be supplemented with a fibre that has that quality.

However, in some cases blends were undertaken to lower the price and 'blend' became associated with cheaper quality. A reversal has now occurred; for example, a high quality fibre such as silk is often added to give a luxury image to wool and to add characteristics to fibres of existing quality. Linen gives wonderful aesthetic qualities and strength to wool/linen blends and mixtures.

Fabric ranges

Blended fabrics usually have a dominant fibre. The fabric ranges produced in mixtures and blends can generally reproduce many of the fabrics produced by that dominant fibre. Blending with other fibres can extend a fabric's range by improving the practical qualities and extending the aesthetic possibilities.

Illustrated fabrics – natural fibres, blends and mixtures

A selection of fabric samples that can be found in a fabric range of blends or mixtures.

Light and thin fabrics

Slub gauze
58% linen 42% silk
Medium drape and shear, low stretch.
A gauze in which the linen fibre gives character to the cloth and shape to the garment pieces.
Main uses: tops – skirts – dresses – scarves.

Single jersey (weft knit)
50% linen 50% silk
High drape, low shear, medium stretch.
A stable knitted fabric, the high drape allows easy cutting of draped styles without distortion.
Main uses: skirts – tops – sweaters – dresses.

Medium fabrics

Boucle
57% linen 43% wool
Medium drape, high shear, medium stretch.
The high shear means that it generally requires some understructure to hold the shape.
Main uses: jackets – coats – overgarments.

Strong weft weave crinkled finish
80% linen 20%cotton
Medium drape and shear, low stretch.
A cool, stable fabric, very suitable for lightweight tailored garments.
Main uses: trousers – skirts – dresses – jackets and suits.

Heavier and thicker fabrics

Creased finish
84% cotton 16% linen
Low drape, shear and stretch.
A very stable fabric that can be cut in many structured pattern shapes. The dominant stripe weave offers design possibilities.
Main uses: jackets – coats – overgarments.

Knop
60% silk 40% cotton
Medium drape, high shear, medium stretch.
The high shear of the fabric requires very simple shapes or some understructure.
Main uses: jackets – overgarments.

Slub gauze

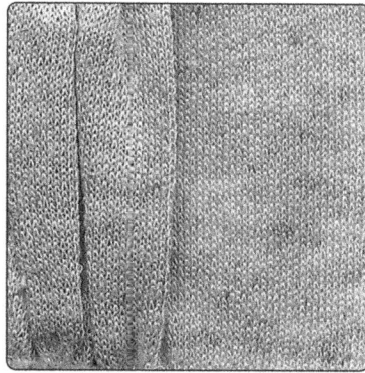

Single jersey (weft knit)

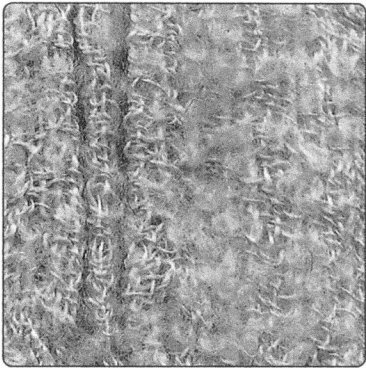

Boucle

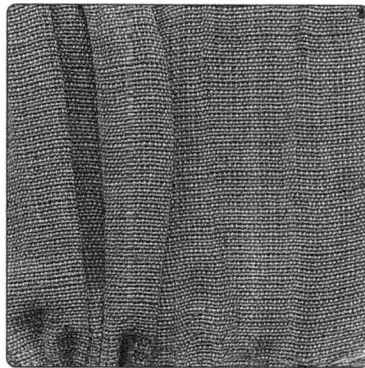

Strong weft weave crinkled finish

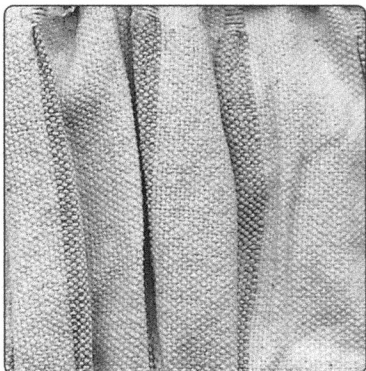

Creased finish

Knop

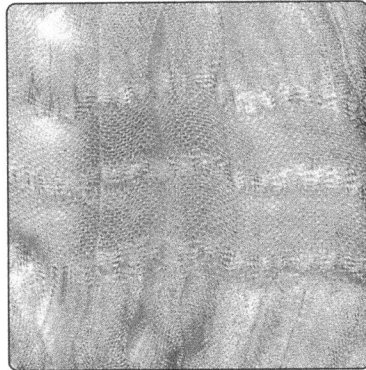

Seersucker

Colorific patterned

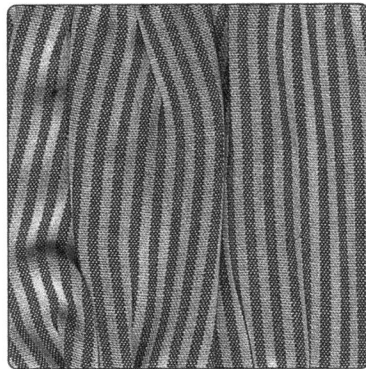

Shirting (lyocell)

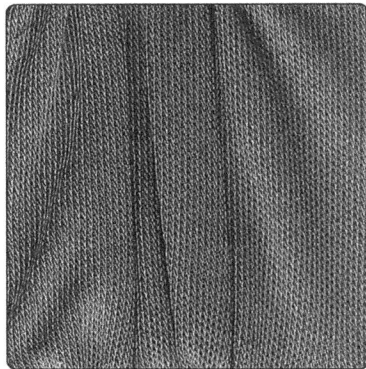

Double jersey (lyocell)

Cord embroidered

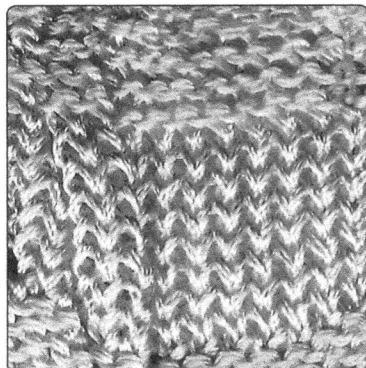

Purl patterned (weft knit)

Man-made fibres and fabrics

Viscose: modal cupro lyocell

Man-made regenerated fibres

Fibre source and fabric production

Viscose rayon: Originally labelled as rayon, it is the oldest of the man-made fibres: cellulose filaments were produced in France in the late nineteenth century. It lost its lead as the primary man-made fibre to polyester, but it is probably the most widely used man-made fibre. Now labelled viscose, new methods of production are now producing fibres that are helping it to regain its popularity, particularly in blends and it is now associated with many quality fabrics.

Viscose rayon is made from regenerated natural sources, cotton linters (waste cotton) or wood pulp. The cellulose is dissolved, forced through a spinneret and wet spun as staple or filament fibre. The shape of the fibre structure can be changed and methods of spinning (for example, inserting crimp and texture) can make the fibre resemble the natural cellulosic fibres, cotton and silk. Modified rayons (modal, cupro) are often blended with cottons to improve the surface of the fabric.

Lyocell (tencel): Lyocell is a fairly new generic 100% cellulosic fibre; its production is made in an environmentally sympathetic process. It has immense strength, yet its 'hand' is soft and lustrous with draping qualities. The strongest cellulosic fibre, it compares well with many polyesters; it also has good washability and moisture absorption. Denim manufacturers, wishing for a soft finish, find it attractive.

Fabric ranges

Viscose: Because of its versatility, fabric ranges produced in viscose are extensive; it was once used mainly in the lower price dress and underwear trade as a cheaper substitute for cotton or silk. Its present versatility means that it is now used across all price ranges and in many different weights, weaves, knits, blends, mixtures and textures. The fabrics produced from cupro fibres have a silk-like appearance, drape well and are mainly of dress weight, whilst fabrics manufactured from modal fibres have some similarity to cotton.

Lyocell: The total fibre production is low but increasing, and the possible ranges are wide. They presently include crepes, twills, poplins, denims, velvets, chambrays and many knitted fabrics.

Illustrated viscose and lyocell fabrics

A selection of fabric samples that can be found within viscose and lyocell fabric ranges.

Light and thin fabrics

Seersucker
High drape, medium shear, low stretch.
This makes it particularly suitable for lightweight garments with fullness. Its weave adds surface texture to a lightweight fabric.
Main uses: nightwear – lingerie – shirts – blouses.

Colorific patterned
High drape, medium shear, low stretch.
The open weave and texture of the fabric limits the pattern shaping of a design unless it is mounted on a supporting fabric.
Main uses: blouses – shirts – dresses.

Medium fabrics

Shirting (lyocell)
High drape, low shear, low stretch.
Lyocell gives a softness and drape and more bulk to a shirting fabric; this widens its range of designs and cutting shapes.
Main uses: blouses – shirts – dresses.

Double jersey (lyocell)
High drape, low shear, high stretch.
A stable useful jersey fabric that can be used in many types of 'jersey cut' garments.
Main uses: skirts – trousers – dresses – sweaters – jackets.

Heavy and thick fabrics

Cord embroidered
High drape and shear, low stretch.
The high shear requires simple pattern pieces or some structure to stabilise the shape.
Main uses: decorative overgarments.

Purl patterned (weft knit)
High drape, low shear, high stretch.
This type of patterned knitwear has its pattern pieces fashioned by fully fashioned knitting machines.
Main uses: sweaters – overgarments.

Acetate diacetate triacetate

Man-made semi-synthetic fibres

Fibre source and fabric production

Acetate, a chemically modified cellulosic fibre, was commercially developed in the 1920s. A lustrous fibre, it became known as 'artificial silk'. Like viscose, the fibre's popularity was undermined by the appearance of polyester, triacetate being the major casualty. Renewed interest in acetate and diacetate has come from the increase in lingerie (body suits and slip dresses) being worn as outerwear and from the tremendous increase in blends.

Acetate, like viscose, is also produced from cotton linters (waste cotton) or wood pulp; however, the cellulose is dissolved in acetic acid and when forced through a spinneret, it is dry spun. Because it is heat-set it is regarded as semi-synthetic; this also means that it is thermo-plastic and can be permanently embossed, crinkled or pleated.

Fabric ranges

Acetate fabric ranges are extensive in woven and knitted fabrics: low absorbency makes it attractive for swim and weather wear; its lustre is used in luxury fabrics (e.g. crepes, velvets and satins); its variability allows it to create novelty fabrics and also crisp embossed fabrics (e.g. taffetas and brocades). It is also widely used for lining fabrics.

Illustrated acetate fabrics

A selection of fabric samples that can be found within an acetate fabric range.

Light and thin fabrics

Faille
Low drape, shear and stretch.
A fabric of great stability with great opportunities for intricate pattern shaping.
Main uses: evening wear – decorative costume.

Spaced leno weave
Low drape, high shear, low stretch.
The high shear of the fabric limits the cut to simple shaping or it requires some understructure.
Main uses: skirts – tops – evening wear.

Medium fabrics

Lurex purl (weft knit)
High drape, low shear, medium stretch.
A fabric that will cut well with pattern drape or fullness.
Main uses: evening wear – tops.

Laquered patterned (weft knit)
High drape, low shear, medium stretch.
A fabric that will also cut well with pattern drape and fullness but has some bulk.
Main uses: tops – dresses – evening wear.

Heavy and thick fabrics

Transfer (weft knit)
High drape, low shear, medium stretch.
A luxury heavy-knit fabric with high sheen. Pattern pieces will be shaped by fully fashioned knitting machinery.
Main uses: sweaters – overgarments.

Heat-set crushed velvet
Medium drape, low shear and stretch.
A very stable luxury fabric. It has wide use, because it can be worked with intricate pattern shapes.
Main uses: skirts – trousers – tops – dresses – evening wear – overgarments.

Faille

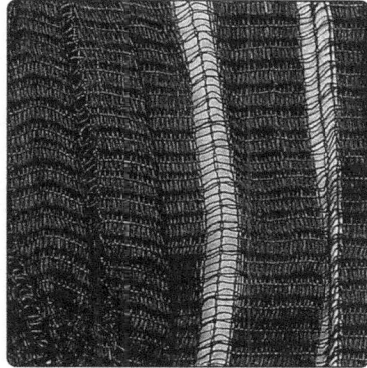

Spaced leno weave

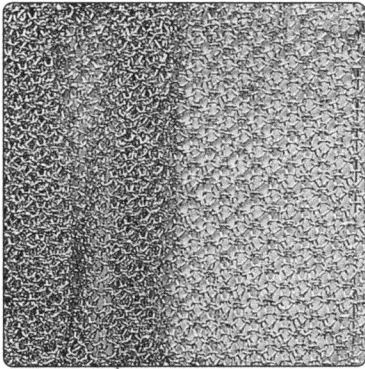

Lurex purl (weft knit)

Laquered patterned (weft knit)

Transfer (weft knit)

Heat-set crushed velvet

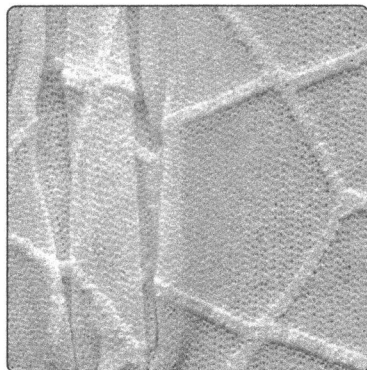

Raschel (warp knit)

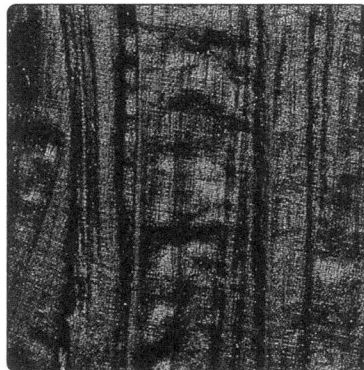

Shreinered finish

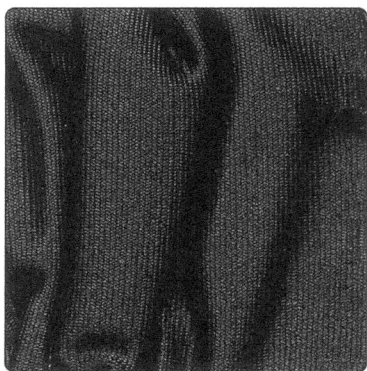

Satin locknit (warp knit)

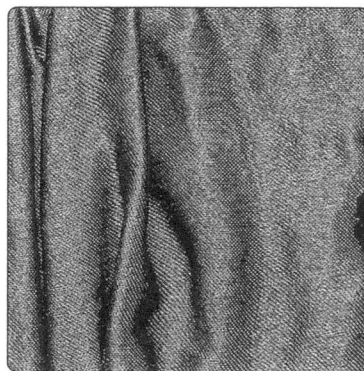

Satin creased finish

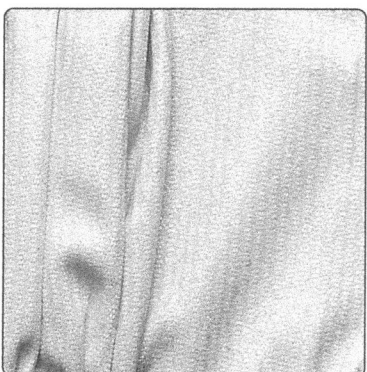

Bedford cord

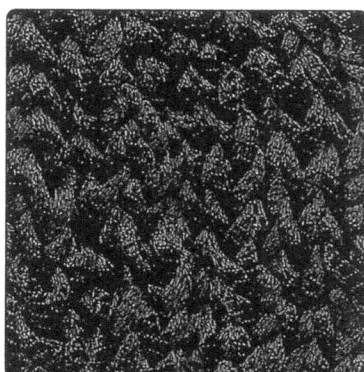

Transfer (weft knit)

Polyamide (nylon)

Man-made synthetic fibres

Fibre source and fabric production

Polyamide (nylon), the first commercial synthetic fibre, went into production in 1939. Nylon's unique strength, stability and fineness gave a truly new dimension to fabrics, particularly in hosiery, underwear and weatherwear. It is still principally identified with these areas of clothing, but the advent of new types of fibre structure, particularly micro-filament yarns, is immensely extending its range.

Coal was the original source for the chemical base of nylon. The fibre is obtained by melt-spinning; molten material is forced through a spinneret and solidifies on cooling, making it very responsive to heat-set finishes. The fibre is produced in filament or staple form. Its important qualities are lightness, strength, easy-care and protection. Polyamide fibres, lighter than cotton or polyester, have the highest strength to weight ratio of any natural or man-made fibre used in clothing manufacture. New polyamide fibres are beginning to be developed from sustainable sources such as castor oil seeds.

Fabric ranges

Nylon is constructed in most fabric forms and blends: delicate sheers and laces; strong, light fabrics for weatherwear and protection, lightweight and bulked fabrics for comfort and athletics; knitted fabrics of wide variations; micro-fibre fabrics with silky or peach-bloom finishes; luxury fabrics, satins, crepes and taffetas, deep pile fabrics and fake furs.

Illustrated polyamide fabrics

A selection of fabric samples that can be found within a polyamide fabric range. There are very few heavy and thick fabrics for clothing produced from polyamide yarns. This is reflected in the list below.

Light and thin fabrics

Raschel (warp knit)
High drape, low shear, high stretch.
A fabric that will cut well with pattern drape or fullness, or for simple lingerie shapes.
Main uses: lingerie – evening wear.

Shreinered finish
Low drape, shear and stretch.
The stability will allow complex pattern shape development.
Main uses: tops – evening wear.

Medium fabrics

Satin locknit (warp knit}
High drape, low shear, medium stretch.
The high drape but stability in a knitted fabric means it is used in much lingerie design.
Main uses: lingerie – tops – evening wear.

Satin creased finish
Medium drape and shear, low stretch.
A fabric of good stability that gives opportunity for cutting creative pattern shapes.
Main uses: tops – dresses – evening wear.

A medium and a heavy thick fabric

Bedford cord
Low drape, shear and stretch.
A fabric weave usually used in tailoring, but its lack of shear means that shaping would have to result from the cut.
Main uses: skirts – trousers – jackets – suits.

Transfer (weft knit)
Medium drape and shear, high stretch.
This type of knitting requires that the pattern is shaped by fully fashioned knitting machines.
Main uses: sweaters – overgarments.

Fibre source and fabric production

Polyester, first produced in the 1940s, is the man-made fibre with the highest production level. Sharing many of the qualities of polyamide, it is cheaper to produce and much research has been focused on its development.

Polyethelene, produced from oil, is used for the chemical base of polyester. The fibre is obtained by melt-spinning; molten material is forced through the spinneret and solidifies on cooling. This makes it very responsive to heat-set finishes. The fibre is produced in filament or staple form. It has many similarities to nylon in its strength, quick drying, heat-setting and easy-care qualities. It also has greater stability than nylon; however, it is not as dense. A new form of polyester (PLA) is now being developed from sustainable sources such as corn starch or tapioca.

Fabric ranges

Polyester fabrics can be found in virtually every type of fabric range: delicate sheers and decorative laces; strong, light fabrics with breathability and wicking for weatherwear and protection, lightweight and bulked fabrics for comfort and athletics; knitted fabrics of wide variations; micro-fibre fabrics with silky or peach-bloom finishes; luxury fabrics, satins, crepes and taffetas, suitings, deep pile fabrics and fake furs. The specific developments are described more fully in Chapter 12.

Illustrated polyester fabrics

A selection of fabric samples that can be found within a polyester fabric range.

Light and thin fabrics

Chiffon
High drape and shear, low stretch.
The delicate weave and high shear requires simple shapes. It is usually cut in quantity or in layers.
Main uses: tops – evening wear – scarves.

Leavers lace
High drape, low shear, medium stretch.
Lace of this complexity requires skilled or specialist cutting.
Main uses: formal and evening wear.

Medium fabrics

Fleece (weft knit)
High drape, low shear, medium stretch.
It has the potential for creative cutting but its appearance may restrict its use to basic shapes.
Main uses: sportswear – casual wear – accessories.

Handmade Torchon lace
Medium drape, high shear and stretch.
Lace of this complexity requires skilled or specialist cutting.
Main uses: formal and evening wear.

Heavy and thick fabrics

Heat embossed velvet
Medium drape and shear, low stretch.
A fabric of good stability that gives opportunity for cutting creative pattern shapes.
Main uses: tops – evening and formal wear – bridal wear.

Ribbon weft insertion
Low drape, medium shear, low stretch.
Fabric of this complex structure requires skilled or specialist cutting.
Main uses: tops – evening and formal wear – bridal wear.

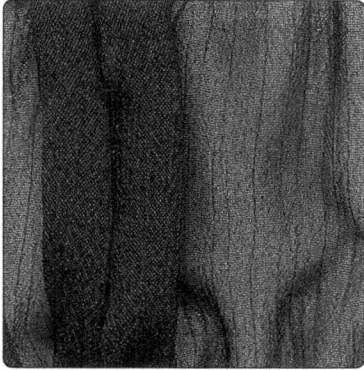

Chiffon

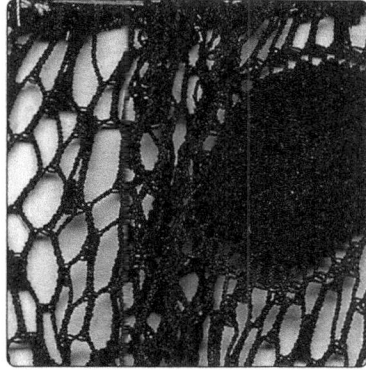

Leavers lace

Fleece (weft knit)

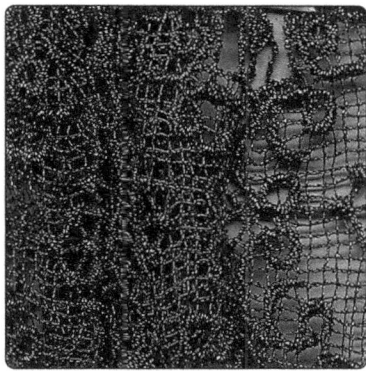

Handmade Torchon lace

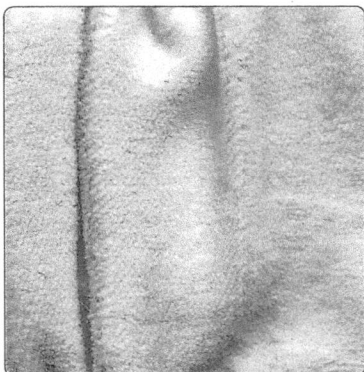

Heat embossed velvet

Ribbon weft insertion

Stripe weave

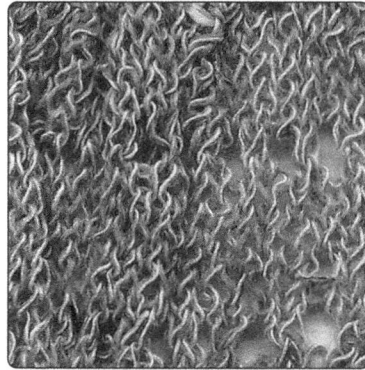

Pointelle (weft knit)

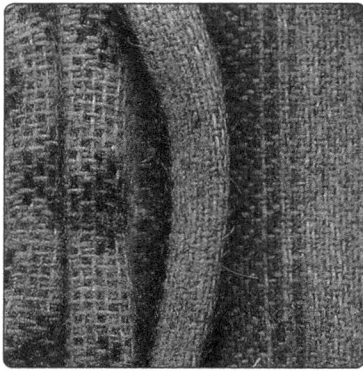

Tapestry

Satin stripe weave

Transfer (weft knit)

High pile warp

Acrylic modacrylic

Man-made synthetic fibres

Fibre source and fabric production

Created from a derivative of natural gas and air, acrylic fibres are dry-spun to produce filament fibres, or wet-spun for staple fibres; the latter form the major part of the production. Acrylic fibres have a good capacity for crimping and are used to produce bulky yarns. The fibres have a low absorption level (and dry easily), good insulation, strength, easy-care and protection qualities. The fibres are heat sensitive and can easily be damaged or distorted, particularly when wet, but new developments have improved its stability.

Commercial production of acrylic fibres began in 1950. Many of the fibres sold today are co-polymers and are placed in the group modacrylics. An inexpensive fibre, it was accepted quickly by the knitting industry. Although it had problems with dyeing, its washability and high bulk yarns made it a fierce competitor for wool. Its use in woven fabrics is principally in blends where it adds softness, texture or bulk. Many of the fabrics illustrated are therefore blends and mixtures. The fibre has also developed a strong market in flocking, particularly in the manufacture of fur fabrics.

Fabric ranges

Lightweight and bulked fabrics for comfort and warmth, knitted fabrics in most weights and in many textures, deep pile fabrics, flocked fabrics and fake furs.

Illustrated acrylic fabrics

A selection of fabric samples that can be found within an acrylic fabric range.

Light and thin fabrics

Stripe weave
100% acrylic
Low drape, high shear and stretch.
An unstable fabric that requires care and structure to hold any body shapes.
Main uses: light overshapes – scarves.

Pointelle (weft knit)
100% acrylic
High drape, low shear and stretch.
This type of patterned knitwear has its pattern pieces fashioned by fully fashioned knitting machines.
Main uses: sweaters – overgarments.

Medium fabrics

Tapestry
60% acrylic 40% wool
Low drape, shear and stretch.
A stable fabric that will hold shape and is used in all types of cutting.
Main uses: dresses – jackets.

Satin stripe weave
38% polyester 35% acrylic 17% viscose 10% wool
Medium drape and shear, low stretch.
A stable fabric that has all types of cutting potential.
Main uses: skirts – trousers – suits – jackets.

Heavy and thick fabrics

Transfer (weft knit)
50% acrylic 50% viscose
High drape, low shear, high stretch.
A textured knitted fabric that if 'cut and sewn' requires simple shapes.
Main uses: sweaters – overgarments.

High pile warp
90% acrylic 10% polyester
Low drape, medium shear and stretch.
The bulk and stability of this fabric requires simple shapes.
Main uses: overgarments.

Elastane

Fibre source and fabric production

The source of elastane is polyurethene. Elastane is always used as an addition to a major fibre to incorporate stretch into the fabric. Although most elastane fibres are produced to stretch to three times their length, they can be extended further. Its greatest characteristic is its ability to recover. It is important because as little as 2% elastane fibre content is enough to change the handle, drape and stretch of a fabric whilst retaining the main characteristics of the dominant fibre. The elastane fibre is rigid when it is sheathed in fibres that are compatible or match the host fibres by core-twisting or core-spinning. The elasticity is regained during the finishing processes. The fabric can have warp-stretch, weft-stretch or two-way stretch (bi-stretch).

DuPont invented the first elastane fibre LYCRA in 1959, but there are now a number of competitors. Used mainly in body form areas of garment production until the last decade, its high extensibility gave a new fashion element to fabrics as well as adding comfort and stability. The growth of knitted fabrics and the use of elastane are bringing about great changes in garment pattern development, (see Chapter 8).

Fabric ranges

Because elastane is embodied in the host fibre, almost any fabric can have added elastane. The main element of choice for its inclusion is the end use and the aesthetic handle that is required. Some designers still believe that the inherent appearance and feel of natural fabrics are diminished when elastane fibres are added.

Illustrated fabrics that include elastane fibres

A selection of fabric samples that show a range of fabrics that contain some elastane fibres.

Light and thin fabrics

Raschel lace (warp knit)
80% acetate 17% polyamide 3% elastane
High drape, shear and stretch.
The elastane stabilises and gives the stretch to delicate fabrics used in body fitting evening and bridal wear garments.
Main uses: lingerie – eveningwear – bridal wear.

Laquered warp
77% polyamide 23% elastane
High drape, low shear, high stretch.
The elastane stabilises the fabric and enables the cutting of more creative body form shapes.
Main uses: eveningwear – bridal wear.

Medium fabrics

Suiting
97% wool 3% elastane
Medium drape, shear and stretch.
The elastane gives the qualities of shape holding and recovery to classic tailored garments.
Main uses: skirts – trousers – dresses – jackets – suits.

Raschel (warp knit)
73% cotton 23% polyamide 4% elastane
Medium drape and shear, high stretch.
The elastane gives extra stability and stretch to enable the cutting of more creative body form shapes.
Main uses: lingerie – eveningwear – bridal wear.

Heavy and thick fabrics

Patterned boucle
95% cotton 5% elastane
Medium drape, low shear, medium stretch.
The elastane gives stability to a type of weave that is usually difficult to pattern shape without structure.
Main uses: coats – overgarments.

Satin faced double cloth
50% polyester 47% cotton 3% elastane
Medium drape, low shear, medium stretch.
The elastane gives stretch to a usually structured fabric and enables a closer body cut.
Main uses: eveningwear – bridal wear.

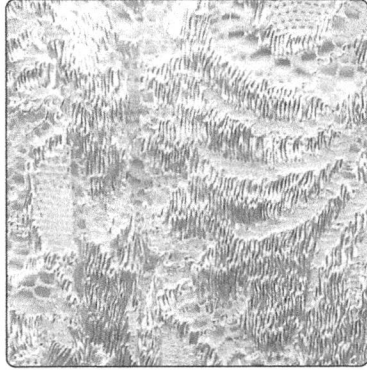

Raschel lace (warp knit)

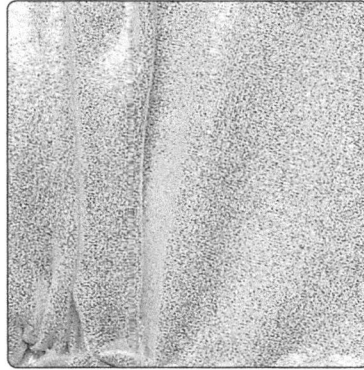

Lacquered warp

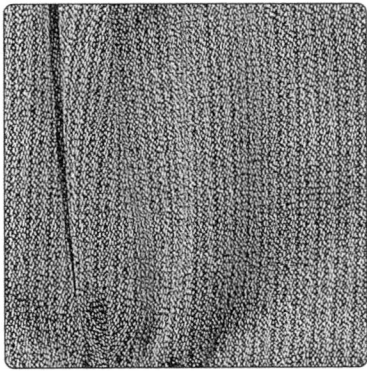

Suiting

Raschel (warp knit)

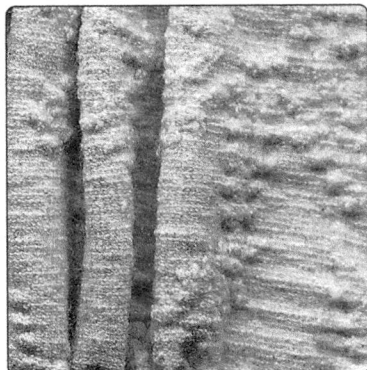

Patterned boucle

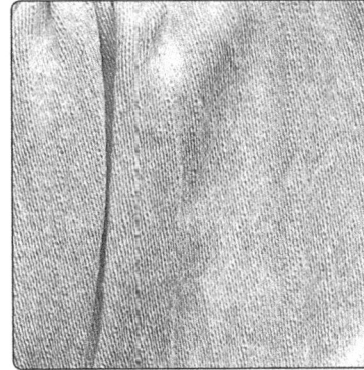

Satin faced double cloth

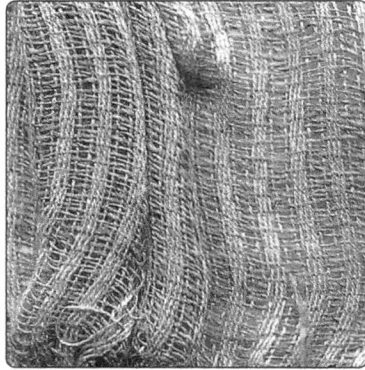

Recycled open stripe

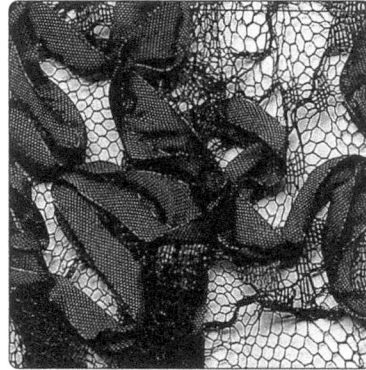

Raschel lace, cornely embroidered

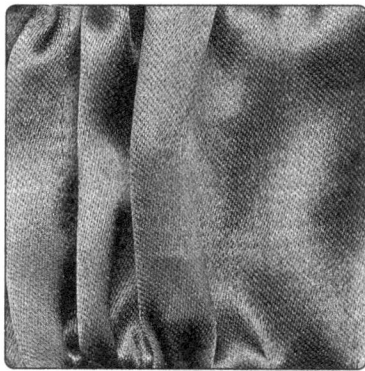

Satin

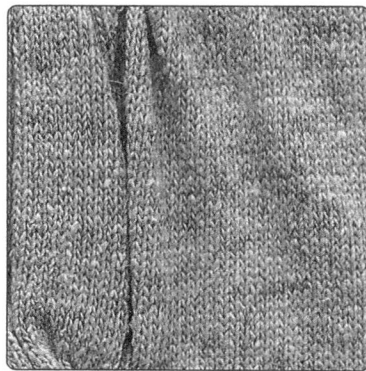

Rib (weft knit)

Recycled tweed

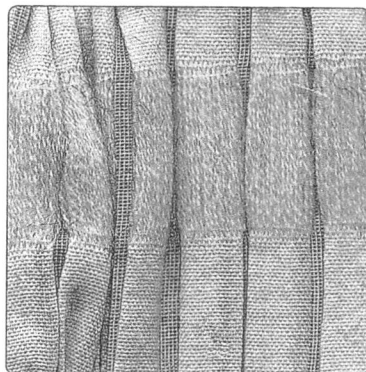

Double cloth

Other fibres and fabrics

Blends and mixtures

Fibre source and fabric production

The blending and mixing of man-made and natural fibres in yarns is common practice. Yarns made of different fibres can be woven or knitted into a fabric. Many high fashion fabrics could only be achieved by the creative marrying of the fibres. Fabrics of unique appearance have been manufactured. Polyamide and polyester give strength and an underlying base to many fabrics, whilst softer and distinctive viscose and acetate fibres offer textural qualities to fabrics. There is now substantial interest in recycling fibres, however the proportions of fibre types in fabrics manufactured from blended or mixed yarns often cannot be

Man-made and natural fibres

guaranteed. The speed of sampling offered by knitting means that many of these new fabrics are knitted. Marrying different man-made fibres or adding man-made fibres to natural fibres creates fabrics that use the special characteristics innate in each of the fibres.

Fabric ranges

The fabric ranges are so great because they cover the span of all fibres. The fabric ranges produced in mixtures and blends can reproduce those fabrics available in the dominant fibre, but also add extra qualities to extend its range by improving the practical qualities and offering new aesthetic possibilities.

Illustrated fabrics – natural and man-made fibres, blends and mixtures

A selection of fabric samples that can be found within a blended and mixed fabric range.

Light and thin fabrics

Recycled open stripe
Cotton linen viscose silk
High drape and shear, low stretch.
The delicate weave and high shear requires simple shapes or layered cutting.
Main uses: dresses – tops – light overgarments – scarves.

Raschel lace, cornely embroidered
80% acetate 20% polyamide
Medium drape, low shear, medium stretch.
Its low shear but high stretch allows it to be used without structure in sleeves or overjackets.
Main uses: formal wear – evening wear – bridal wear.

Medium fabrics

Satin
50% acetate 50% viscose
Medium drape, shear and stretch.
Satin can distort if cut too closely to the body. It is often cut on the cross to maximise the drape.
Main uses: underwear – tops – skirts – blouses – dresses.

Rib (weft knit)
50% cotton 37% mohair 13% viscose
High drape, low shear, high stretch.
A jersey fabric with a textured finish that gives it the bulk to be cut into dresses.
Main uses: sweaters – tops – dresses.

Heavy and thick fabrics

Recycled tweed
Cotton acrylic silk wool
Medium drape, shear and stretch.
Although it appears that the coarse weave would give problems, it is a stable fabric and used mainly for outerwear and the understructure holds the shape.
Main uses: overgarments – jackets – coats.

Double cloth
90% wool 10% polyamide
Low drape, shear and stretch.
A very stable fabric. In double cloth the uneven thickness can restrict some designers but can also give new opportunities for creative cutting.
Main uses: overgarments – jackets – coats.

Coatings and laminates

Coated and laminated fabrics

Many coated and laminated fabrics are created by spraying or bonding plasticised coatings made from polyurethane or polyvinyl choride (PVC) onto fabric backings. Most are impermeable to water and air. Many of the coatings or fabric additions are made from chemicals or processes which are described in Chapter 12.

Fabric ranges

Originally, their main use was for waterproof garments, but as other synthetic breathable membranes have been realised, they are used increasingly for fashionable effects, fantasy clothing, stage costume and particularly accessories. Metal foils sandwiched in plastic film (e.g. Lurex) are used in many decorative fabrics.

Illustrated coated fabrics

The fabrics show the types of effects that can be found within a coated fabric range. Their use, as described above, is limited to structured pattern shapes because most have low shear or stretch, but it is useful to note the drape quality of some coated fabrics.

Light and thin fabrics

Coated net
50% polyamide 50% polyurethene
Medium drape, low shear and stretch.

Metal transfer
90% polyester 10% metal
High drape, low shear and stretch.

Medium fabrics

Coated embossed
70% polyester 30% polyurethene
Low drape, shear and stretch.

Coated hologram
68% viscose 30% polyurethene 2% metal
Medium drape, low shear and stretch.

Heavy and thick fabrics

Coated
68% polyester 32% polyurethene
Low drape, shear and stretch.

Embossed 'snakeskin'
80% polyester 20% polyamide
Medium drape, low shear and stretch.

Coated net

Metal transfer

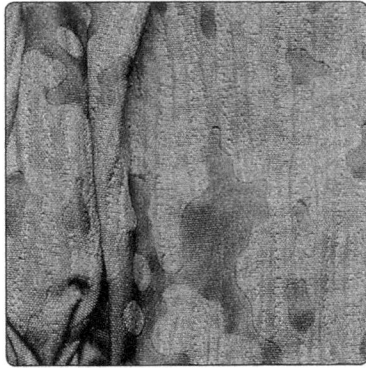

Coated embossed

Coated hologram

Coated

Embossed 'snakeskin'

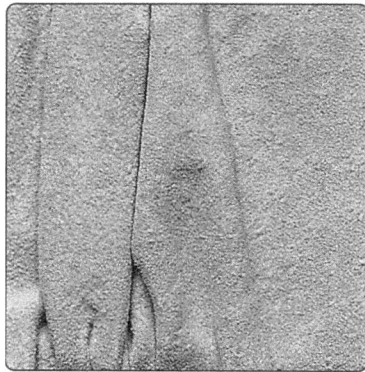

Suede (pig)

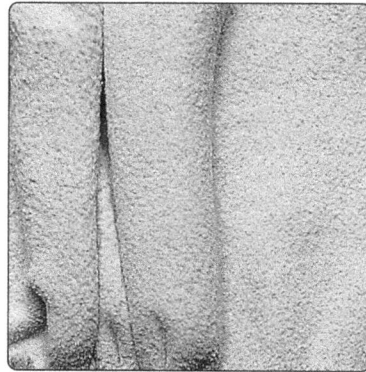

Chamois (calf)

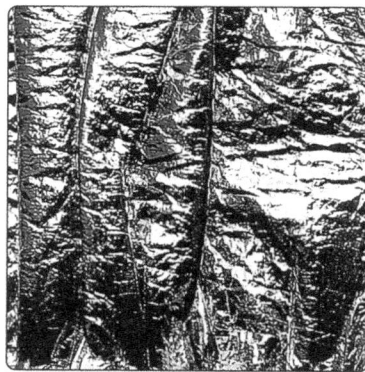

Foil transfer (calf)

Foil embossed (calf)

Leather: fur

Leather

Clothing leather is available in a wide range of weights and handle. Nappa leather can be printed to resemble the skins of exotic animals that are under threat of extinction. Antique, distressed, metallic, printed, decorated and waterproof finishes are now major factors in the market. This is the result of the high fashion focus on shoes, bags and accessories.

Whilst the UK still produces some quality leather in its tanning industry for clothing, shoes and accessories, its production has reduced dramatically. Spain and Italy are still renowned for their quality leathers. However, since environmental restrictions have come into force in Europe, production is being moved to less developed areas of the world where restrictions are more lax.

Fur

A very effective campaign against fur some twenty years ago almost decimated the industry. But there has been a strong revival in the use of fur in high fashion by a number of the couturiers and this has created some conflicts. Their sales are high in very cold countries where fur and sheepskin are essential 'weather' clothing. A competing environmental argument has also been offered that fur is degradable whilst many of the synthetic furs are not.

Working with fur is a very specialised skill, creating larger shapes from small animal skins of varying texture, thickness, handle, and cannot be associated with mainstream pattern cutting and is not covered in this book.

Illustrated leather

Most leathers for clothing are of medium or heavy weight. Some of the leathers shown have special finishes. Leather varies in thickness between skins and also in different areas of the skin. Therefore cutting leather garments is a specialist trade. The structure and handle of most clothing leathers also varies. This requires skilled pattern cutting to develop the shaping and styling that is required by the present fashion market.

Clothing leather

Suede (pig)
A leather of medium weight and thickness with low drape, shear or stretch.
Main uses: skirts – trousers – jackets – coats.

Chamois (calf)
A leather of medium weight, thickness, drape, shear and stretch.
Main uses: jackets – skirts – accessories.

Speciality leather

Foil transfer (calf)
A decorative leather of medium weight and thickness, but low drape, shear and stretch.
Main uses: novelty clothing – accessories.

Foil embossed (calf)
A decorative leather of medium weight and thickness, but low drape, shear and stretch.
Main uses: novelty clothing – accessories.

Fabric names and finishes

Names of major garment fabrics

Fabric glossaries

This glossary appears to be a historical list of mainly traditional fabric names, but it also includes new terms that are becoming standard names to recognise at trade fairs or on fabric swatch samples. Fabric names originate from many sources. The principal source of a fabric name is the name of a weave or knitted structure. However, this name is often used liberally and may incorporate a group of fabrics; for example, woven and knitted fabrics or fabrics in natural and man-made fibres. Other names have historical significance or geographical attachments where a particular fabric trade has flourished. Some fabrics now require a close inspection to decide their structure. Although many new fabric names appear, particularly in the area of man-made fibres, many are trade names that are linked to the fibre source, or simply rather exotic range names given for a fashion fabric, which may disappear after a season.

Lace: Many of the names of lace refer to the places where the lace techniques were created. Only a small selection of popular laces and lace type fabrics are listed. Their placing is only a guide; they will vary with the density of the design, the yarns used and other decorative features. A large amount of fabric that is sold under the heading 'lace' is warp-knitted; for example, raschel lace.

Excellent fabric glossaries can be found in most textile books that give full descriptions of these fabrics. The purpose of this glossary is to give a guide to their weight and thickness. This is very approximate, because fabrics in man-made fibres bearing traditional names (for example, gabardine woven in modal) can be much lighter than the medium weight that one expects in cotton or wool gabardine fabrics.

Light and thin fabrics

AFGHALAINE	HONAN	ORGANDY
ALENÇON (lace)	JAPPE	ORGANZA
ANGORA	JERSEY (SINGLE)	PAPER TAFFETA
BATISTE	LAWN	PEAU DE SOIE
BRODERIE ANGLAISE	LEAVERS (lace)	PLISSÉ
BURNT OUT FABRICS	LENO	POPLIN
CAMBRIC	LININGS	RATINE
CHALLIS	LUREX	SEERSUCKER
CHANTILLY (lace)	MADRAS	SHANTUNG
CHARMEUSE	MAROCAIN	SHIRTINGS
CHEESE CLOTH	MARQUISETTE	SLIPPER SATIN
CHIFFON	MESH	STOCKINETTE
CHINZ	MICROFIBRE	SURAH
CIRÉ	MILANESE	THAI SILK
CRÊPE DE CHINE	MOUFFLON	TRICOT
CREPON	MOUSSELINE	TULLE
CRINOLINE	MUSLIN	VANISSE
DIMITY	NAINSOOK	VOILE
DOTTED SWISS GAUZE	NET (lace)	VALENCIENNES (lace)
FILET (lace)	NINON	VYELLA
HABUTAI	NUNS VEILING	WARP KNITS

Medium fabrics

ALPACA
BAGHEERA
BARATHEA
BARK CRÊPE
BATTENBERG (lace)
BEDFORD CORD
BENGALINE
BOUCLÉ
BROCADE
BUTCHER
CALICO
CANDLEWICK
CASHMERE FABRICS
CAVALRY TWILL
CHEVIOT
CHINO
CLOQUE
CORDUROY (MEDIUM)
COVERT
CRÊPE BACK SATIN
DAMASK
DENIM
DONEGAL TWEED
DRILL
DUCHESSE SATIN

DUNGAREE
DUPION
FACONNE VELVET
FAILLE
FLANNEL
FLANNELETTE
FUSTIAN
GINGHAM
GABARDINE
GROSGRAIN
HAIRCORD
HOMESPUN
HONEYCOMB
IRISH TWEED
JAQUARD FABRICS
JEAN
JERSEY (DOUBLE)
KNOP
LAMÉ
LLAMA FABRICS
METALLIC (lace)
MOLESKIN
OTTOMAN
OXFORD

PANAMA
PANNE VELVET
PERCALE
PIQUÉ
POINTELLES
PVC
REPP
RIBBON (lace)
SAILCLOTH
SATEEN
SATIN
SAXONY
SCHIFFLI (lace)
SERGE
SHARKSKIN
SHETLAND
SUITINGS
TAFFETA
TARTAN
TIE FABRICS
TORCHON (lace)
TUSSORE
WINCEYETTE
WORSTED

Heavy and thick fabrics

ASTRAKAN FABRIC
BEADED (lace)
BEAVER CLOTH
BROADCLOTH
BRUSSELS (lace)
BUCKRAM
BURLAP
CAMEL HAIR FABRICS
CANVAS
CHENILLE
CLUNY (lace)
CORDUROY (HEAVY)
CROCHET
DOUBLE CLOTH
DOUBLE KNIT

DOUBLE PIQUÉ
DUCK
DUFFLE
DUVTEYN
EMBROIDERED (lace)
FELT
FLEECE
FLOCKED FABRICS
FUR FABRICS
FUSTIAN
GUIPURE (lace)
HARRIS TWEED
INTARSIA
LEATHER CLOTH
LODEN CLOTH

MACRAMÉ
MELTON
PLUSH
QUILTED FABRICS
RIB KNITS
SUEDE CLOTH
TAPESTRY
TERRY CLOTH
TICKING
TWEED (HEAVY)
VELOUR
VELVET
VELVETEEN
VICUNA
ZIBELIN

Names of leather and fur

Leather: Terms used to describe the most popular types of leather used in garment production are listed. Leather is a term used when the outer part of the animal or reptile skin has the hair removed and is finished for production; the term suede is used when the inside is finished. Sheepskin and lambskin are skins with the fleeces unshorn. Skins from the same type of animal can vary in weight, thickness, handle and drape, and different areas of the same skin can also vary.

Fur: The name fur refers to the skin when the animal fur or hair has been retained, therefore the skins vary in density and weight in different parts of the skin. This variation occurs mainly in heavier and thicker fur.

Leather names

ANTELOPE	DEERSKIN	PATENT
BUCKSKIN	DOESKIN	PIGSKIN
CABRETTA	GOATSKIN	SHARKSKIN
CALFSKIN	HORSE	SHEEPSKIN
CHAMOIS	KID	SHEERLING
COWHIDE	LAMBSKIN	SNAKESKIN
CROCODILE	NAPPA (LAMB)	SPLIT SKIN

Fur names

ASTRAKHAN	LYNX	RABBIT
BEAVER	MARTEN	RACOON
CALF	MINK	SABLE
CHINCHILLA	MUSKRAT	SEAL
ERMINE	OCELOT	SQUIRREL
FOX	OTTER	
LEOPARD	PERSIAN LAMB	

Names of interlinings

Interlinings are used to give strength, structure and shape to different parts of a garment. A wide range is available and some are listed below. Most of the interlinings used in the garment ready-to-wear industry are fusible, whilst bespoke tailors or couturiers still rely on many of the conventional non-fusible cottons and canvasses (see page 149 for further descriptions).

Interlining names

COTTON PLAIN WEAVE (also fusible)	JERSEY (also fusible)	PERMULL
CRINOLINE	LAWN (also fusible)	SILK-PLAIN WEAVES
DOMETTE (also fusible)	LINEN CANVAS (also fusible)	TARLATAN
FELTS (also fusible)	MULL	WADDING
HAIR CANVAS (also fusible)	NET	WOOL (also fusible)
HOLLAND	NON-WOVENS (also fusible)	
	PAPER TAFFETA	

Fabric finishes and pattern cutting

All fabrics are finished to some degree; the finishes may have a marginal or a very significant effect on the finished fabric. The original characteristics of the fibre or the fabric structure may be suppressed, enhanced or distorted. A particular finish (example: embroidered, flocked, plasticised coated) will make a substantial difference according to the degree of change. The designer has to see and handle the fabric, and in many circumstances has to make an intuitive judgement of the fabric. *The following finishes are the type of examples that can change the character of the fabric and care should be taken when cutting patterns.*

Some finishes are completed after the garment has been constructed. When this is the case, thorough fabric tests have to be made to identify the measure of the changes in the fabric, so that the garment patterns can have the necessary allowances or adjustments made.

Many of the new finishes that are produced by highly technical processes are described in Chapter 12.

Major fabric finishes

BEADED	FLAME PROOFED	RESINATED
BLEACHED	FLOCKED	RUBBERISED
BRUSHED	GLAZED	SANDED
CREASE RESISTANT	GRANITE	SANDWASHED
CREPE	IRIDESCENT	SCHREINERED
CRINKLED	LAMINATED	SEQUINNED
CRUSHED	LAQUERED	SHOWERPROOFED
CURED	MERCERISED	SILICONED
DEVORÉ	METALLIC	SOAPED
DISTRESSED	MILLED	STONEWASHED
DYED	OILED	TEFLONED
EMBOSSED	PATENTED	WADDED
EMBROIDERED	PLASTICISED	WASHED
EMERISED	PLEATED	WATERPROOFED
FADED	PRINTED	WAXED
FELTED	QUILTED	WRINKLED

PART TWO: FABRICS AND SIMPLE PATTERN CUTTING

Chapter 4   Simple 'flat' cutting

Pattern cutting – basic information

(1) There are no seam allowances on the blocks or adaptations.

(2) All the pattern shapes in this book were made from basic geometric shapes or from the blocks in Chapter 14 (all available at wiley.com/go/fabrics).

(3) Light thin lines are used to show original block shapes and dotted lines used where there may be confusion or lines are close together. Heavy lines are used for completed pattern shapes.

(4) The patterns are developed to show how the garment shape was created and illustrate the hang of the fabric. Details of finishes such as waistbands, collars or facings can be found in *Metric Pattern Cutting for Women's Wear*.

(5) Further information on adapting from blocks to patterns is also available in the book *Metric Pattern Cutting for Women's Wear*.

(6) The instructions in the book are to help students understand a sequence of working. Many students learn techniques or principles in isolation; the examples of practice are to help them to develop their own procedures.

Simple 'flat' cutting

This chapter begins by demonstrating how 'flat' geometric shapes, such as the rectangle or triangle, can be transformed into 3D shapes. It also uses variations of the simple kimono block, to demonstrate how basic 'flat' blocks, without bust darting, can envelop the body shape or create their own sculptural forms. This use of simple 'flat' body shapes is often the most effective way of cutting when the designs use complex woven, printed or embroidered fabrics. Simple 'flat' cutting is the basic method used for most designs that use knitted fabric.

Many of the beautiful garments that are displayed in costume museums are based on only small modifications of a basic geometric shape, and so they can be a good basic reference for students.

Very basic shapes

Simple geometric shapes: the bell and the balloon

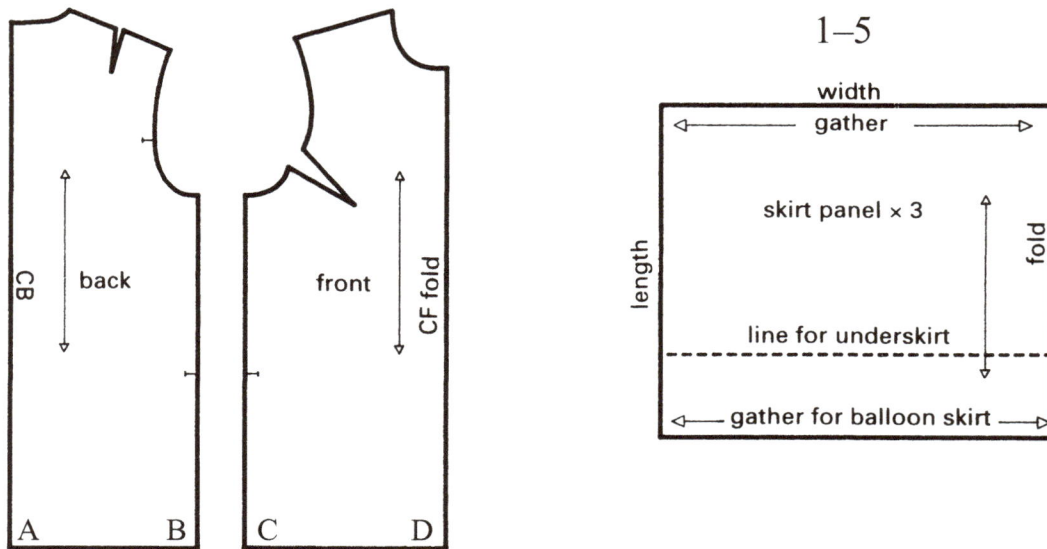

1–5

Garment shapes

Many garment shapes created through flat pattern cutting are based on simple shapes or simple adaptations of the body block. More complex shapes can be achieved by adding, inserting and overlaying shapes. The designer's selection of the fabric is crucial in achieving the finished shape of a garment design. This chapter concentrates on simple 'flat' pattern cutting techniques that create quite different shapes.

The examples of creating basic shapes on this page and pages 63–67 are shown as skirt shapes, attached to a basic body block (shown above) just below the hip level. Although the examples shown can be attached to a band or yoke to create a separate skirt, the techniques can also be used for creating cuffs, frills or overlays, or used to change the shape of basic blocks.

1–3   The bell shape

The bell shape is created by simple rectangles of fabric. It is usual to cut the rectangle with the length running parallel to the warp of the fabric, because it is generally the strongest yarn. This means that the rectangle is cut in panels depending on the width of the cloth.

Occasionally the rectangle is cut in one piece, with the width running down the selvedge of the cloth. This depends on the patterning or structure of the fabric.

Skirt panels Decide the amount of fullness required with reference to the fabric's characteristics.

This example is cut in three panels and is three times the measurement A–B + C–D on the body block. Measure the base of the body block A–B + C–D.
Example = 46 cm
Construct a rectangle:
length = length required.
width = A–B + C–D on the body block = 46 cm

Images 1–3 (opposite page) The images show the effects of cutting bell shapes of the same dimensions in quite different fabrics.

(1) The fabric fullness looks acceptable in a polyamide warp knit; (2) because of its thickness the fabric appears to have reached its limit in polyester suiting; (3) it looks scant when cut in cotton organdy.

4 and 5   The balloon shape

Overlaying the main skirt onto a shortened underskirt creates the balloon shape.

Skirt panels Repeat the instructions as given for the bell shape.
Underskirt The underskirt requires only one panel piece with the length reduced by approx. 10 cm.

Images 4 and 5 (opposite page) They show the effects of cutting bell shapes of the same dimensions in quite different fabrics.

1
*Polyamide
(warp knit)*

2
*Polyester
suiting*

3
*Cotton
organdy*

4
*Polyamide
(warp knit)*

5
Acetate/cotton

1

*Cotton jersey
(weft knit)*

2

*Medium weight
calico*

3

*Hemp/
cotton/wool*

4

Acetate/lurex

5

Sandwashed silk

Simple geometric shapes: the triangle

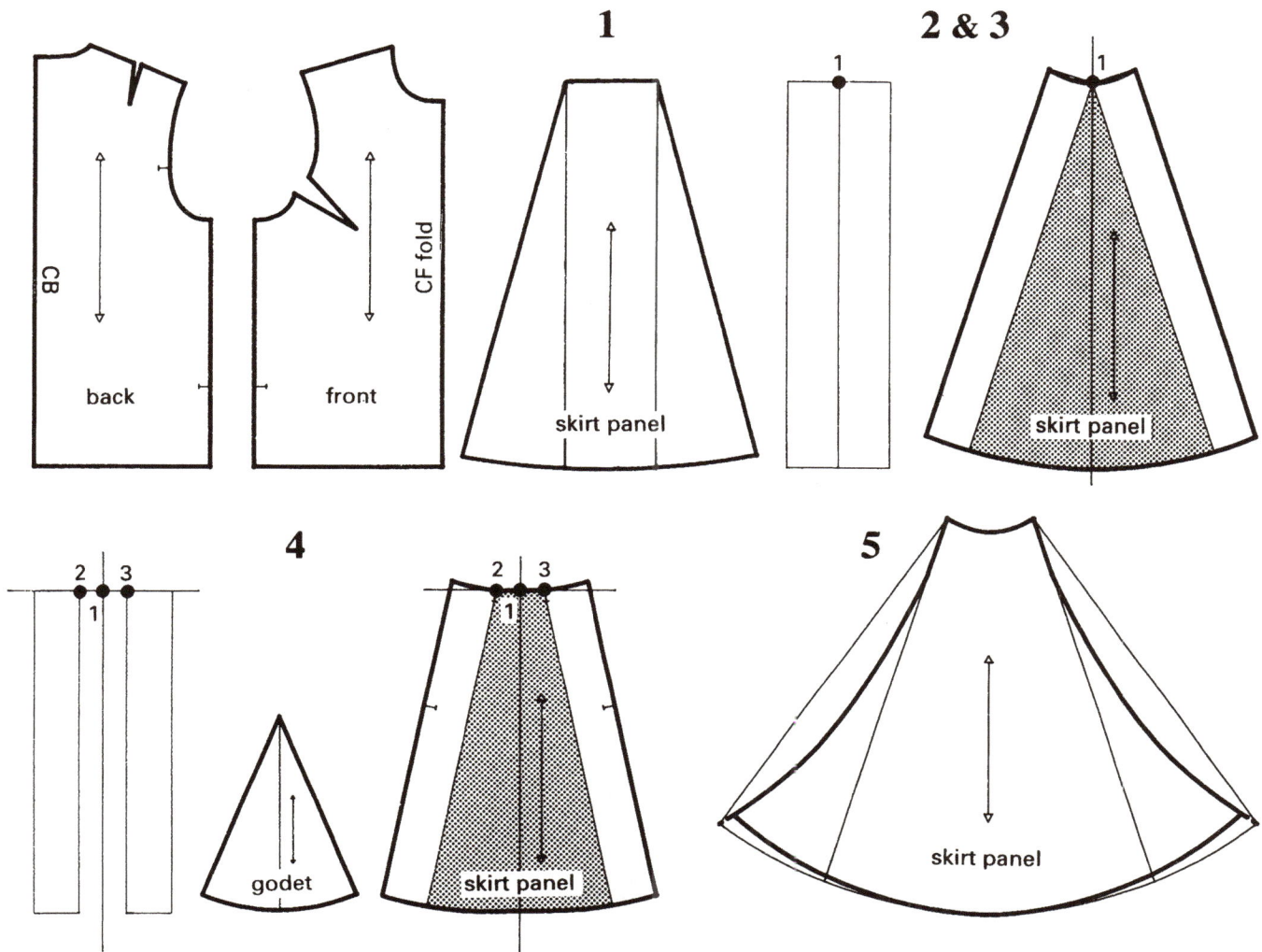

1

2 & 3

skirt panel

skirt panel

4

godet

skirt panel

5

skirt panel

back

front

CB

CF fold

This page shows groups of triangles attached to a basic body shape (size 10) just below the waistline. The full measurement of the lower edge of the bodice is 92 cm.

1   A simple triangle

Skirt sections Decide the number of gores (e.g. 8). Construct a rectangle: length = the required length; width = full measurement of the bodice divided by 8. Add the required amount of flare to the hem. Make the diagonal line the same length as the vertical line. Join lower edge with a curve.

Image 1 (opposite page) This simple triangle works best in knitted fabrics or fabrics with high drape.

2 and 3   A triangle – 'cut and spread'

'Cut and spread' is a basic method of achieving flare.
Skirt sections Construct a rectangle (ref. 1).
Divide into two equal sections. Cut out the pattern and cut the sections almost to the top of the centre line at 1. Lay the sections on the paper.
'Cut and spread' the hemline out the required amount each side of the vertical line (e.g. 10 cm).
Draw in a new waistline and hemline with curves.

Images 2 and 3 (opposite page) The images show how different fabrics create different outlines.

4 and 5   Triangles – tucks and godets

Tucks and godets can change skirt shapes.
Skirt sections Construct a rectangle.
Cut out and divide into two equal sections.
On a separate piece of paper draw a vertical line with a horizontal line at the top, mark point 1.
Mark 2 and 3 (positions of the tucks, e.g. 4 cm).
Lay the sections on the paper at points 2 and 3.
'Cut and spread' the hemline out the required amount each side of the vertical line.
Extra flare (5) Extend width of the flare (e.g. 15 cm); draw panel line in a curve. The curve length depends on the fabric's 'drop', see note image 5 below.
Draw in new waistline and hemlines with curves.
Fold the tucks before cutting out the waistline.
Godets Godet triangles can be inserted in seams.

Images 4 and 5 (opposite page) They show the effects of cutting the pattern shapes in different fabrics. (5) The skirt hemline will drop in high drape fabrics; this has to be remedied by reducing the length of the curve.

Geometric cutting: shaped overlays

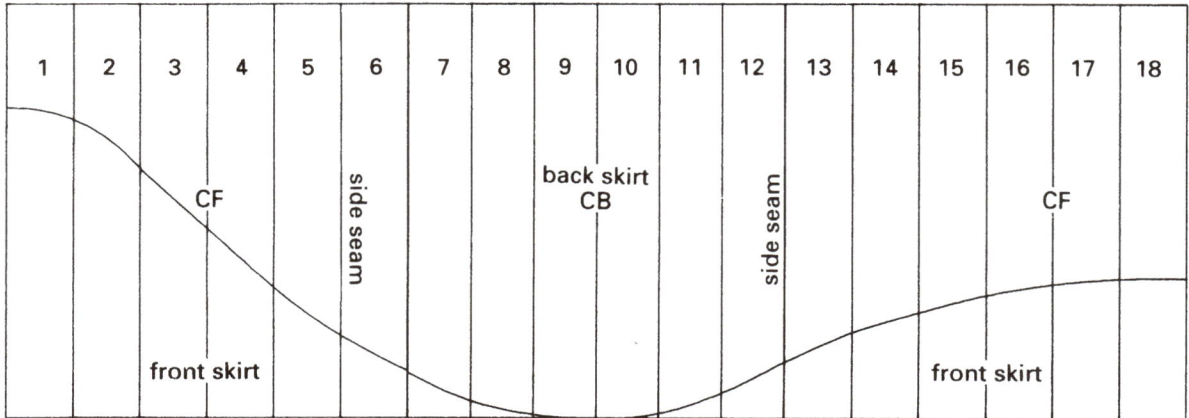

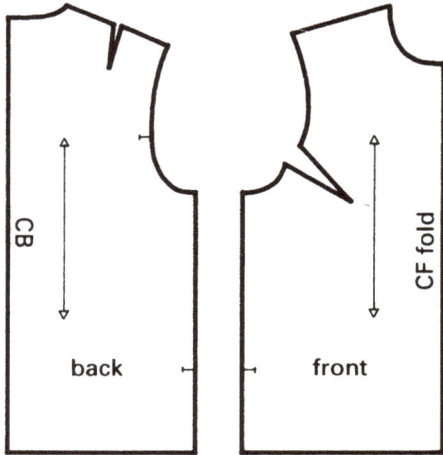

1	2	3	4	5	6	7	8	9	10	11	12	13	14	15	16	17	18

CF

side seam

back skirt
CB

side seam

CF

front skirt

front skirt

1–3   Shaped 'cut and spread'

Skirt section   Draw a rectangle; width = $1\frac{1}{2}$ times the full measurement of lower edge of the body pieces (92 cm). Length = centre back length.
Divide the rectangle into three sections. Mark side seams.
Mark the centre section, back; the side sections, front. Mark side seams.
Draw a shaped line as shown, touching the centre back hem.
Divide the sections into 18 parts. Cut out the pattern piece.
Cut up the vertical lines and 'cut and spread' the hem unevenly.

CB

CF fold

back

front

1–3

CF

CF

front skirt

front skirt

side line

side line

1

CB

back skirt

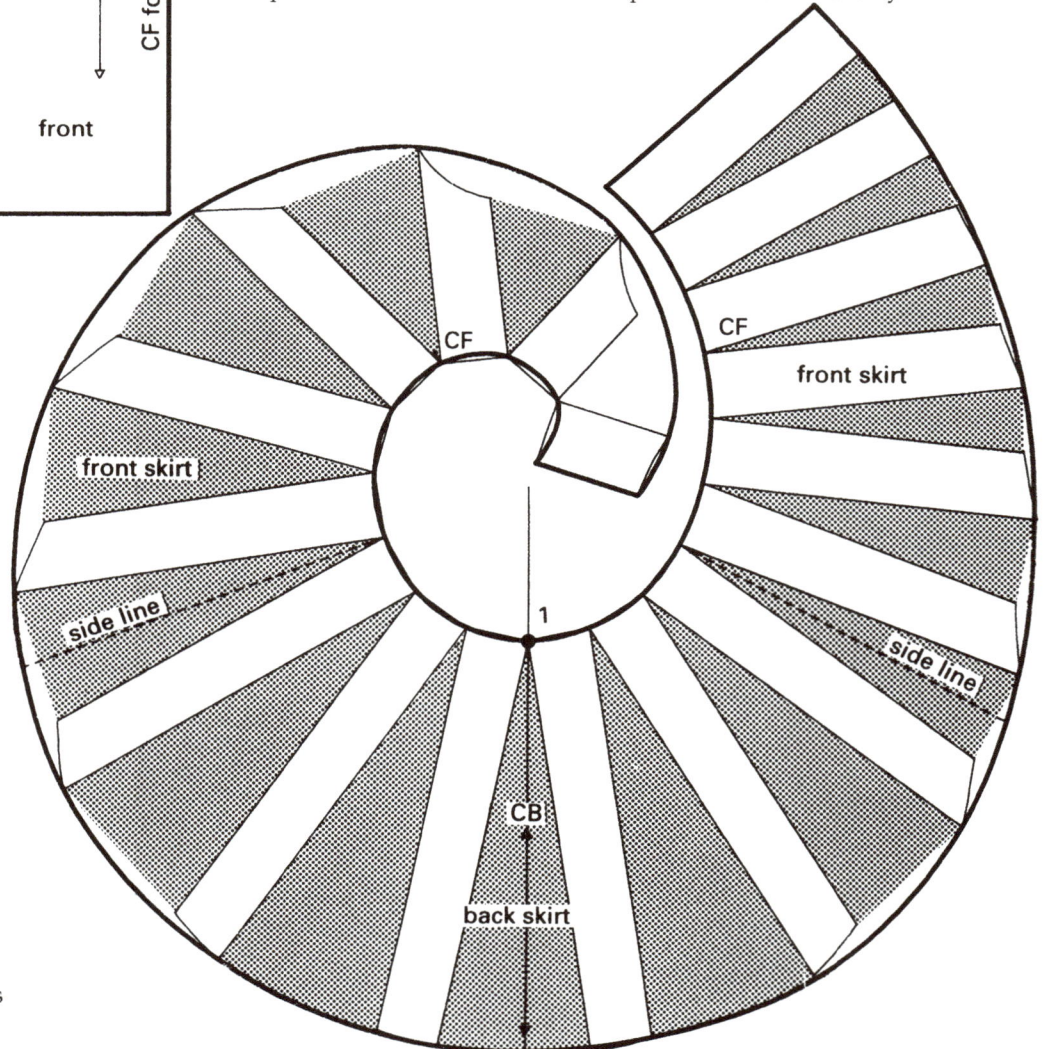

Different shapes can be made by cutting and spreading the hem of a shaped pattern piece, evenly or unevenly.

Images 1 and 2
(opposite page)
The images show how the different fabrics create very different shapes.

1

Silk georgette

2

Acetate/lurex

3

Fabric

3   *Silk velvet (devore)/silk crepe*
The main fabric has medium drape, but low shear and stretch. The fabric has dual thickness; the devore (burnt out areas) are very thin and delicate. This delicacy means that a sympathetic fabric, silk crepe, is needed to give some support to the shape.

Pattern cutting

The uneven texture of the fabric makes the layered cut very attractive. The design on the model uses the pattern shown on the stands, but has a lowered neckline. Because the main fabric is delicate and see-through in areas, the garment is cut with an underbody and simple underskirt in silk crepe.

1

2

Fabric

1 Hemp /cotton/viscose
The fabric is of medium weight, thickness, drape, shear
and stretch giving structure to the trousers.

2 Polyester micro-fibre
A lightweight, thin fabric with high drape and sheer
but low stretch. An ideal fabric for draped designs.

Pattern cutting

A simple geometric base can create many different
trouser shapes. The use of the 'cut and spread'
technique can give dramatic shapes. Note that the first
fabric gives the pants the appearance of a divided skirt,
but the second fabric creates obvious wide trousers.

Geometric cutting: trousers

1&2

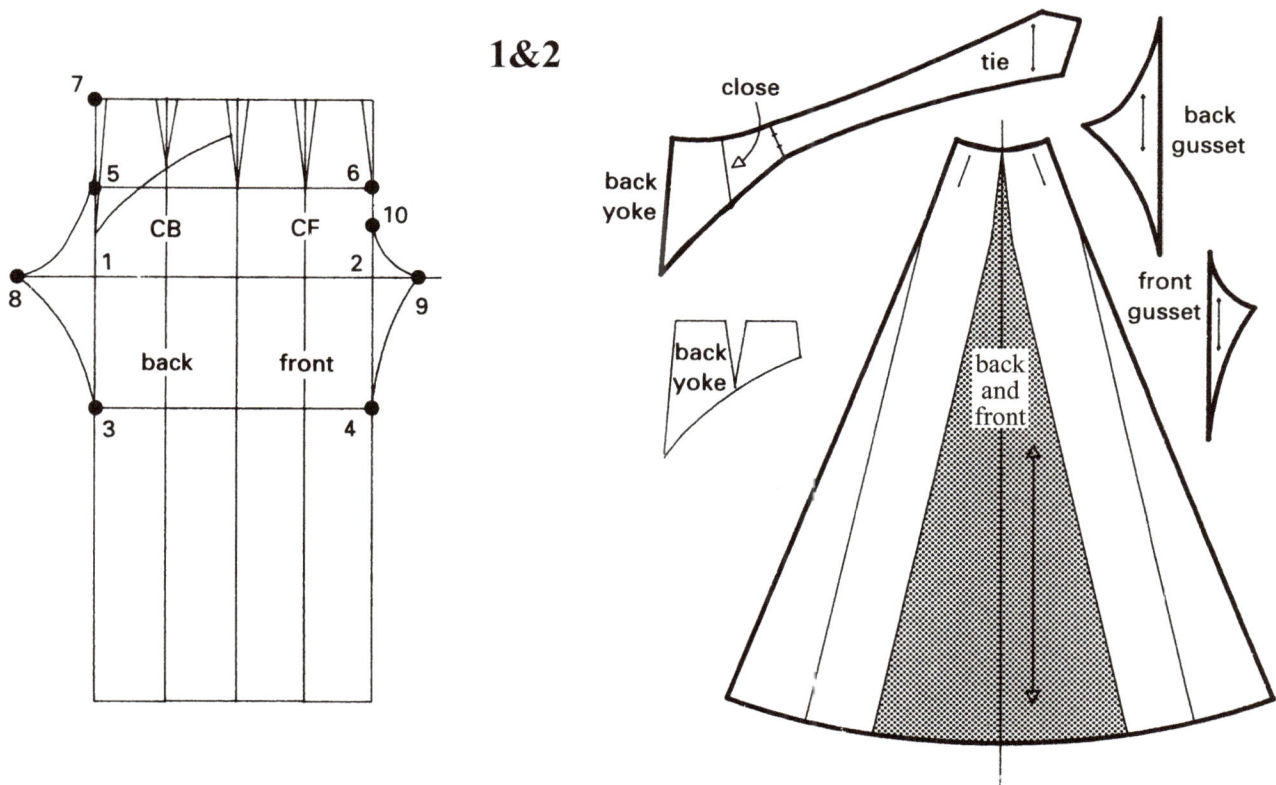

1 and 2   Trousers: geometric shape

The trousers shown on the opposite page are cut from the same pattern in different fabrics. They are cut in four equal panels; the top back yoke is overlaid onto the back panel. The tie on the extended yoke is threaded through slits in the front panel.

Main sections Construct a rectangle:
length = length required;
width = ½ hip meas. plus 5 cm.
Draw a low hipline line approx. 30 cm from the top edge.
Draw a low crutch line 50 cm from the top edge.
Divide into back and front sections.
Draw a vertical line through each section.
Mark points 1, 2, 3, 4, 5, 6 on the horizontal lines
1–8 = ½ the width of the back section;

2–9 = ½ 1–8 plus 1 cm.
10 is midway between 2–6; 5 is midway between 1–7.
Draw in gusset shapes as shown.
Construct darts on each vertical line:
length = 13 cm; width = 3 cm.
Shape in CF and CB 1.5 cm.
Draw in back overlaid yoke line.
Trace off overlaid yoke section. Cut out back, front and gusset sections.
Add approx. 10 cm flare to hemline of each side of back and front trouser sections. Join to hip line.
Cut and spread the centre line of front and back sections the amount required.
Overlaid yoke with tie Close back dart.
Extend the yoke with a shaped tie, length approx. 50 cm.

Simple 'flat' body shapes

Geometric cutting: the basic grid

Many geometric shapes are used in a simple form for loosely woven fabrics with high shear or drape.

1   Circular shapes

Loose fitting body shapes can be cut by basic measurements. The basic circular shape can be used as a base for all types of garments; for example, evening wraps, ponchos and capes.

The image shows the garment cut in two simple pieces.

Body sections Construct a quarter circle of the required length. Bisect the quarter circle.

Draw in front neckline.

Draw in the hemline to the bisecting line at the length required. Shape the hem line upwards towards the side seam to prevent fabric 'drop'.

Mark sleeve length required on the bisecting line.

Draw in the sleeve hemline parallel to the hem; but at half the distance, square up to the top line.

Mark the underarm slit.

The basic grid

The basic grid (ref. page 195) marks important points and lines of the body; for example, neck, shoulder line and waistline. It allows freedom for the designer to create innovative loose fitting shapes.

The simple kimono blocks are drafted from the basic grid.

2   Geometric shaping

Trace off the rectangular simple kimono block (ref. page 195).

Widen the body sections at the side seam.

Lengthen the body the amount required.

Extend the sleeves to the extended length required.

Draw a narrow rectangle at the base; width approx. 12 cm, length ½ distance to side seam.

Join the sleeve rectangle to a point below the waist.

Draw in any style lines (e.g. yoke lines).

Trace off all pattern sections.

Extend the yoke line on the back to create gathers.

Fabric

1 Silk/cotton
The heavy fabric is of medium thickness, drape and stretch; its high shear requires simple shape cutting.

2 Polyester micro-fibre
A lightweight, thin fabric with little stretch. The high shear and drape create the soft folds in the design.

Pattern cutting

Constructed geometric shapes or simple patterns, developed from the basic grid, work well with loosely woven fabrics with high shear or drape. Design 2 demonstrates how a simple wide shape can work if the correct fabric is selected. The fabric is held in position by the yokes and the tight lower sleeves.

1

Fabric

1 Polyester (warp knit)
A lightweight, thin fabric. Although it has medium shear and stretch, it has very high drape. This is essential for the design.

Pattern cutting

The simple kimono blocks are very useful for constructing patterns for designs using knitted fabrics. The model illustrates the subtle figure shaping that can be achieved, when using a simple pattern. The design's success relies on the fabric choice and the use of ties.

The simple kimono block: angled sleeve

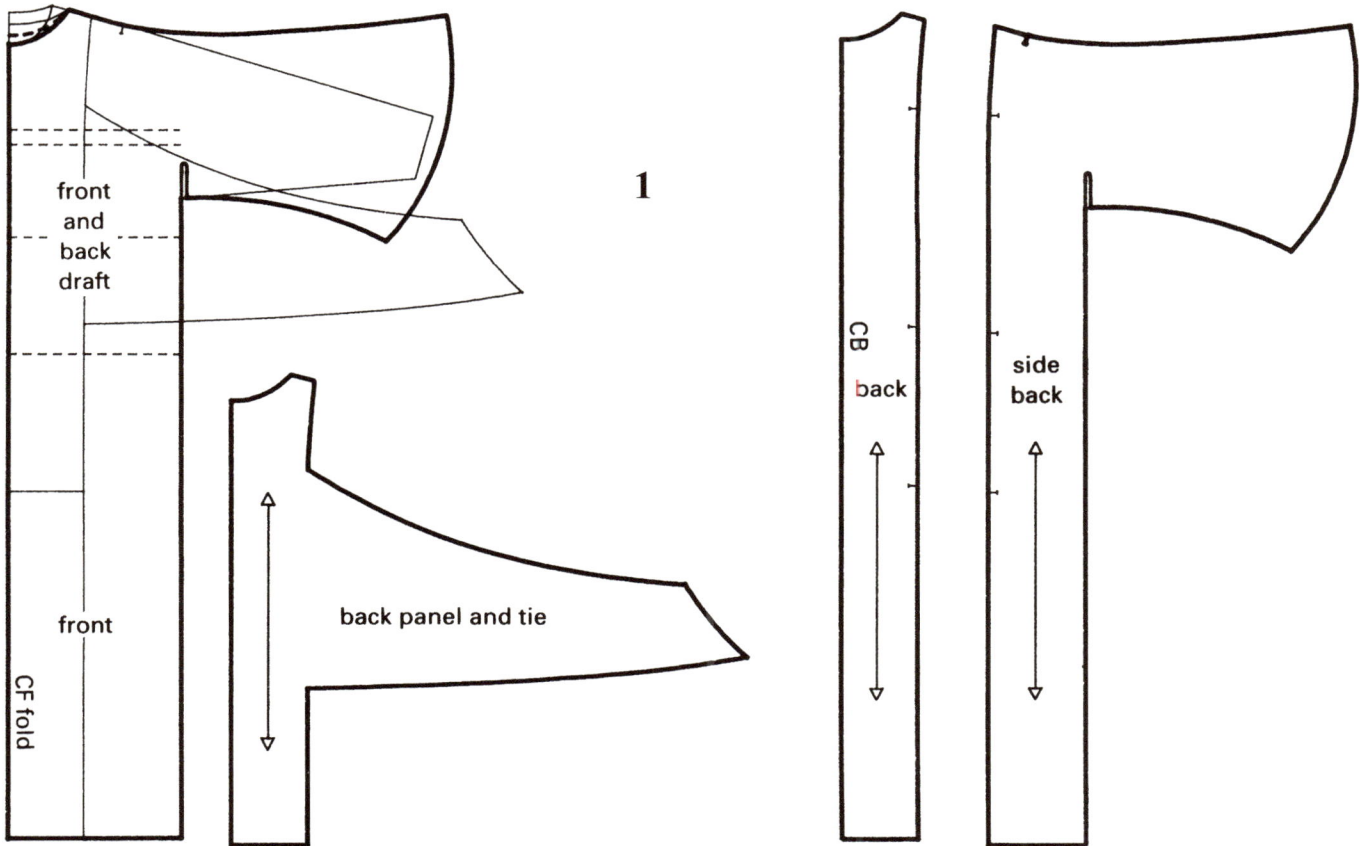

Labels in diagram: front and back draft, front, CF fold, back panel and tie, CB back, side back

1

The simple kimono with angled sleeve

The simple kimono block with the angled sleeve option is the most popular kimono option for simple flat shapes. The following pages demonstrate some of its possibilities to create quite different designs.

Note: It is a common practice in companies using mainly 'flat' cutting on CAD systems, to have back and front pieces facing the same way. This practice reduces the number of grading points needed on the pattern pieces when producing a size range.

1   Simple kimono: wide sleeve

The design has a back over panel with a tie.
Trace off the simple kimono block with the angled sleeve option (ref. page 195).
Body sections Draw in a lowered neckline.
Lengthen the body the amount required.
Draw in a wide sleeve shape as required. The sleeve hem is shaped up at the inside seam to prevent 'drop'.
Mark a slit at the underarm.
Draw in the back style lines and the tie.
Front Trace round the front pattern.
Back panels Trace off the centre back and side back panels.
Tie Trace off the back over panel with tie.

The simple kimono block: widened sleeve angle

1

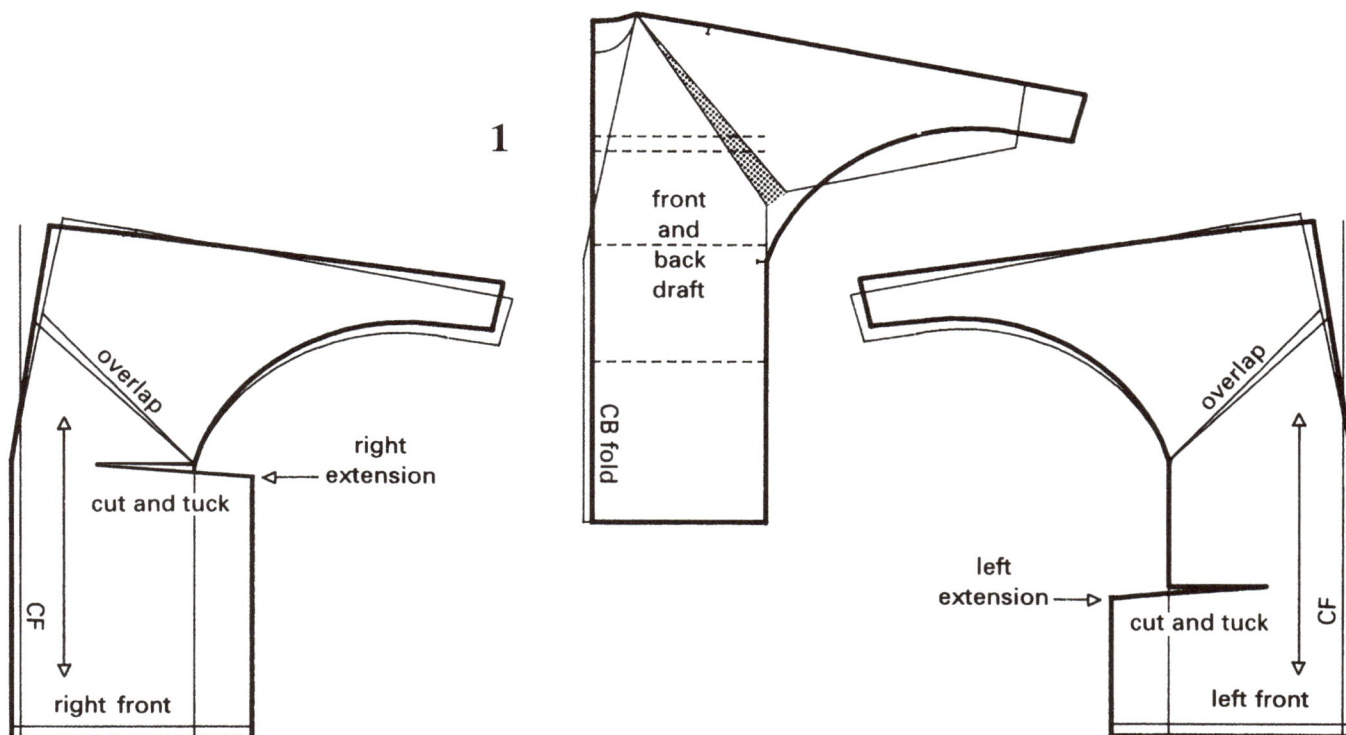

Widening the sleeve angle

Widening the sleeve angle creates extra movement for the arm. It works best with high drape fabrics.

1 Simple kimono: narrowed sleeve

The front of the garment illustrated is cut and tucked at different levels to give a changed outline.
Trace off the simple kimono block with the angled sleeve (ref. page 195).
Body sections Lengthen the body amount required.
Draw a line from the underarm to the neck point, and open the required amount.
Extend the sleeves. Narrow at the wrist.
Join to the waist with a curve as shown.
Add a buttonstand to the centre front line; draw in front neckline.

Back Trace off back section (heavy black line).
Front Trace off front section.
Draw a line from the neckline to the waistline; cut and overlap 1–2 cm (to prevent neck sag).
Lengthen front 2 cm.
Trace off and mirror left front.
Add an 8 cm side seam extension from the waist of the right front, midway on the side seam on the left front.
Dart the side seam 2 cm at each extension.

Note The front patterns are shown as if they were laid on the wrong side of the fabric as required for manufacturing production.

1

Fabric

1   *Polyester/polyurethene (warp knit)*
A lightweight, thin fabric. Although the polyurethene gives it more structure than the fabric on the previous page, it still has high drape. This is essential for the design.

Pattern cutting

The wider sleeve angle creates dramatic outlines to a design and extra arm movement. The high drape fabric needed for the design is also required for the extended 'ruffled' sleeves.

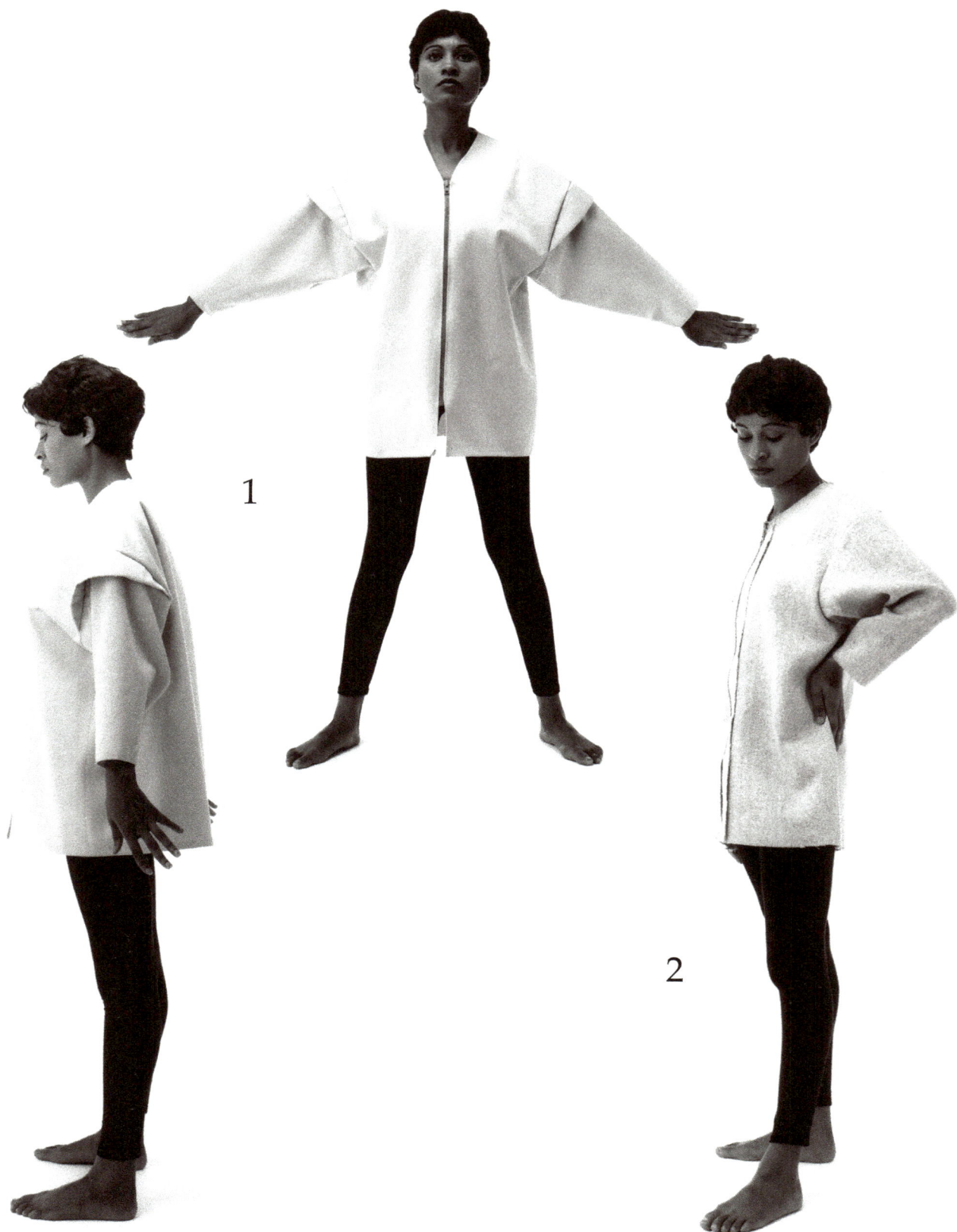

1

2

Fabric

1   Polyester
A fabric of medium weight, thickness, shear and drape but low stretch. A very stable fabric.

2   Hemp/cotton/wool
The thick fabric is of medium weight, drape and stretch, but high shear.

Pattern cutting

Design 1 illustrates how stable fabrics can produce defined shapes, folds and angles. The gusset insertion adds to the defined geometric cut.

Design 2 uses the dolman sleeve (diagram page 78) with subtle body shaping at the waist and sleeves. Although a thicker fabric is used, it creates a different slimmer profile.

The simple kimono block: gussets

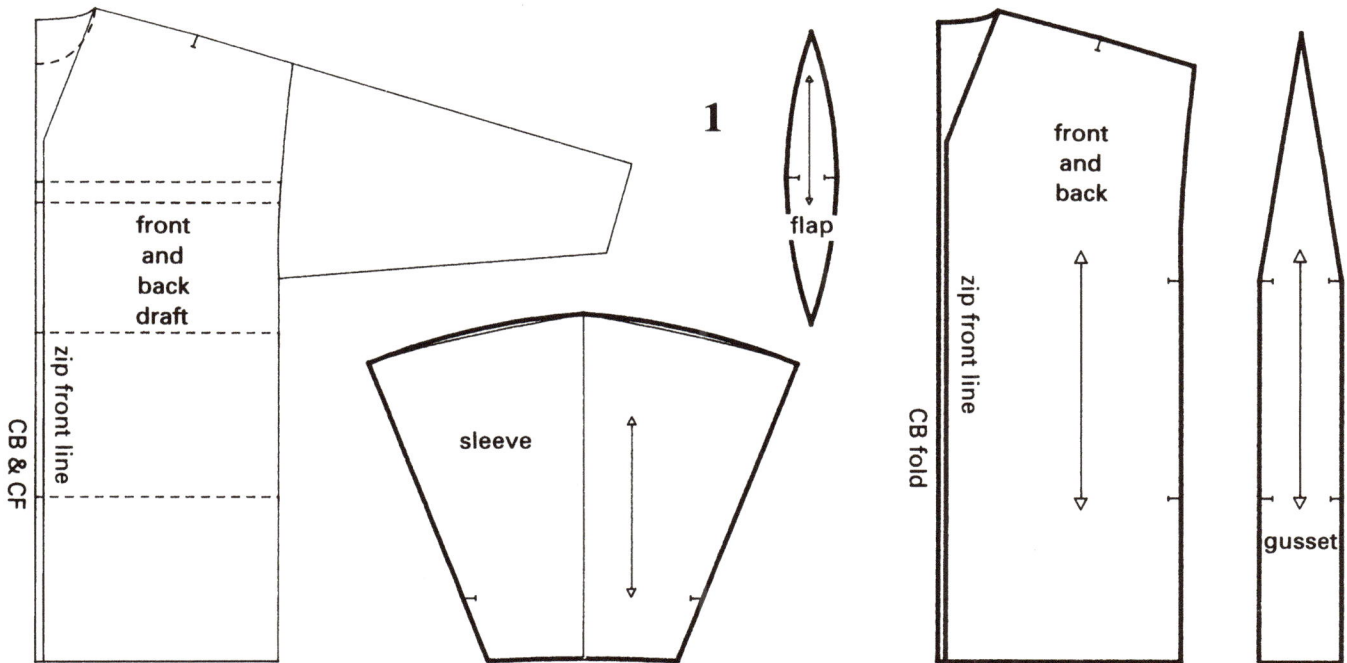

Gussets

Gussets are pieces that are inserted into flat shapes to give extra movement, particularly where the fabric has little stretch. They can also be used to create a 3D boxy shape using structured fabrics, as shown by the front and side views of image 1 on the opposite page.

1   Simple kimono: side seam gusset

A simple flat design can be changed into a box shape.
Body sections Trace round the simple kimono block with angled sleeve to length required (ref. page 195).
Draw in the zip front line; width = ½ width of zip teeth.
Draw in front 'V' neckline to zip line.
Draw in armhole line.
Trace off separate back, front and sleeve pattern sections.

Sleeve Draw a soft curve at the sleeve head.
Gusset Construct a rectangle:
length = side seam length, width = approx. 10 cm.
Extend the rectangle a point (the length must measure less than underarm seam).
Flap Construct any shape of flap as required.

Note 1 The instructions for the Simple kimono: Dolman sleeve are given on the following page.

Note 2 It is a common practice in companies using mainly 'flat' cutting on CAD systems to have back and front pieces facing the same way. This practice reduces the number of grading points needed on the pattern pieces when producing a size range.

The simple kimono block: dolman sleeve

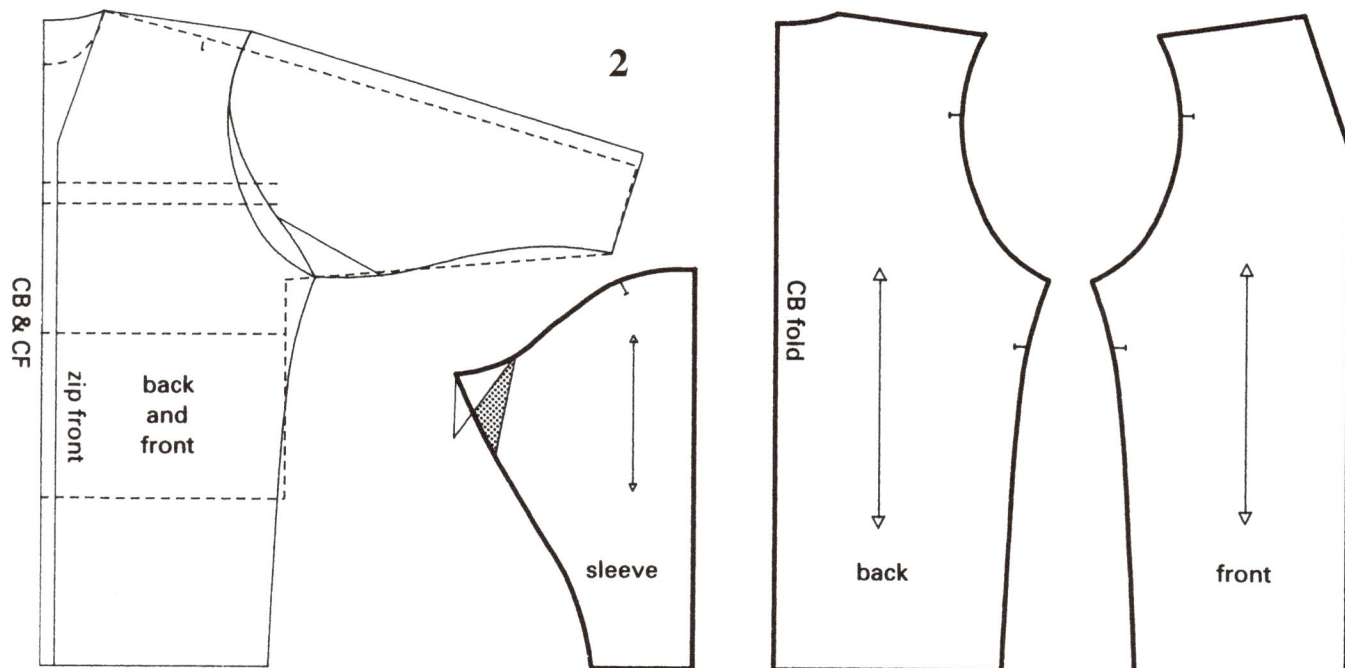

Dolman sleeves

This simple shape is often known as the 'dolman sleeve' and provides the base for many casual jacket designs. The gusseting ease is inserted into the sleeve seam to allow for extra movement.

The process works best in fabrics with some drape qualities. It is useful for thick fabrics because some of the bulk is removed from the armhole area. Because of its simplicity, it is often used for weatherwear with over panels. When a structured fabric is used, stiff folds can appear in the armhole area.

2   Simple kimono block: dolman sleeve

Body sections Trace round the simple kimono block with angled sleeve to length required (ref. page 195).

Lengthen the body section the amount required.
Raise the shoulder and widen the body at the underarm; narrow slightly at the hemline.
Draw a curved side seam.
Draw in the zip front line; width = ½ width of zip teeth.
Draw in front 'V' neckline to zip line.
Draw in a curved armhole line.
Draw in sleeve line making a shaped dart ¾ the length of the seam, approx. 2 cm wide.
Draw a gusset line from the armhole (approx. ¼ of armhole length) to approx. 7 cm down the sleeve seam.
Trace off the pattern sections.
Sleeve Open the gusset line approx 4 cm: re-draw underarm seam.
Draw a new sleeve head line with a soft curve.

PART TWO: FABRICS AND SIMPLE PATTERN CUTTING

Chapter 5 Simple 'form' cutting

Simple 'form' cutting
The bust and shoulder darts

Darts

Blocks that do not include bust darts are mainly used for styles that do not fit the body or where high drape or stretch fabrics are used. When more body fitting designs are created in other fabrics, bust darting becomes necessary. Examples of this were shown in Chapter 1 (ref. page 12).

The bust dart creates the shaping for the bust area, the shoulder dart for the prominence of the shoulder blades.

The dart position can be moved to different places. For example:
1. It can be moved temporarily, if it gets in the way of drawing a style line;
2. It can be moved permanently if it is required in a new position;
3. It can be integrated into a seam.

Many blocks and styles eliminate the back shoulder dart. This is done by substituting ease in the back shoulder length.

The examples in this chapter show the different role that the bust dart can play in simple designs. It demonstrates how the bust dart creates a balanced bodice for attached skirts or a balanced shift shape for the insertion of other pattern pieces. The bust dart can also be integrated into flared shapes.

1 Transferring the bust dart position

Trace round the front bodice block.
Draw a line from the centre shoulder to the bust point.

Cut up the line, close the original dart and secure with tape. The bust dart is now in the centre shoulder.
Transfer the dart to other positions using the same method.

2 Transferring the bust dart to style lines

Trace round the required bodice block.
If the dart interferes with the style line, transfer it to a new position.
Draw in the style line; the style line should be within a 5cm circle around the bust point or back dart point, if the conventional shaping needs to be retained.
Move the dart point to the style line.
Cut up the style line. Close the dart; the dart will become integrated into the style line.

3 Transferring the shoulder dart to ease or a style line

(a) Mark point 1 at the neck point.
Mark point 2, 0.5cm in from the armhole edge along the shoulder line. Draw a line from 1–2.
Draw in a new armhole line from 2 to armhole notch; 0.5cm ease will remain in the shoulder line.
(b) Draw in the yoke line.
Cut along the yoke line.
Close the shoulder dart; the dart will become integrated into the style line.

Transferring the bust and shoulder darts

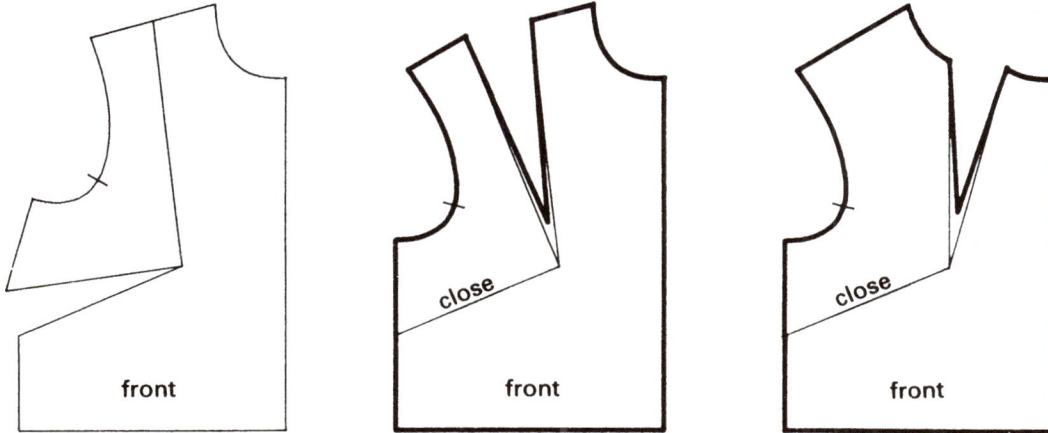

1 Transferring the bust dart position

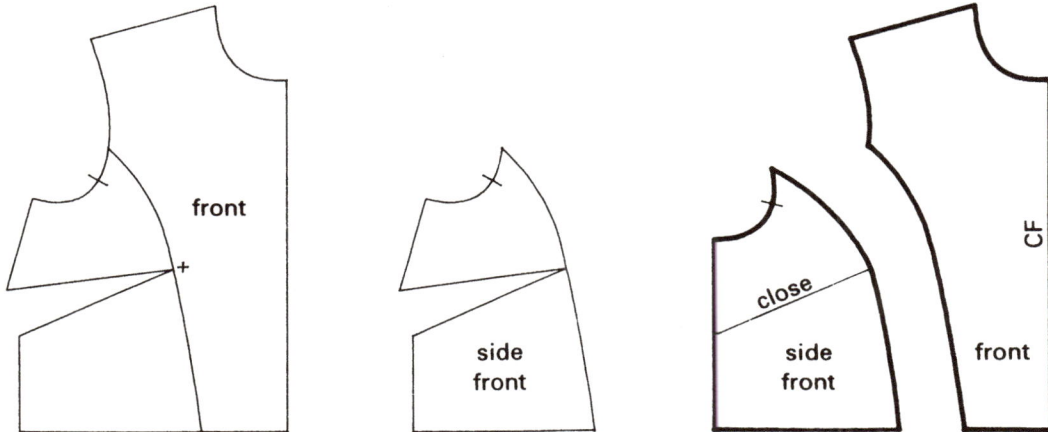

front

close
front

close
front

2 Transferring the bust dart to style lines

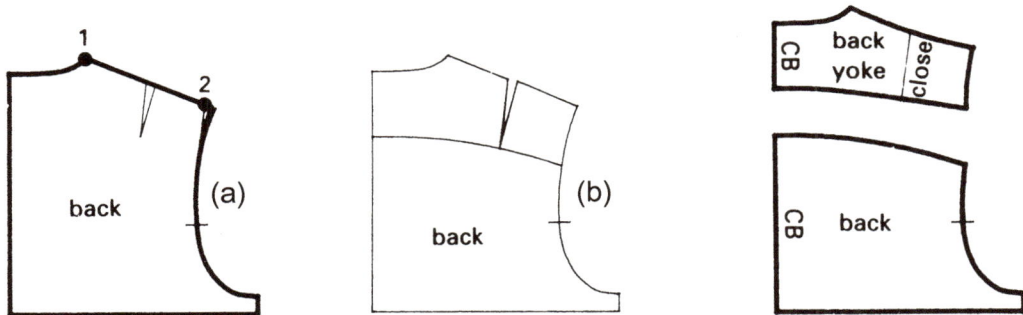

front

side
front

close
side
front

CF
front

3 Transferring the shoulder dart to ease or a style line

1

2

back

(a)

back

(b)

CB
back
yoke
close

CB
back

Darts and the balanced body shape

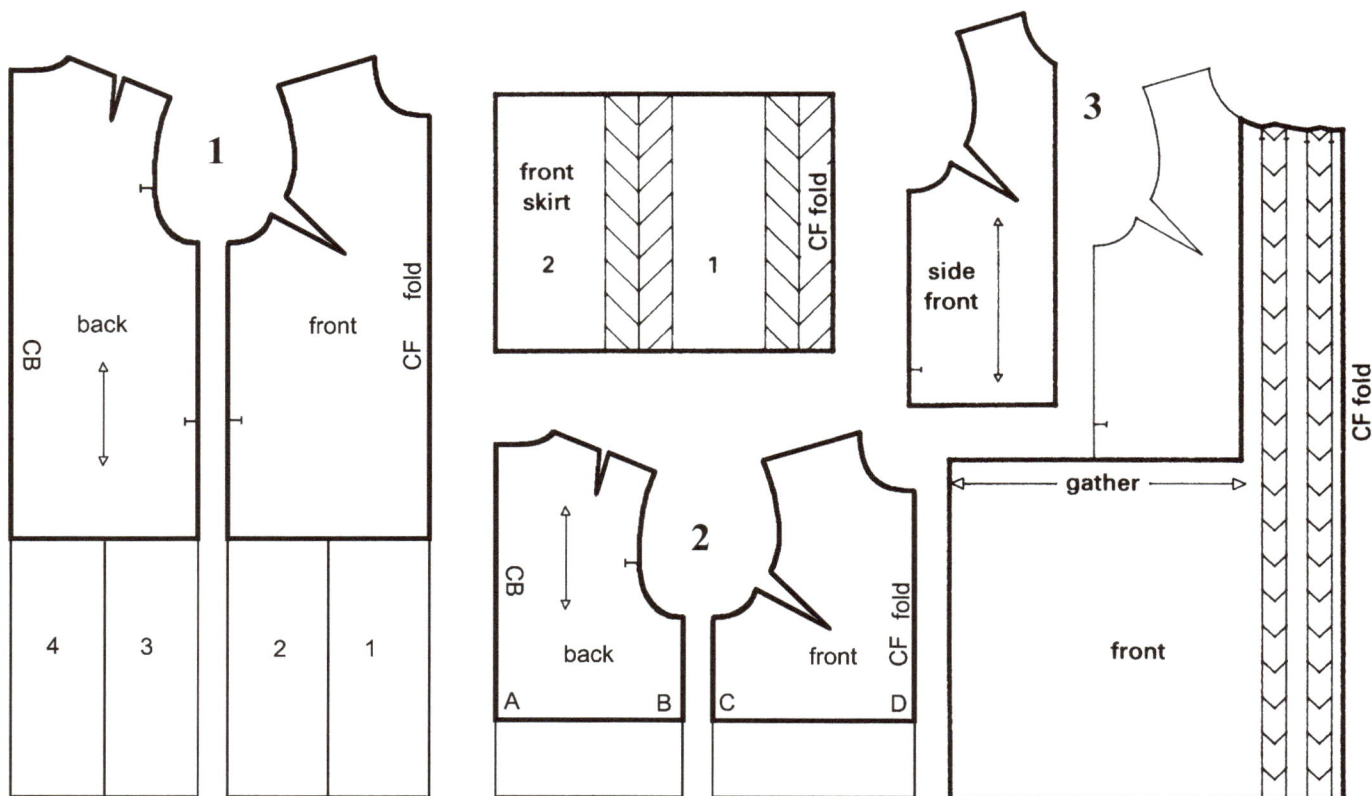

Balanced body shapes

Using the close fitting bodice (dress) block (ref. page 208), examples on this page show how the bust dart creates a balanced 'shift shape' (see page 12).
Further pattern adaptations with the bust dart transferred to the armhole are described below.
For example:
it can be divided at different lengths, to add skirts;
the basic shape can also be used to insert panels.

1 Dress with box pleated skirt

Trace close fitting bodice (dress) block to length required.
Draw horizontal skirt lines at the box pleat position.
Divide skirt into four panel sections.
Trace of front and back bodice.
Front skirt Cut out the skirt panels.
Extend the centre front of panel 1 twice the width of the centre pleat.
Draw vertical lines to indicate the pleats.
Extend the side of panel 1 twice the width of side pleat.
Draw vertical lines to indicate the pleats.
Place panel 2 to the inside line of the side pleat.
Draw round pattern.
Back skirt Repeat the above instructions.

2 Dress with a simple pleated skirt

Trace close fitting bodice (dress) block to length required.
Draw in a high waistline. Trace off pattern.

Back skirt Construct a rectangle: length = the length required; width = 6 × the meas. A–B on bodice back.
Front skirt Construct a rectangle: length = the length required; width = 6 × the meas. C–D on bodice front.
The simple pleats must be stitched to different lengths, to give an uneven profile.

3 Dress with inserted pleated panel

Extend the close fitting bodice block to length required.
Front and side front Draw in panel shape on the block.
Trace off side front and main front patterns.
On the main front, draw vertical lines at pleat positions.
Cut up the vertical lines and open the width of the pleat.
Extend the front skirt the required amount for gathers.
Draw round pattern.
Back Trace off the back bodice at the skirt position.
Back skirt Construct a rectangle: length = the length of front skirt; width = the required amount for gathers.

Technical drawings and fabrics

It is important that the images are drawn to show clearly how the design would look in the selected fabric.
For example:
Image 1 A fabric of medium weight and thickness, with low drape, shear and stretch.
Image 2 A lightweight thin fabric with medium drape, shear and stretch.
Image 3 A lightweight thin fabric with low drape, shear and stretch.

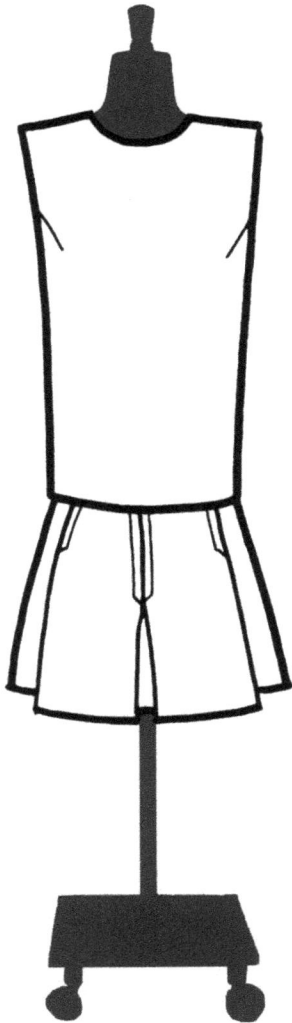

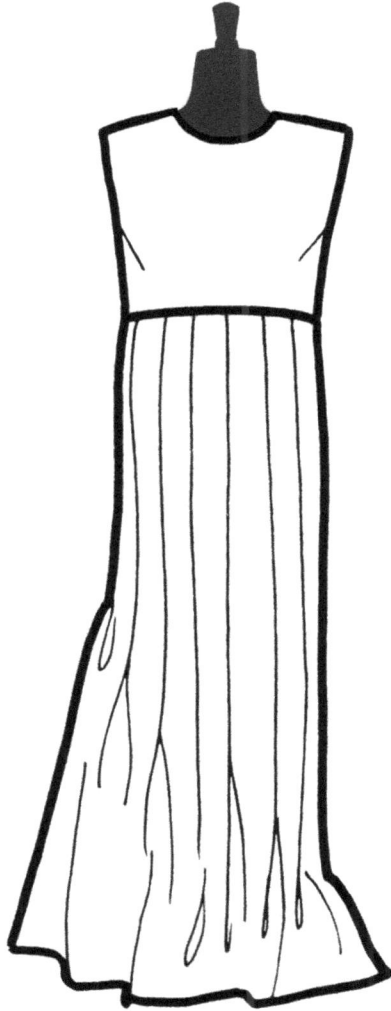

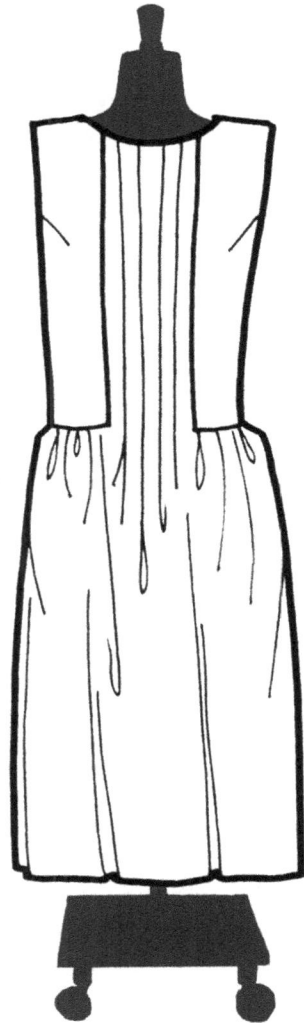

1

2

3

back

1

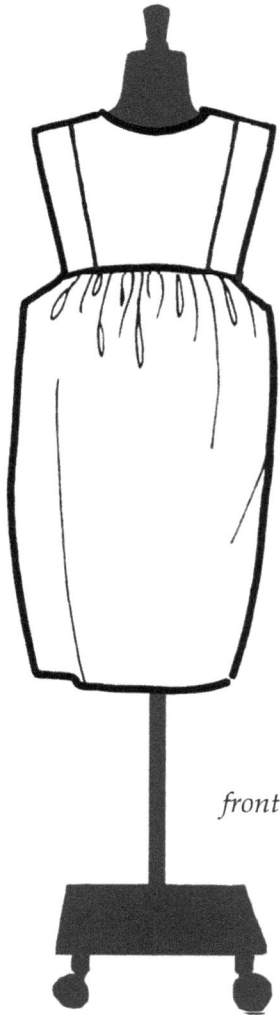

front

Darts in seams

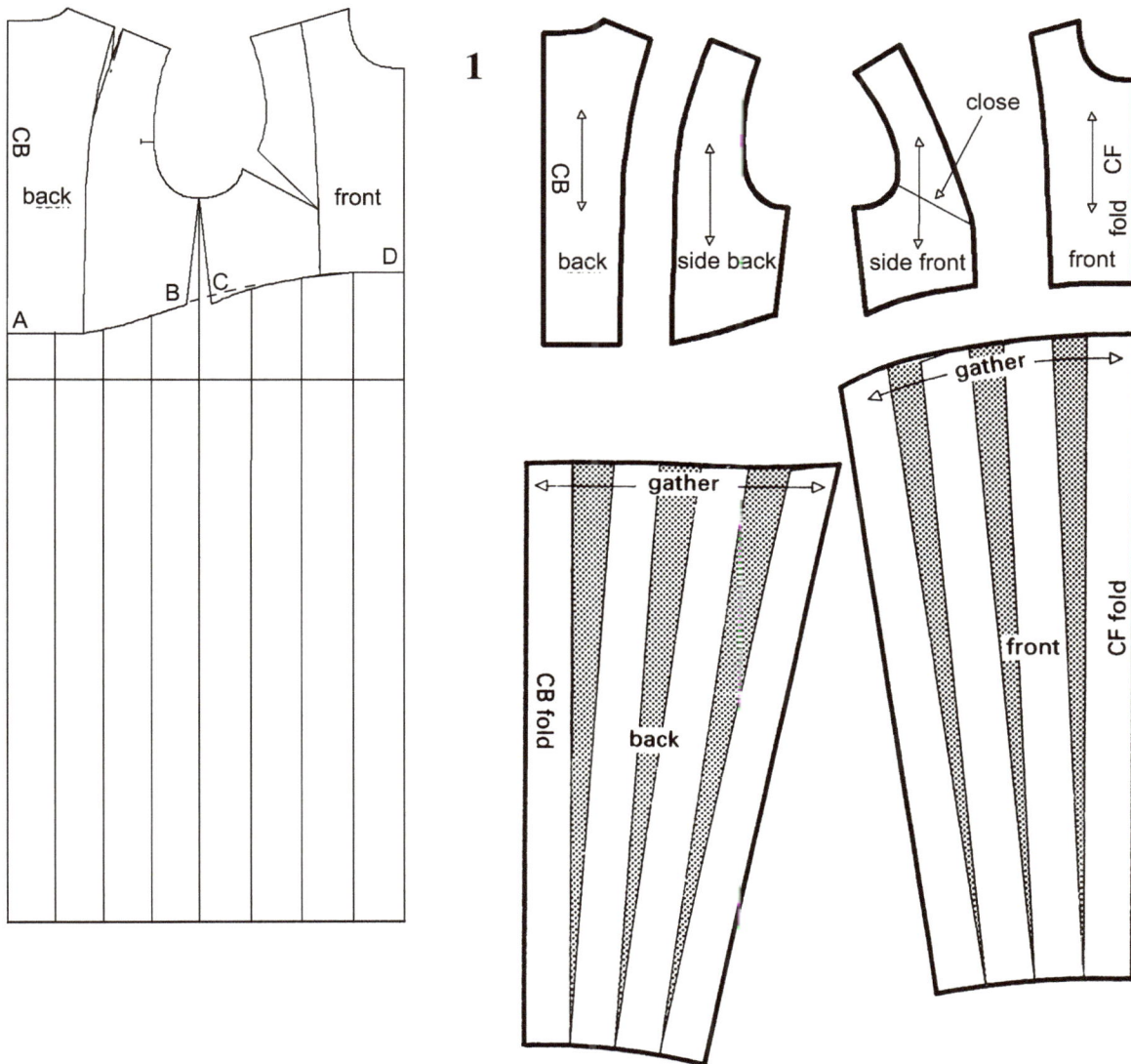

The design demonstrates the transfer of darts to seams in the bodice. This process can be done on any block.
It also combines the shaped bodice with a 'peg top' skirt using the technique of 'cut and spread'.

1 Darts in seams

Body sections Trace the close fitting bodice (dress) block (ref. page 208).
Draw in a high shaped waistline.
Shape in the waistline at the side seams approx. 1.5 cm.
Ensure that the side seams are of equal length.

Draw in style lines on the bodice: from the back shoulder dart to the waist; from the front shoulder through the bust point to the waist.
Divide both the back and front skirt into four sections as shown.
Trace off the bodice sections. Close bust dart.
Skirt Trace off the skirt pattern pieces and cut up the section lines.
Open the skirt sections at the waist the required amount.
For extra width, the sections can also be opened at the hemline.

The bust dart in 'cut and spread'

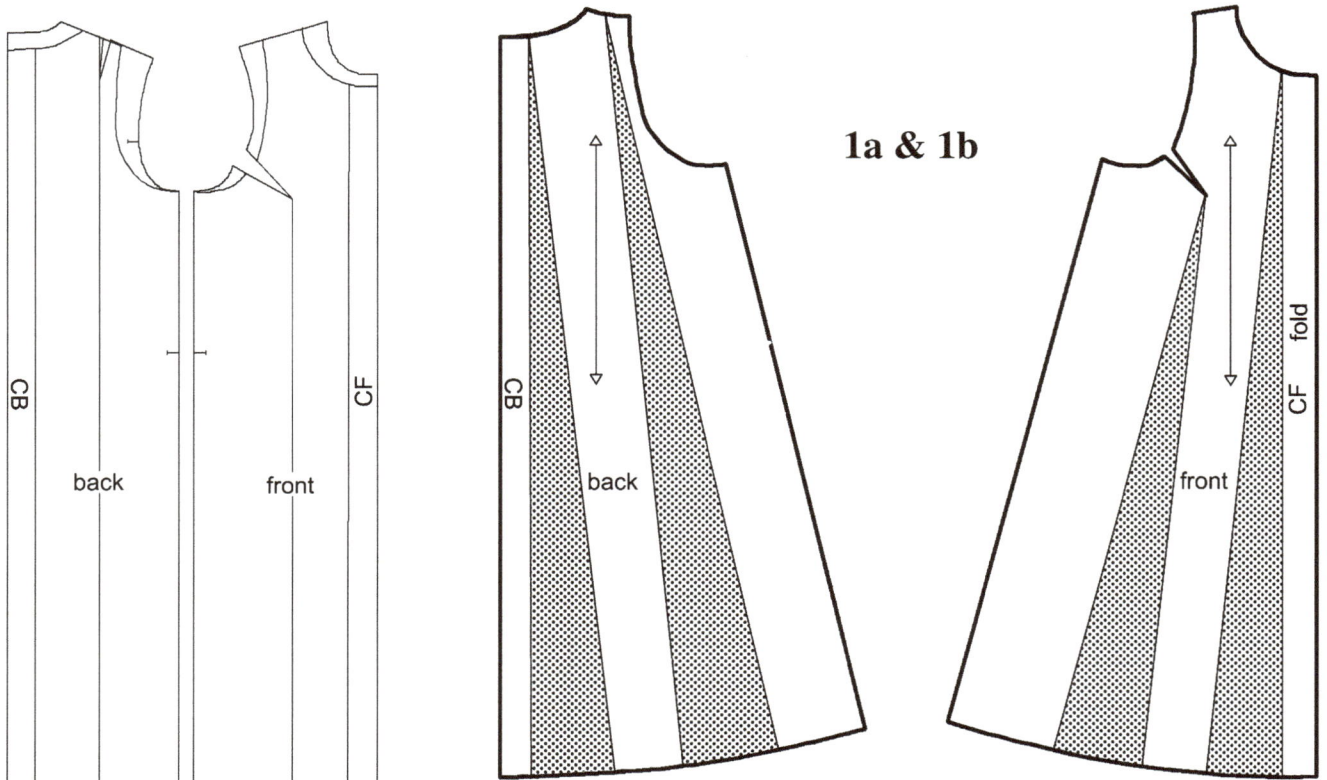

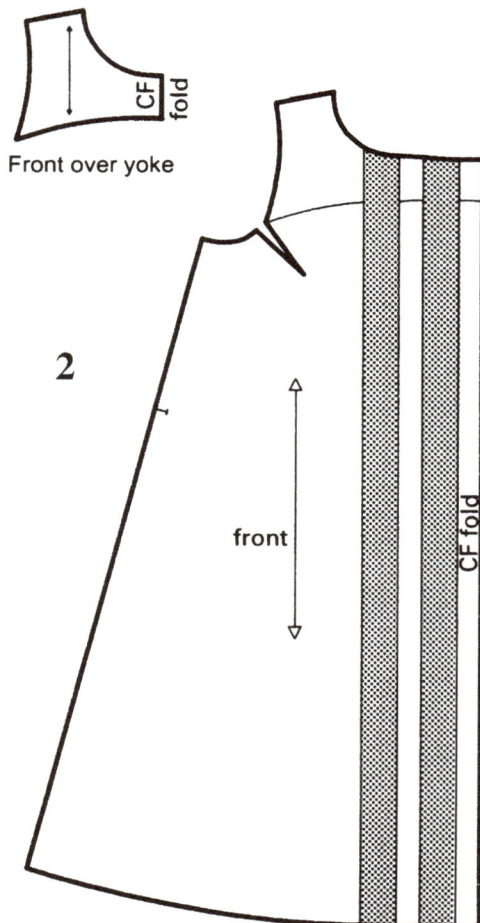

1a & 1b

Front over yoke

2

front

The bust dart can be incorporated into the process of 'cut and spread' on any bodice, jacket or overgarment block to create a well balanced 'A' line shape. This basic shape can be used for many further pattern developments. The profile changes depend on the amount of flare inserted and the fabric selected.
Image 1a Shows the adapted close fitting bodice (dress) block with a basic 'cut and spread' adaptation.
Image 1b Shows how the same shape can be altered with a lowered elasticated waistline.

1a and 1b basic 'A' line adaptation

Body sections Trace off the block required.
Draw in the neckline and armhole shape.
Divide the body into sections; one vertical line should be dropped from the bust dart point.
Trace off the divided sections.
Cut up the vertical lines and spread at the hem; the bust dart should half close.
Draw hemline with a smooth curve.

2 'A' line adaptation – extra gathered fullness

Body sections Repeat the instructions for a basic 'A' line shape as above.
Draw in an over yoke line on back and front sections.
Trace off the front and back over yokes.
Draw two vertical lines from the back and front neckline.
Cut up the lines and open the necklines the required amount as shown.

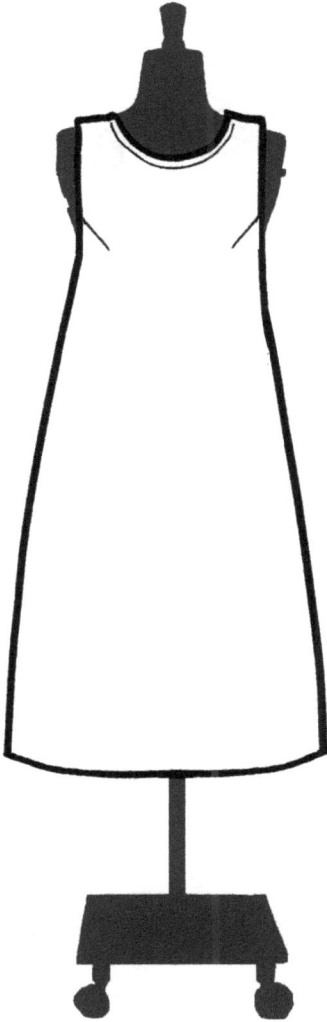

1a

1b

2

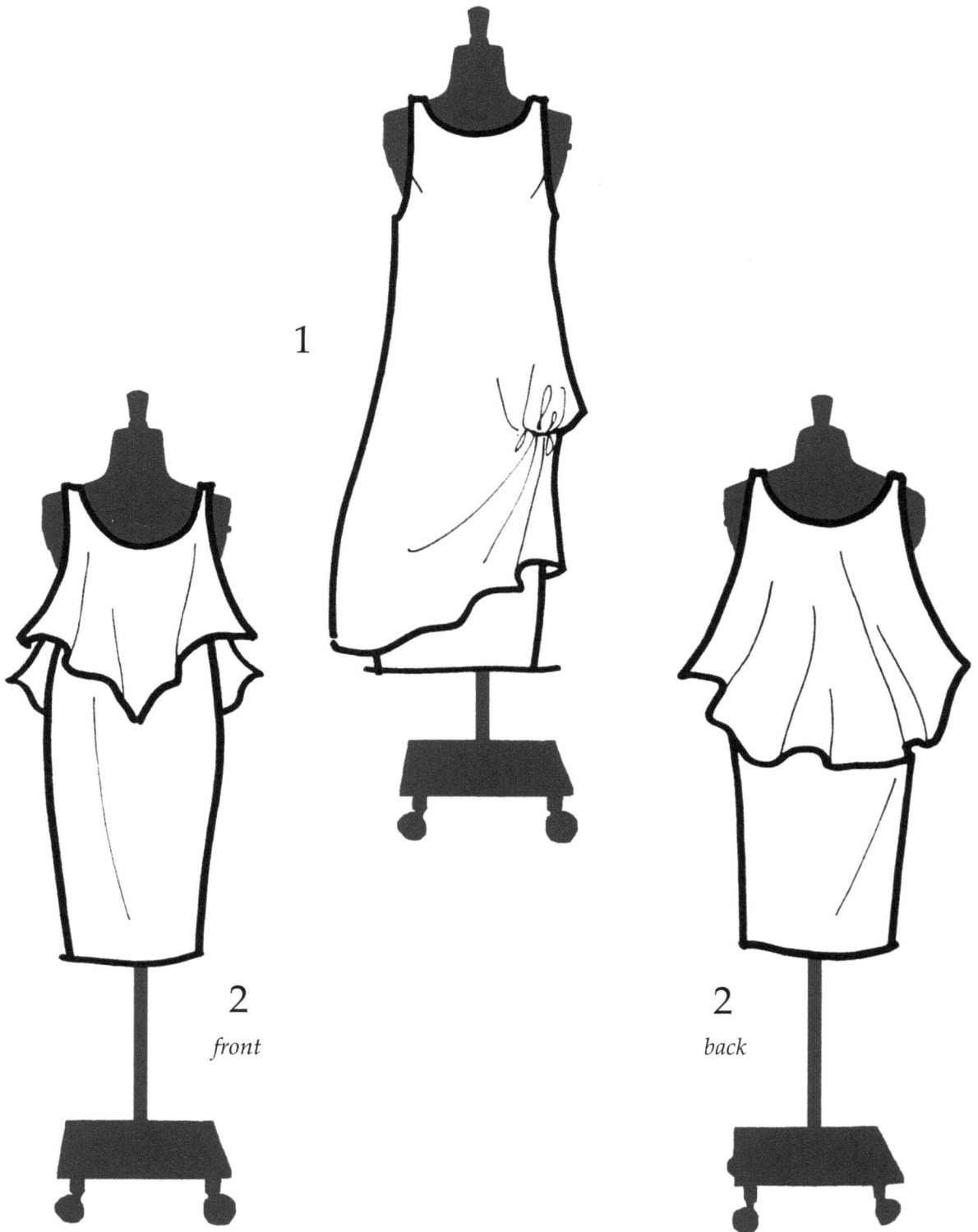

1

2

front

2

back

The bust dart in overlays

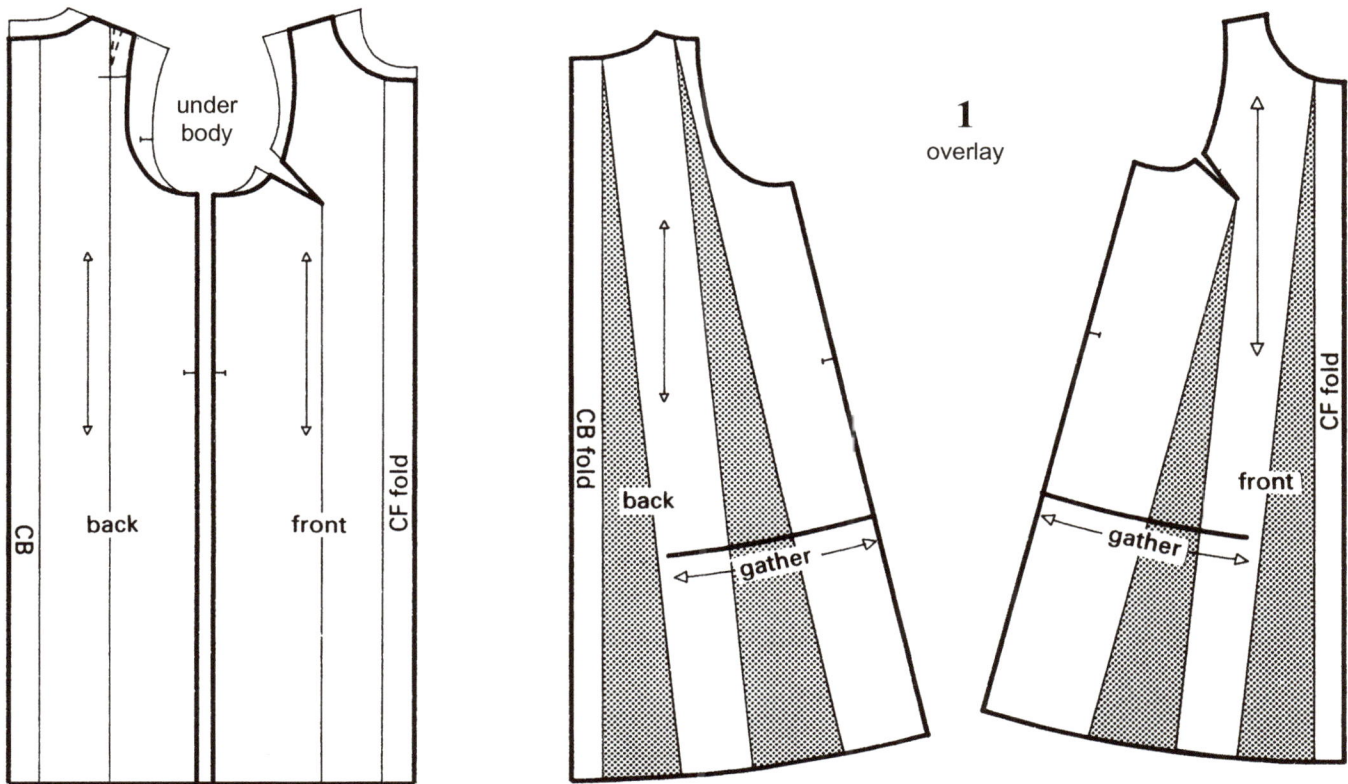

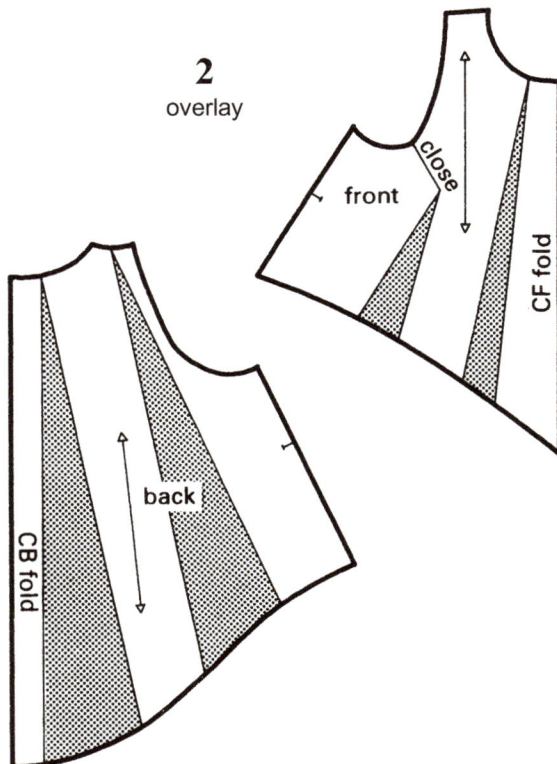

The basic body shape can provide a base for overlays of different 'A' line shapes cut in the same or contrasting fabrics.

The first image shows the basic body shape with a 'cut and spread' overlaid shape. This is gathered and stitched to the underlying body shape. The second image is a shorter top with extra flare in the back body overlay. This style of cutting requires fabrics with a high drape.

1 Stitched overlay

Body sections Trace off the close fitting bodice (dress) block (ref. page 208).
Draw in the neckline and armhole shape.
Divide the body into sections; one vertical line should be dropped from the bust dart point.
Under body Trace off the basic under body back and front sections.
Overlay Trace off the divided sections.
Cut up the overlay sections and spread at the hem. The bust dart should half close.
Draw in the gather line.

2 Overlay – extra flare

Body sections Repeat the first instructions as above, but draw the required overlay line on the main body section.
Cut up the overlay sections and spread at the hem with more flare. The bust dart should fully close.
Open the back sections further to add extra flare.
Redraw the hemline of the overlay.

The easy fitting overshape block: simple jackets and coats

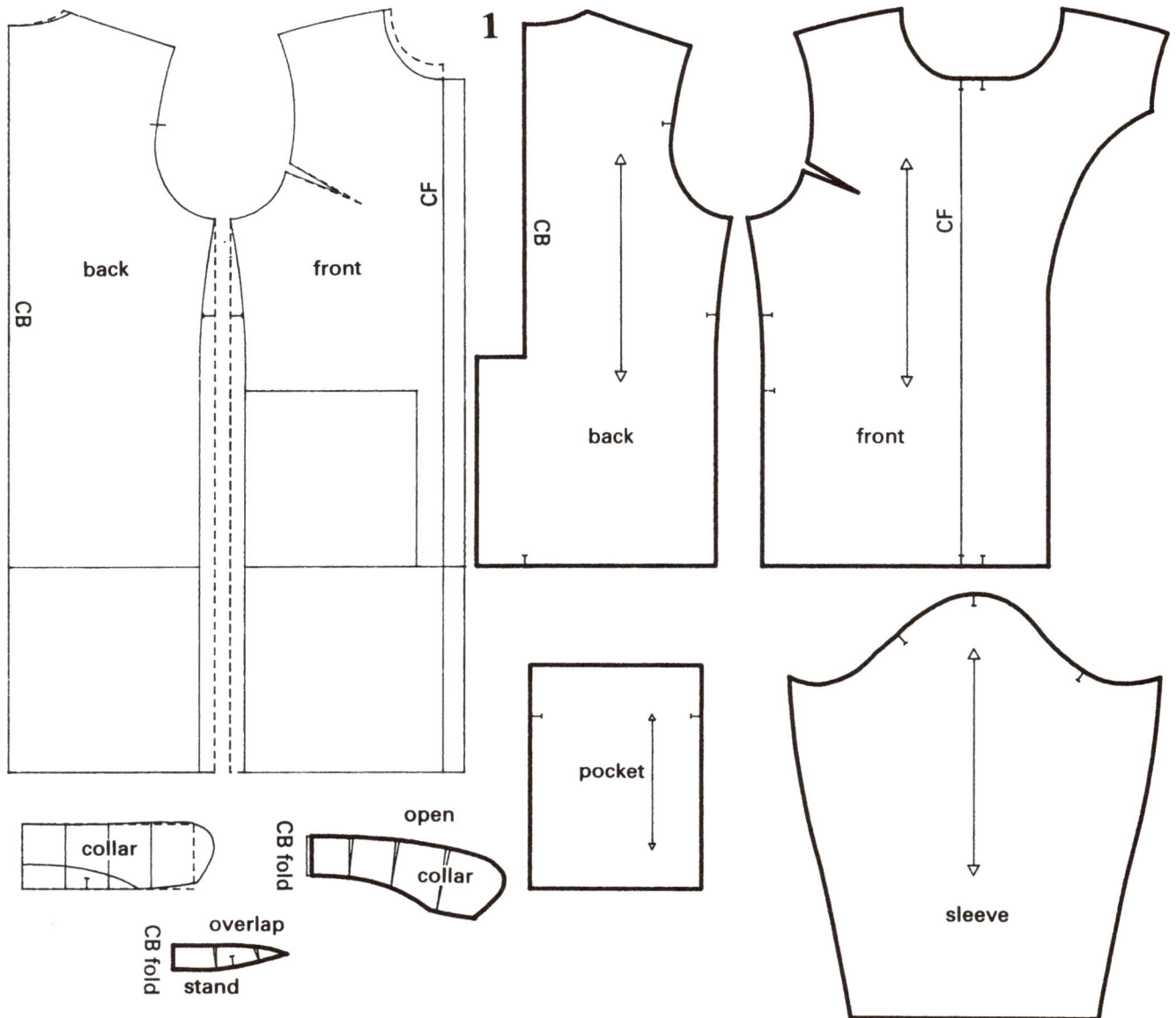

1

back

front

CF

CB

back

CB

front

CF

collar

open

CB fold

collar

pocket

sleeve

CB fold

overlap

stand

The easy fitting overshape block

The overshape block (ref. page 205) is useful for simple shapes, very wide shapes and can be adapted easily into more ambitious designs. It has a reduced bust dart, but a dart remains necessary to give a balanced shape to a classic design.

The jacket is an illustration of its basic shape. The block length can be extended to create an easy fitting coat block.

1 Basic loose shapes

Body sections Trace round the easy fitting overshape block. Extend the length.

Lower neckline slightly. Add buttonstand.

Swing dart to armhole. Shorten the dart.
Shape in side seam 1.5cm.
Draw in pocket shape.
Back Trace off back pattern.
Add back vent (approx. 6cm) if required.
Front Create an extended facing – fold the pattern paper along the front edge of the pattern.
Trace the shoulder and part of the armhole.
Draw a curved line from armhole to hem.
Pocket Trace off the pocket sections.
Add a facing to the top edge.
Collar Construct a shirt collar with back stand (ref. *Metric Pattern Cutting for Women's Wear*; collar section).

1

Fabric

1 Linen/cotton

The fabric is of medium weight, thickness, drape and shear, but with low stretch.

Pattern cutting

Medium to heavy fabrics with low drape or shear will produce a boxy shape. This fabric with medium drape and shear gives a softer, 'slouchy' profile.

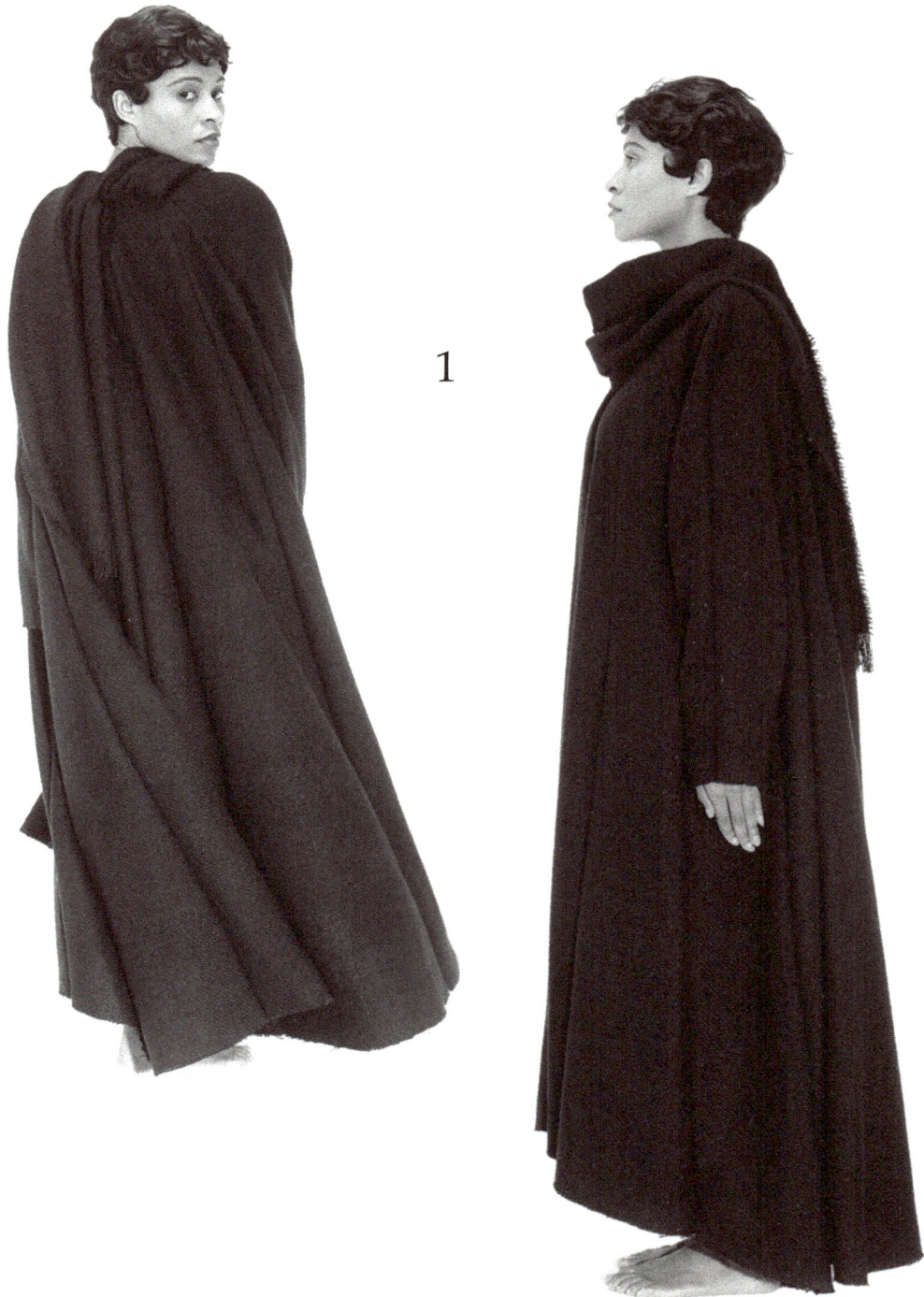

1

Fabric

1   *Wool*
The fabric is of heavy weight, medium thickness, drape
and shear, and low stretch.

Pattern cutting

The heavyweight woollen fabric, which has medium
drape and shear, will hang in folds with a narrow
outline until the body moves; then, its weight will make
it swing dramatically to produce many different
shapes. Fabrics with low drape would hang
geometrically, and swing in distinct panels.

The easy fitting overshape block: extravagant flare

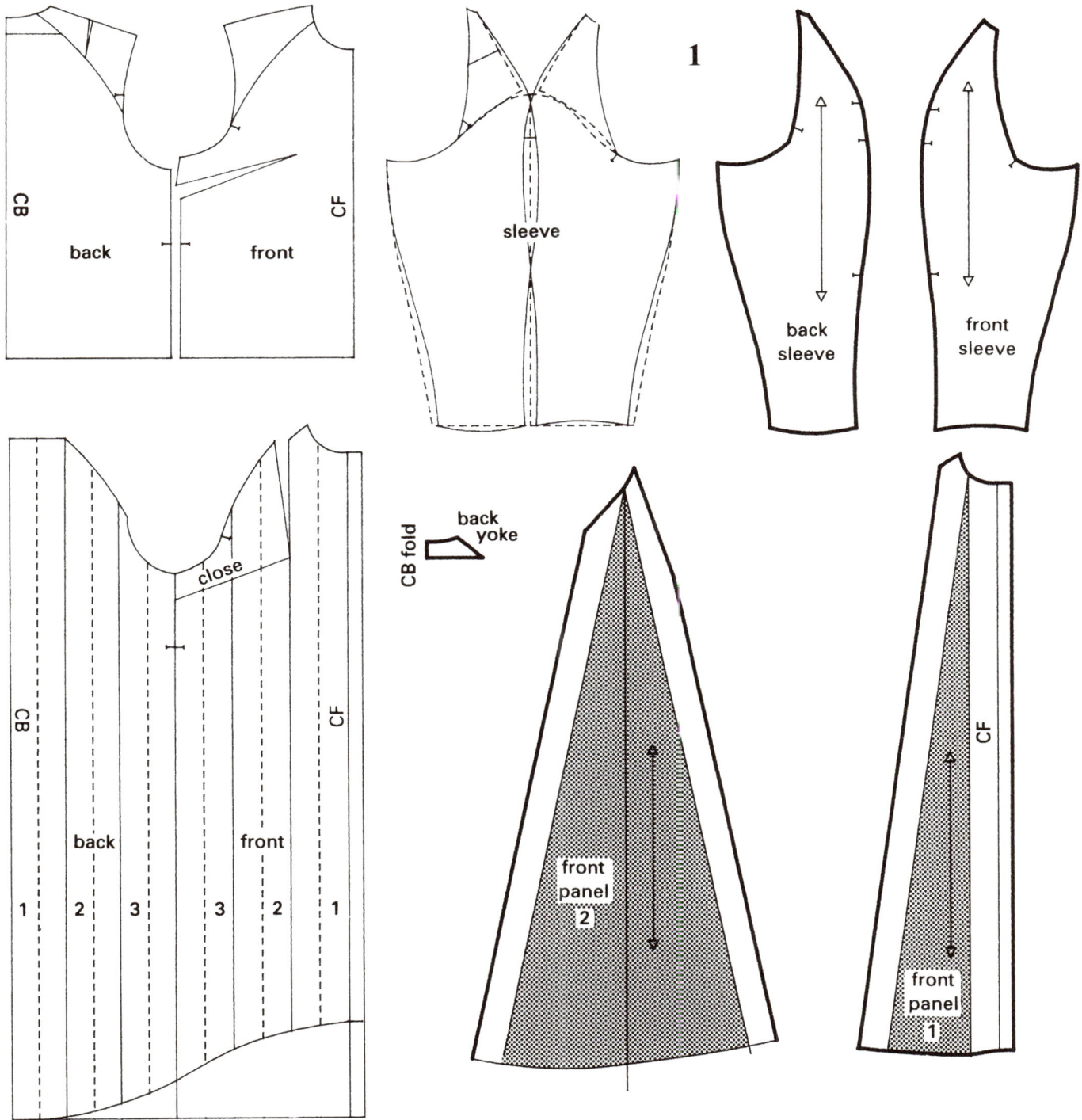

1

back

front

sleeve

back sleeve

front sleeve

CB fold
back yoke

close

CB

CF

back

front

1 2 3   3 2 1

front panel 2

front panel 1

CF

1 Darts in wide flared shapes

Body sections Trace the easy fitting overshape block
(ref. page 205).
Draw in raglan lines. Draw in back yoke line.
Draw back shoulder dart to replace ease allowance.
Trace off the body sections.
Front and back Transfer the bust dart to the raglan line.
Place patterns together, draw in a shaped hemline.
Add buttonstand.
Divide patterns into sections as shown.
Divide each section with a vertical line.
Cut up sections.
'Cut and spread' all the sections the required amount.

The 'cut and spread' amount can vary on each section,
as shown on the front panels 1 and 2.
Sleeves Trace off raglan sections from the body block.
Add raglan sections to the sleeve heads, matching
balance points. Leave some gap at the sleeve head for
ease.
Re-draw centre lines overlapping at the top sleeve,
shaping in at the bottom.
Shape in the underarm seam with a curve.
Trace off back and front sleeve.
Scarf Cut long straight lengths of fabric for the scarf.
Back yoke Trace off back yoke.
The scarf was inserted in back yoke.

PART THREE: FABRICS AND THE BODY FORM
Chapter 6 Cutting to fit the body form (woven fabrics)

Fitting the body

Fitting the body in woven fabrics that do not stretch over the body curves presents great challenges for pattern cutters. These skills have to be developed. Many couturiers are masters of 'cut'. Cutting fitted shapes in woven fabric for the mass market is very difficult: that is why there has been such a growth in fabrics with stretch characteristics either in the yarn (e.g. elastane) or the construction (e.g. fancy crepe weaves or knitted fabrics). The use of these fabrics has solved some problems, but has created others.

These will be discussed in Chapter 8. This chapter concentrates on the creation of patterns for garments made in woven fabrics with little stretch ability. It illustrates the types of blocks available for achieving different shapes and the different types of 'fit'.

'Fit' is a word that is used quite often in a very loose way and it can be ambiguous. The word 'fit' should be used more precisely in terms such as 'close fitting', semi-fitting or easy fitting.

Basic close fitting waist shaping (dress blocks)

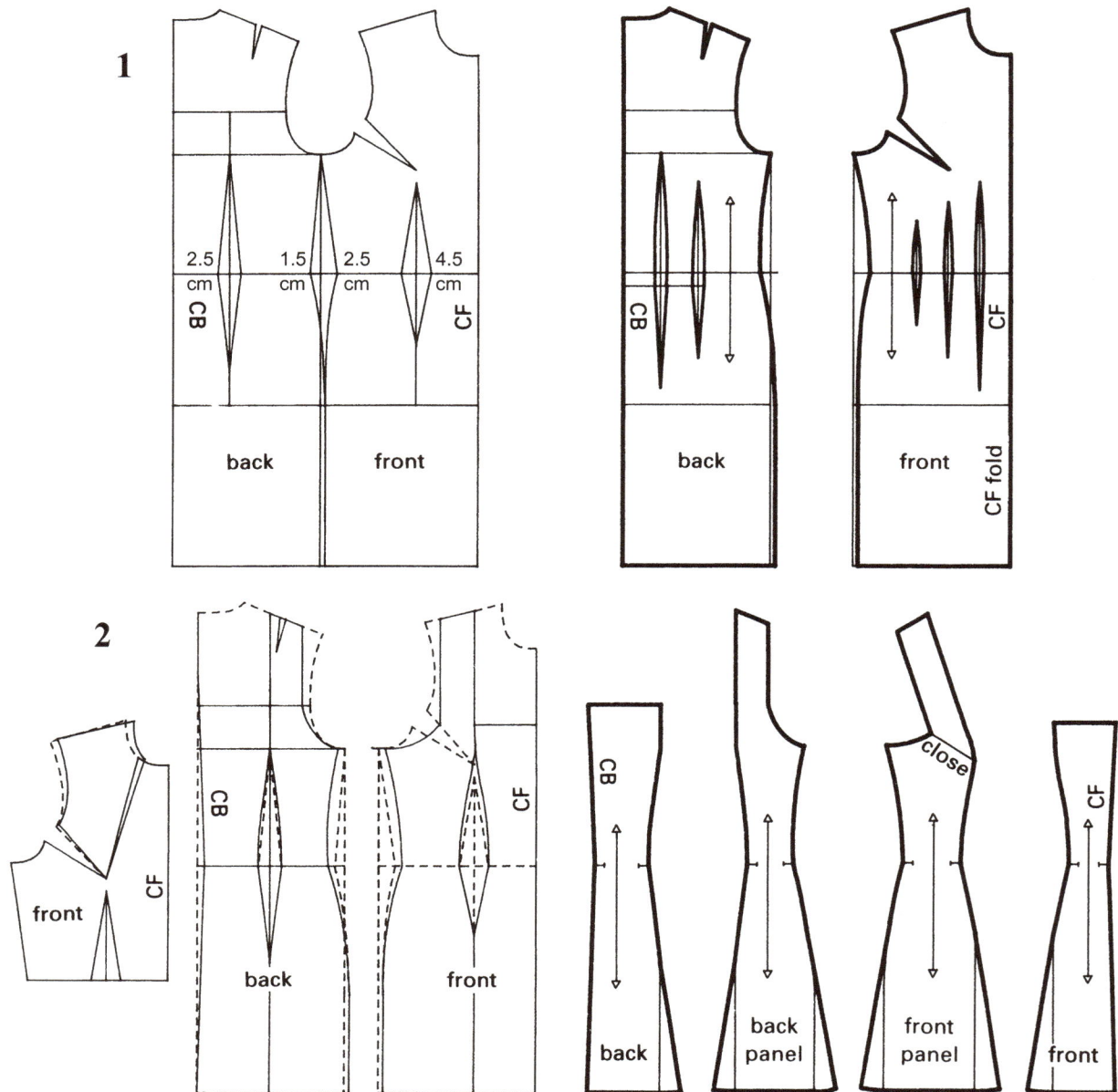

1

2.5 cm | 1.5 cm | 2.5 cm | 4.5 cm

CB

CF

back | front

CB

back

CF

front

CF fold

2

front

CF

CB

back

CF

front

CB

back

back panel

close

front panel

CF

front

1 Basic close fitting waist shaping

The basic waist shaping for a close fitting body shape with ease for movement is approx. 11-12cm.
Body sections Trace the close fitting bodice (dress) block (ref. page 208): extend to length required.
Swing bust dart to the armhole; join the side seams.
Draw in front and back darts as shown.
The darting amount can be divided differently as shown.

Equalise the side seam The front bodice is wider than the back bodice; the side seam is placed in the centre to create a better balanced shape.
Divide the hemline into two equal sections.
Square up to the hipline for a new side seam.
Shape in the bodice waist side seam as shown.
Draw in the hip shaping to the new skirt side seam.

Low necks

Dresses with a low neck will sag at the front unless the

neck is tightened.
On the bodice front, draw a line from neck to bust point.
Cut out the dart, cut up the line, overlap approx. 1cm (depending on the depth of neck).

2 Sleeveless dress with vertical seams

Body sections Trace the close fitting bodice (dress) block.
Tighten the front neck: see low neck instructions.
Draw in front neck shape.
Draw in darting and side seam shaping as (1).

Sleeveless instructions Reduce side seam by 1cm at the underarm; 0.5cm at the waist; join to the hip point.

Draw in new armhole shape.
Square down from base of darts.
Curve darts slightly. Shape in back waist 0.5cm.
Trace off the body sections. Close bust dart.
Add flare to the hem of the seam lines.

2

1

1

Horizontal close fitting body shaping (dress blocks)

1

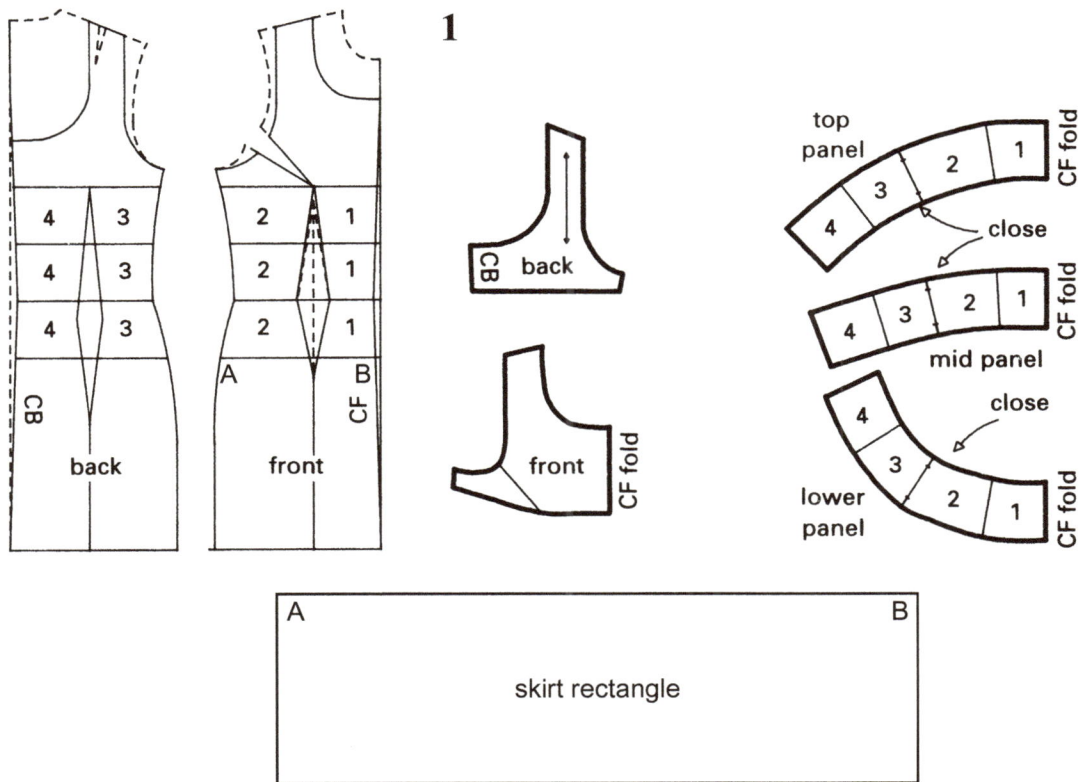

top panel

mid panel

lower panel

CF fold

close

skirt rectangle

A B

back front

CB back

CF fold

front

1 Horizontal waist shaping

Body sections Trace off the close fitting bodice (dress) block (ref. page 208) to the length required.
Construct the basic waist shaping and sleeveless adaptation (ref. 1 and 2 page 96).
Draw a horizontal line across the bodice at the bust dart.
Draw a horizontal line across the waistline.
Draw a horizontal line midway between the two lines.
Draw the fourth horizontal line across the high hipline at an equal width.
Number all the sections.

Upper body sections Trace off all the upper body sections. Close the bust dart.
Body panel sections Trace off the horizontal panel sections.
Close the darts and seam shaping to create four horizontal shaped panels.
Skirt The skirt can be created in any skirt shape, see Chapter 4, pages 62–66.
The skirt illustrated is a simple gathered skirt created by four rectangular panels.
Length = length required.
Width of a skirt panel = 4 × measurement of A–B.

Classic semi-fitting waist shaping (jacket blocks)

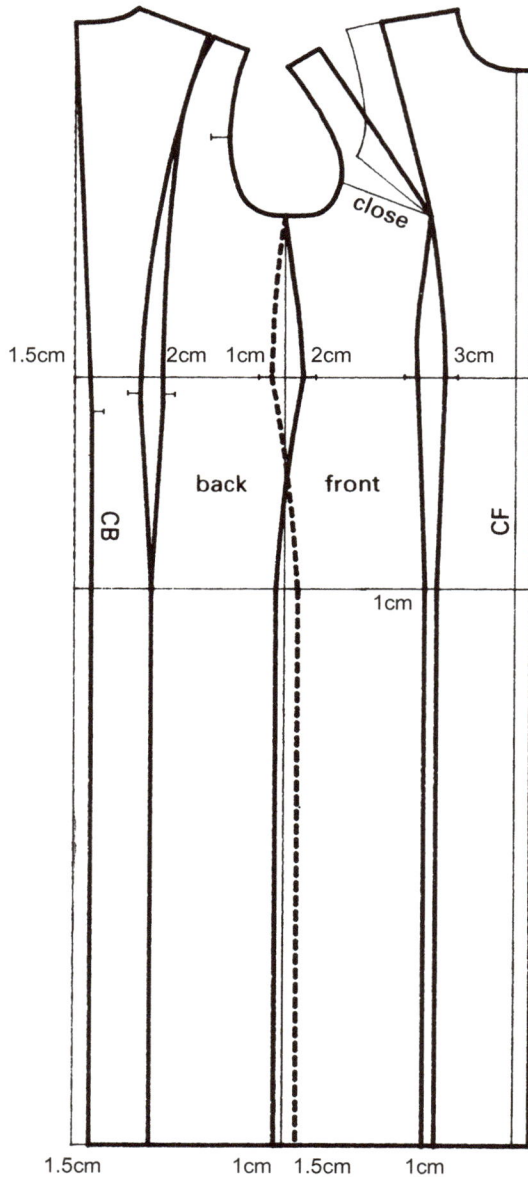

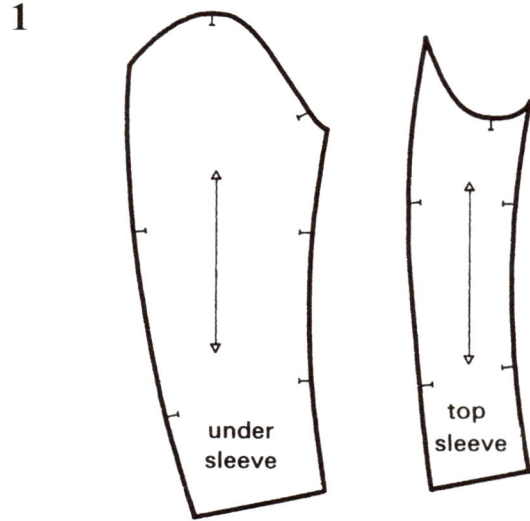

1.5cm 2cm 1cm 2cm 3cm

back front

CB CF

close

1cm

1.5cm 1cm 1.5cm 1cm

1

under sleeve

top sleeve

1 Semi-fitting waist shaping in vertical seams

Body sections Trace round the close fitting jacket block (ref. page 203). Extend the length.
Remove the rever shape; redraw higher neckline.
Add buttonstand.
Swing bust dart to armhole; join side seams.
Lower back waist approx. 2cm.
Shape in back waist 1.5cm; square down to hemline.
Draw in a style line from centre front shoulder to hemline.
Draw in a style line from back shoulder dart to hemline.
Shape in panel lines as shown in diagram; make smooth curves on all shaping.
The hip shaping that is reduced at front seam and the centre back seam is added to the side seams.
Close bust dart to swing the bust darting to the panel line.
Trace off the pattern sections.

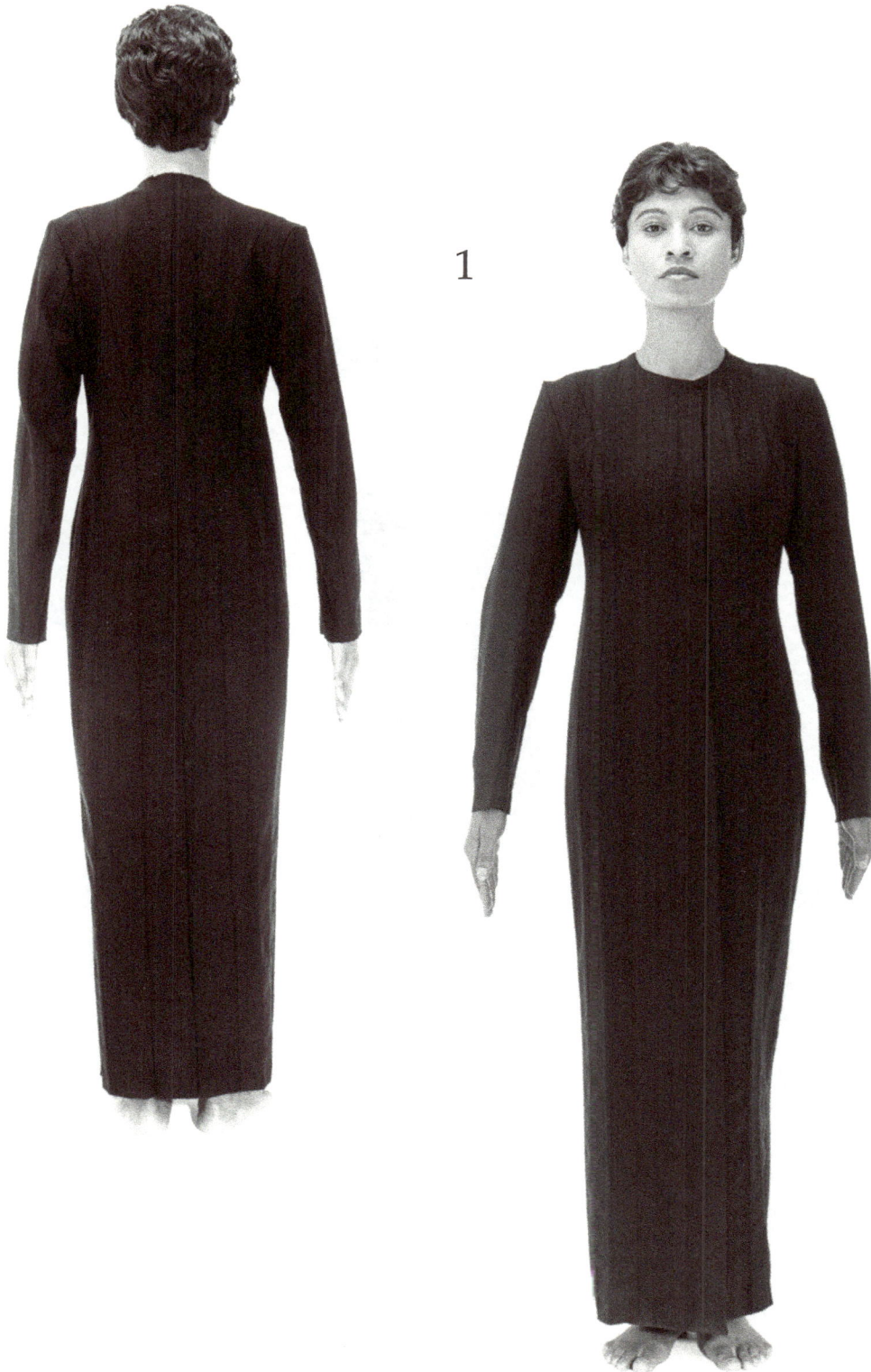

1

Fabric

1 Wool/polyester/elastane

The fabric is of medium weight and thickness, low drape and shear, and medium stretch.

Pattern cutting

The small amount of elastane in the cloth is used only as a 'comfort' factor. Using the close fitting jacket block with high shear, loosely woven fabrics, would result in distortions, unless the fabric was supported. The easy fitting jacket block should be used for thick fabrics.

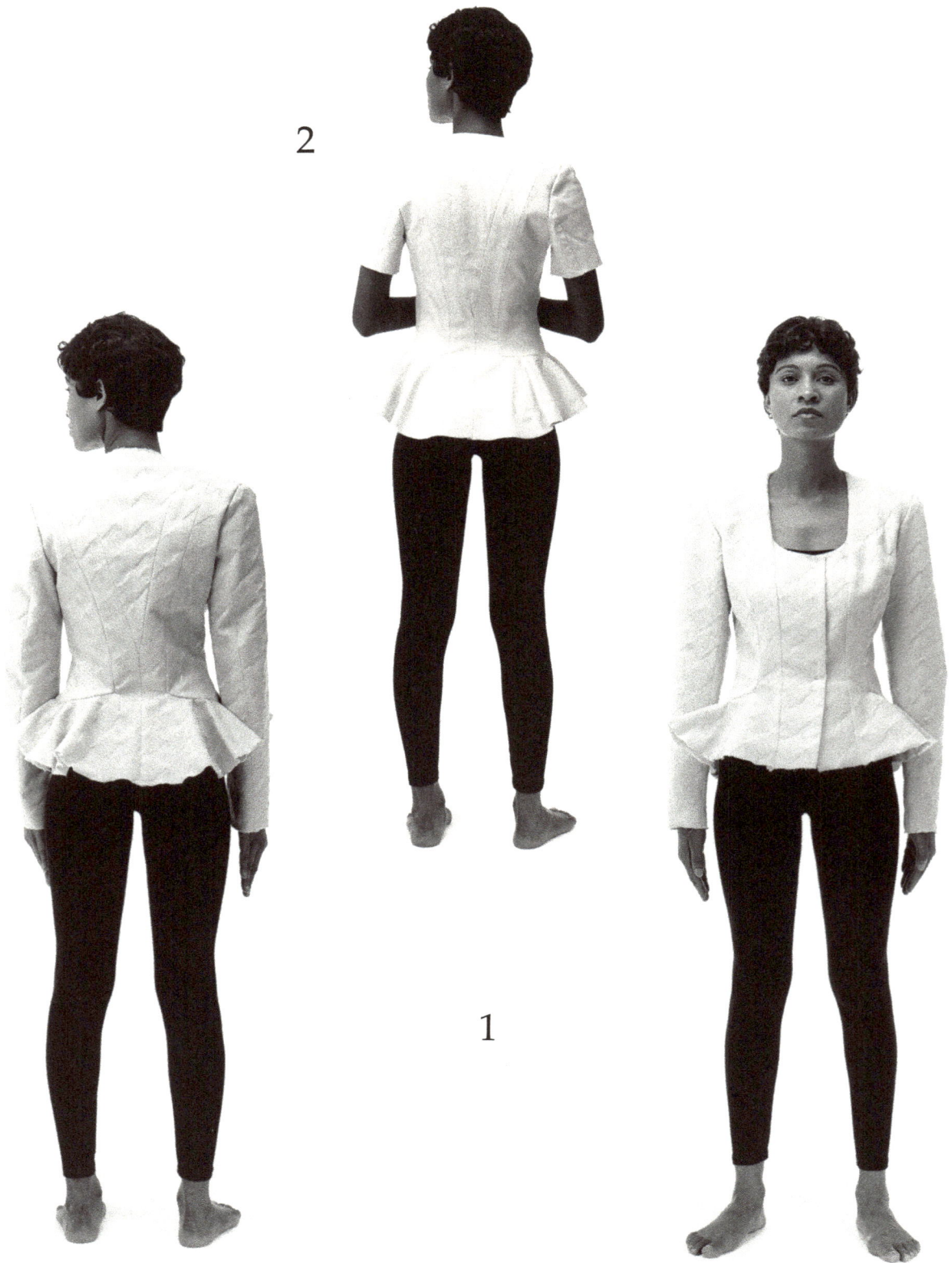

Fabric

1 Polyester
The fabric is of medium weight and thickness, and low drape, shear and stretch.

2 Nappa leather (calf)
The fabric is of heavy weight, medium thickness and drape, and low shear and stretch.

Pattern cutting

The images illustrate a different example of waist shaping; more style lines and close waist shaping will give a sculptured look to designs. Particularly, if low shear and low drape fabrics are used (1). The higher drape of the nappa leather (2) softens the design.

More complex close body shaping (jacket and dress blocks)

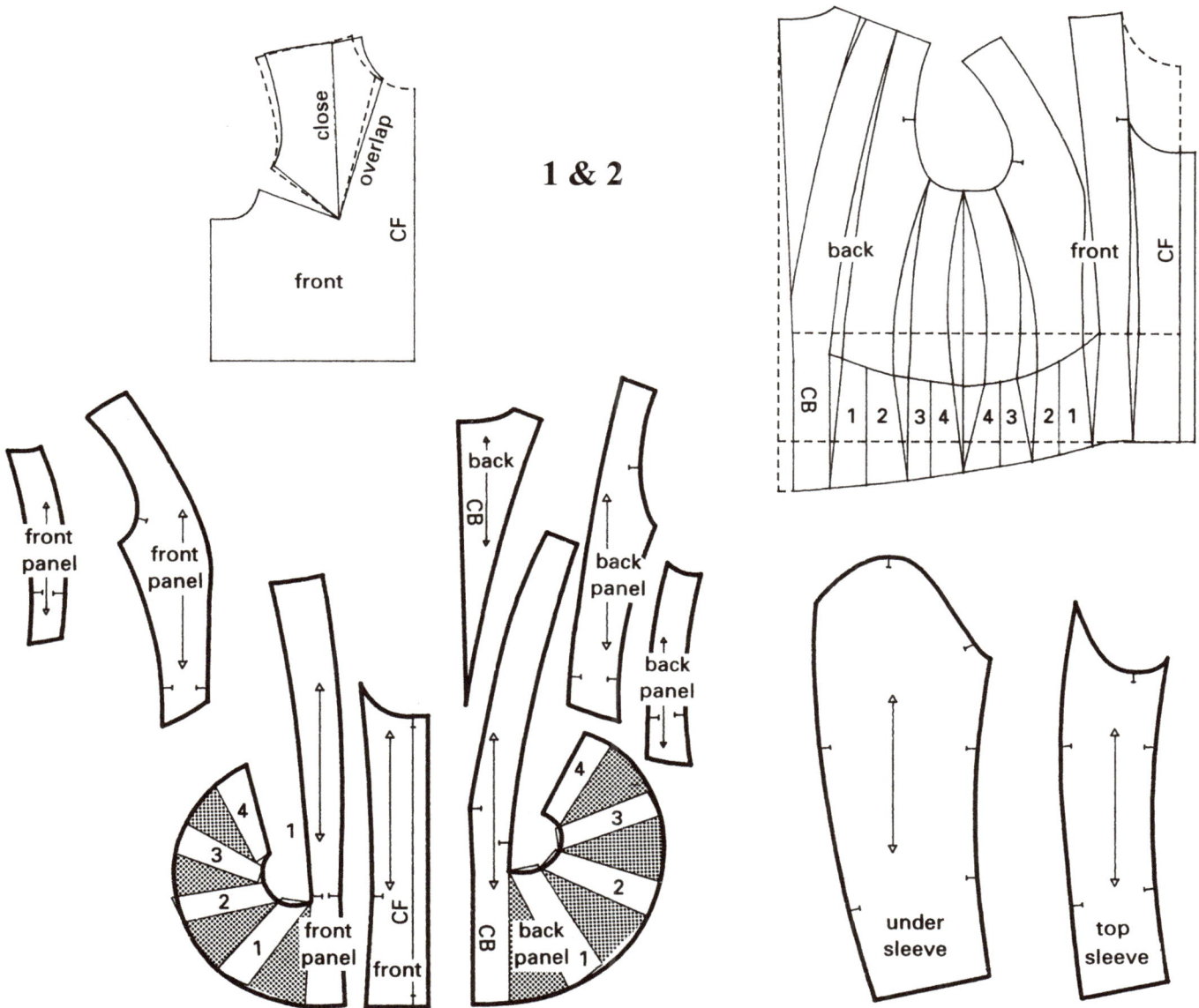

1 & 2

1 and 2 Complex body shaping

The diagram illustrates a different example of waist shaping; more style lines and very close waist shaping (example 14cm) that give a sculptured look to designs, particularly when low drape, low shear fabrics are used.
Image (1) is cut from the close fitting jacket block (ref. page 203).
Image (2) is cut from the close fitting dress block (ref. page 208).
Body sections Trace off the selected close fitting jacket or dress block.
Tighten the front neckline to prevent sag.
On the bodice front draw a line from neck to bust point.
Cut out the dart, cut up the line, overlap approx. 1cm (depending on the depth of neck).
Transfer bust dart to the centre shoulder.
Draw a vertical line from the neck point.
Draw in front neckline. Add buttonstand.

Draw a seam line from the front shoulder dart.
Shape in the back seam 1.5cm at the back waist; square down to the hem line.
Draw curved panel lines and a curved side seam.
Distribute 14cm of darting, taking more from the front than the back bodice in shaped panel lines as shown.
Draw a curved seam line below the waistline from the back panel to the dart panel.
Number all the lower panels created.
Top body sections Trace off top body panels.
Main front and back panel sections Trace off the front. Trace off the front and back panel; add the lower panels, cutting and spreading the hemline.
Sleeves image (1) Cut from the close fitting jacket block, it has a two-piece sleeve.
Sleeves image (2) Cut from the close fitting dress block, it has a one-piece short sleeve.

Classic easy fitting body shaping (jacket block)

1 & 2

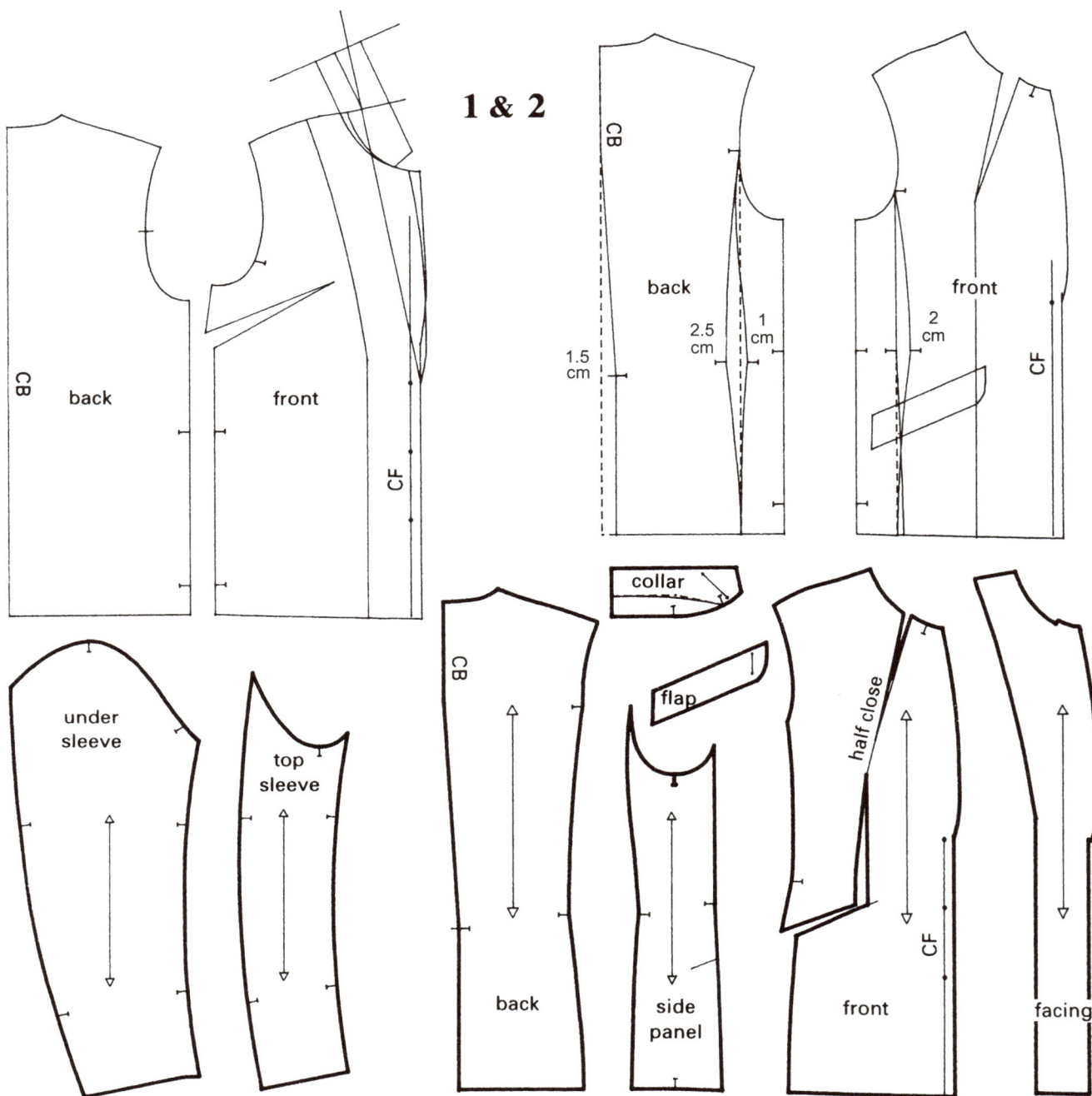

CB back

front

CF

CB back

2.5 cm

1 cm

front

2 cm

CF

1.5 cm

under sleeve

top sleeve

collar

flap

CB

back

side panel

half close

front

CF

facing

Easy fitting jacket block

The easy fitting jacket block (ref. page 204) is a basic shape. The semi-fitted waist shaping retains an easy fitting image. The jacket shoulder includes enough ease for a light thin shoulder pad.
The back views of the jacket are on page 106.

1 and 2   Classic easy fitting waist shaping

Body sections Trace round the easy fitting jacket block. Extend to the length required.
Construct a 'gents' collar and facing; (ref. *Metric Pattern Cutting for Women's Wear,* collar section).

Swing the bust dart to the neckline.
Draw in the pocket line.
Lower back waist approx. 2cm.
Shape in back waist 1.5cm; draw a vertical line to the hemline.
Draw in vertical lines from sleeve points and bust point.
Shape panel lines as shown in diagram.
Trace off the pattern sections.
Cut along pocket line and the vertical line to bust point.
Half close the bust dart at the neck to create bust darting to the pocket. Shorten dart.
(The neck dart can be fully closed to give a wider dart at the pocket.)

Front views

Fabric

1 Linen/lurex
A medium weight, thin fabric with medium shear, but low drape and stretch.

2 Wool double jersey (weft knit)
A fabric of medium weight, thickness, drape and stretch, but low shear.

Pattern cutting

The designs have no interlinings and the style is one that needs a minimum amount of under structure. However, compare the different natural profile of the 'sharp' linen jacket (2) and the knitted wool jersey jacket (1), which drapes around the figure giving a softer, easier outline.

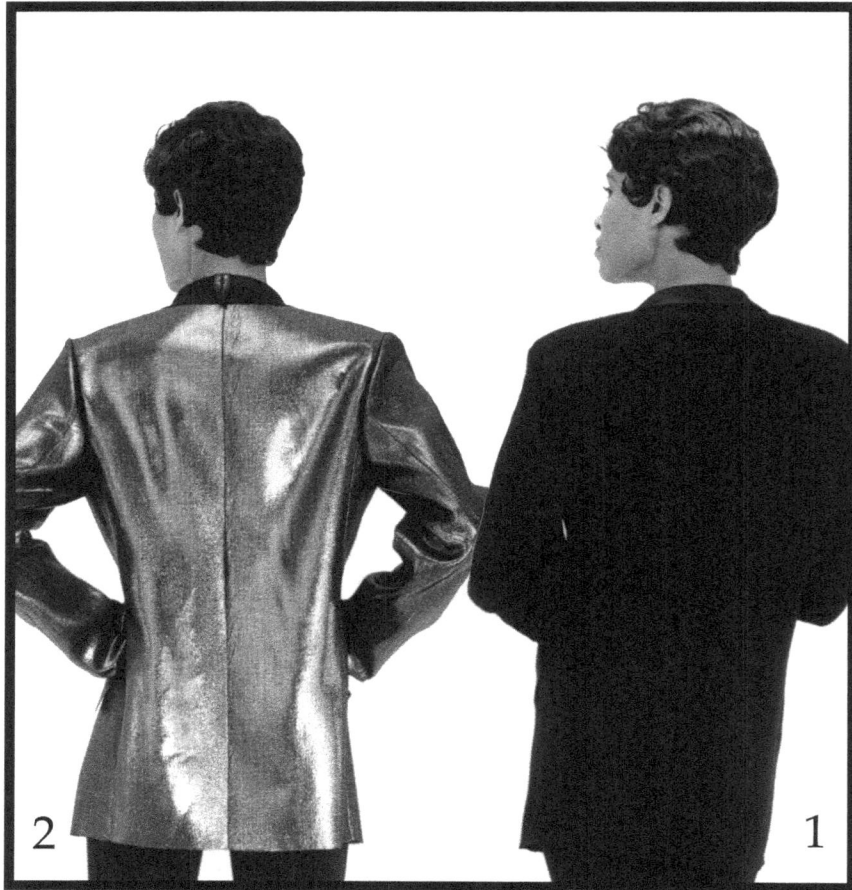

Back views

PART THREE: FABRICS AND THE BODY FORM

Chapter 7 Crossway cutting

Crossway cutting

Crossway cutting fabric can produce garments that fit in a sensual way around the figure, and drape in soft fluid folds. It also gives bounce and life to folded frills and other decorative features. Crossway cutting is cutting directly across the fabric. This means that the vertical hang of the material is at the crossway intersection of warp and weft. Cutting in this way takes full advantage of any drape or shear characteristics. However, very open weave, high shear fabrics can become uncontrollable. Cutting geometrically and cutting correctly on the true bias can help to retain some control.

Crossway cutting is found mainly in expensive garments; because to obtain a perfect final shape some preparation of the fabric usually takes place. Fabric pieces are cut wider than the pattern shape, then left to hang for three days; this is done so that the major 'vertical drop' of the fabric will take place before the garment is cut out. This method was used for all the garments shown on the following pages.

Crossway cut garments have become more fashionable at 'High Street' level. However, the quality control of crossway cut garments is difficult in mass production. Garments reach the stores having dropped in crossway areas of fabric, they then become distorted in shape, and wrinkle at the seams.

Crossway cutting: classic shaping

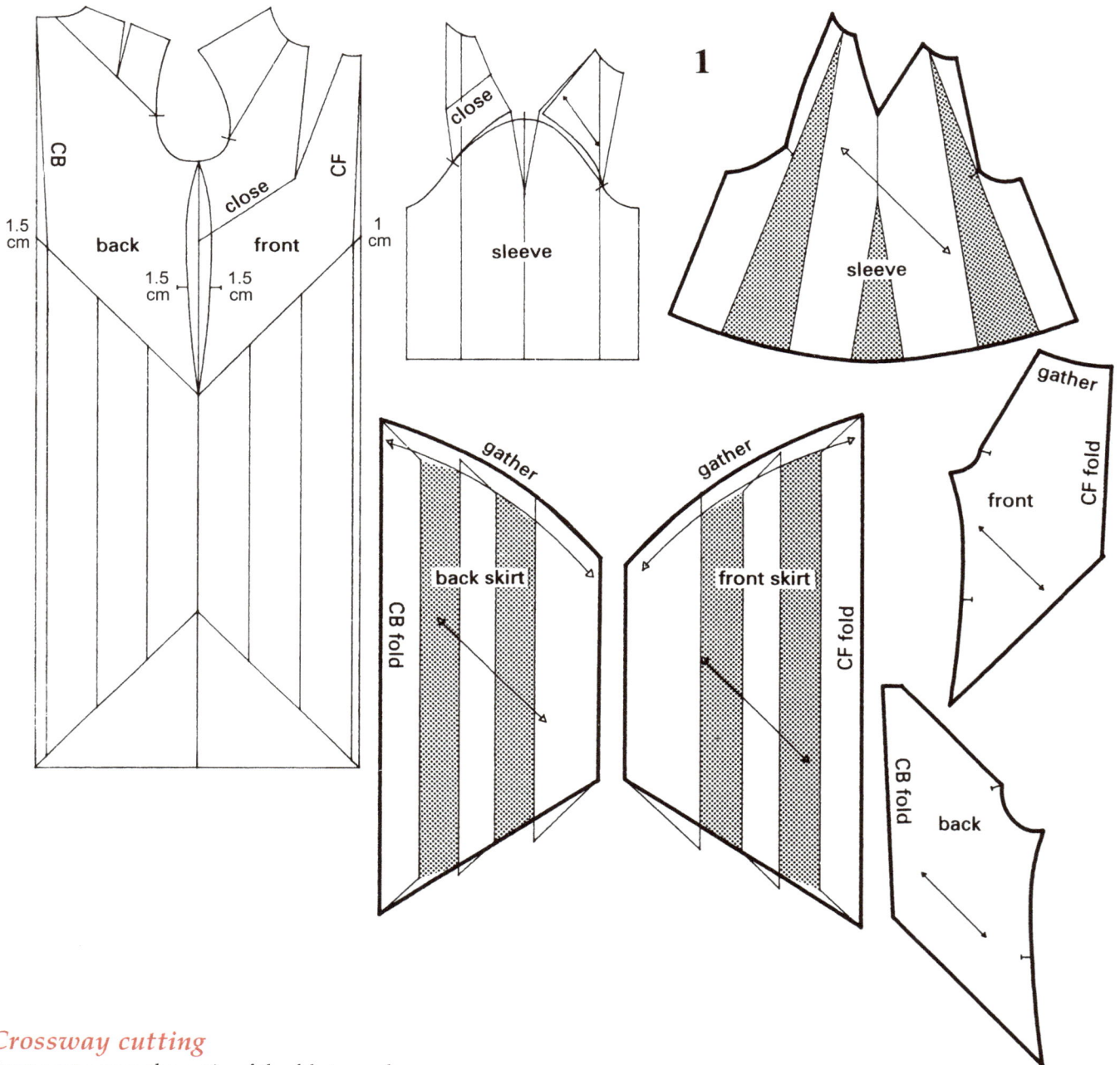

Crossway cutting

Seams cut across the grain of the fabric can become buckled. One of the techniques of crossway cutting is to have seams drawn at a true 45° angle, so that the main seam lines are on the straight grain. The dress is cut from the close fitting bodice (dress) block (ref. page 208).

1 Classic crossway dress shape

Body sections Trace round the block. Extend the length. Place back and front sections together.
Shape in back and front side seams as shown to give a high waist shaping.
Draw in raglan sleeve lines (from balance points), skirt seam lines and hemlines at a 45° angle.
Swing the bust dart to the neckline.
Divide each skirt into three sections.

Back and front bodices Trace off bodice sections.
Change neckline dart into a curved line for gathers.
Sleeves Trace off raglan sections.
Place the raglan sections to the sleeve head, matching balance points. Leave a gap at the sleeve head for ease.
Divide the sleeve into four sections.
Cut up sections. Cut and spread the required amount.
Skirt Trace off the back and front skirt pattern sections.
Cut up the sections.
Cut and open the required amount.
At the top of the skirt, draw a smooth curve between the centre line and the side seam.

1

Fabric

1 Wool crepe
A fabric of medium weight, thickness and shear, but high drape and low stretch.

Pattern cutting

Wool crepe, which has a medium weight and high drape, hangs beautifully when cut on the cross. Used in cutting with classic close fitting blocks, it gives subtle shaping to the body.

1 & 2

Fabric

1 & 2 Modal

A lightweight, thin fabric with high drape and shear, but low stretch.

Pattern cutting

Cutting very close to the body, with a fabric of high shear and high drape, allows the design to shape to the body in a fluid way. The variety of man-made fabrics with these characteristics has made lingerie styles fashionable for day wear.

Crossway cutting: cutting closer to the body

1   Simple 'lingerie' style top

Body sections Trace round the close fitting bodice (dress) block (ref. page 208). Extend the length.
Complete the sleeveless adaptation (ref. 2 page 96).
Swing the bust dart to the neck point.
Draw in the style lines for the top of the bodice and hemline.
Shape in the centre front and back seams and the side seams the amounts shown.
Draw vertical lines from the front dart and centre of the back bodice.
Trace off the pattern sections. Cut up sections.
Close the front dart to spread the hem.
'Cut and spread' the back sections the required amount.
A slight amount of ease will remain over the bust area; this will be eased into the top binding.

2   Simple four gore skirt

Trace round the skirt block (ref. page 207). Extend the length.
Front skirt Eliminate the front dart: take the dart amount out of the front seam.
Add flare to hemline on each seam. Make smooth curves.
Back skirt Eliminate back darts. Create a new dart at the centre, the width of one dart.
Take the second dart amount out of the centre back seam.
Add flare to hemline on each seam. Make smooth curves.

Crossway cutting: closer fitting cowl back

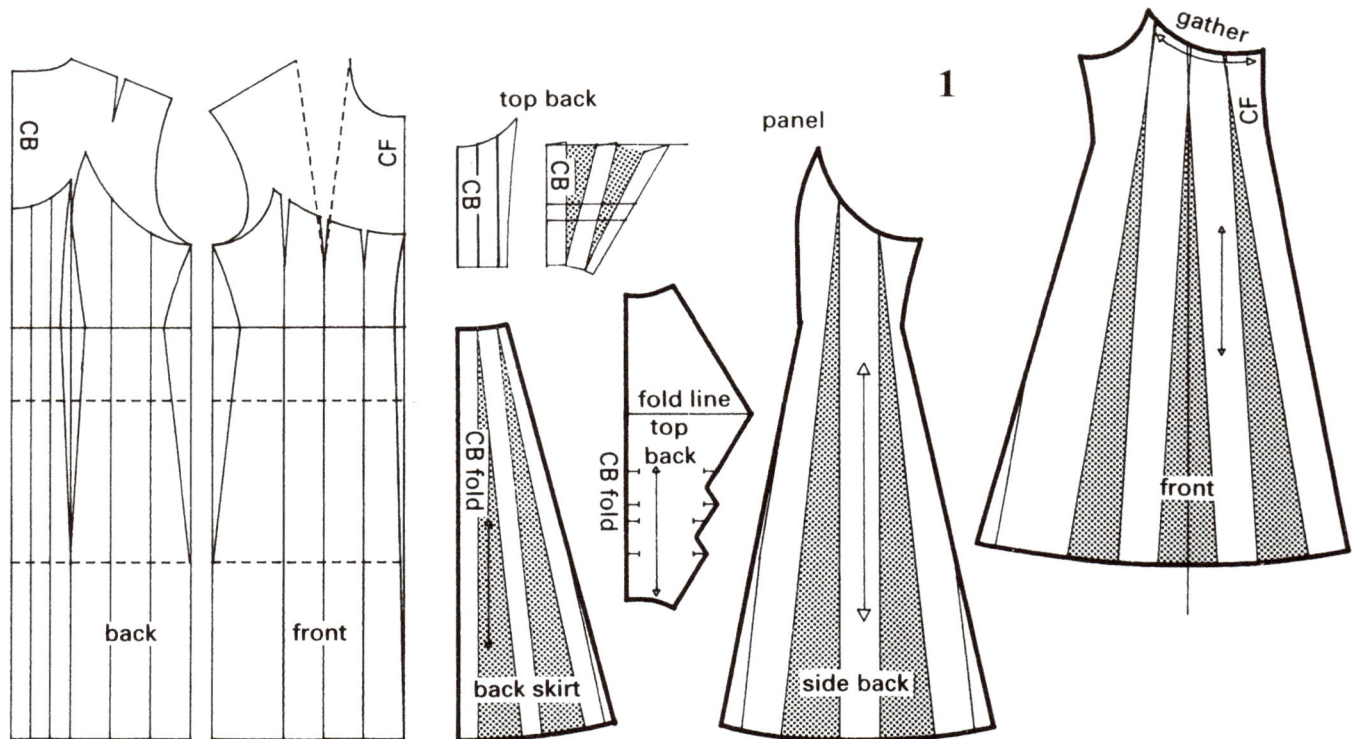

1 Closer fitting cowl back

Body sections Trace round the close fitting bodice (dress) block (ref. page 208). Extend the length.
Complete the sleeveless adaptation (ref. 2 page 96).
Swing the bust dart to the neck point.
Draw in the style lines for the top of the bodice.
Shape in the centre front waist 1cm.
Shape in back and front side seams approx. 3.5cm.
Draw in a back panel line; shape at the waist approx. 3.5cm. Create a small dart at the top edge.
Draw vertical lines to divide the three body sections as shown.
Create three 1cm darts along the front top edge on the section lines.
Trace off the three pattern sections.

Cut across the back panel at the waistline.
'Cut and spread' the front, side front and back skirt sections, closing the front bust darts.
Top back Divide the top back into three vertical sections.
Cut and spread the sections at the top, so that the top is a horizontal line.
Draw a curve at the bottom seam line.
Draw two horizontal pleat lines across the lower pattern.
Mirror the piece to create the back facing.
Using a new piece of paper make two folds for the horizontal pleats.
Lay the main panel piece on top of the paper matching the pleat lines.
Trace round the pattern and cut out.

1

Fabric

1   *Polyester (micro-fibres)*
A lightweight thin fabric, with high drape and shear,
but low stretch.

Pattern cutting

Micro-fibres have a unique quality of high drape and
high shear. Although of low stretch, they drape closely
to the body. and have a high recovery from creasing.
The design, although cut with a flared skirt and a cowl
back, still drapes softly with folds around the body.

1

Fabric

1 *Wool crepe*
A fabric of medium weight, thickness and shear, but high drape and low stretch.

Pattern cutting

When loose shapes are created by crossway cutting, a softer, narrower outline is obtained. The image also illustrates how, when high drape fabrics have large amounts of flare in the pattern, the narrow silhouette still remains.

Crossway cutting: easier fitting

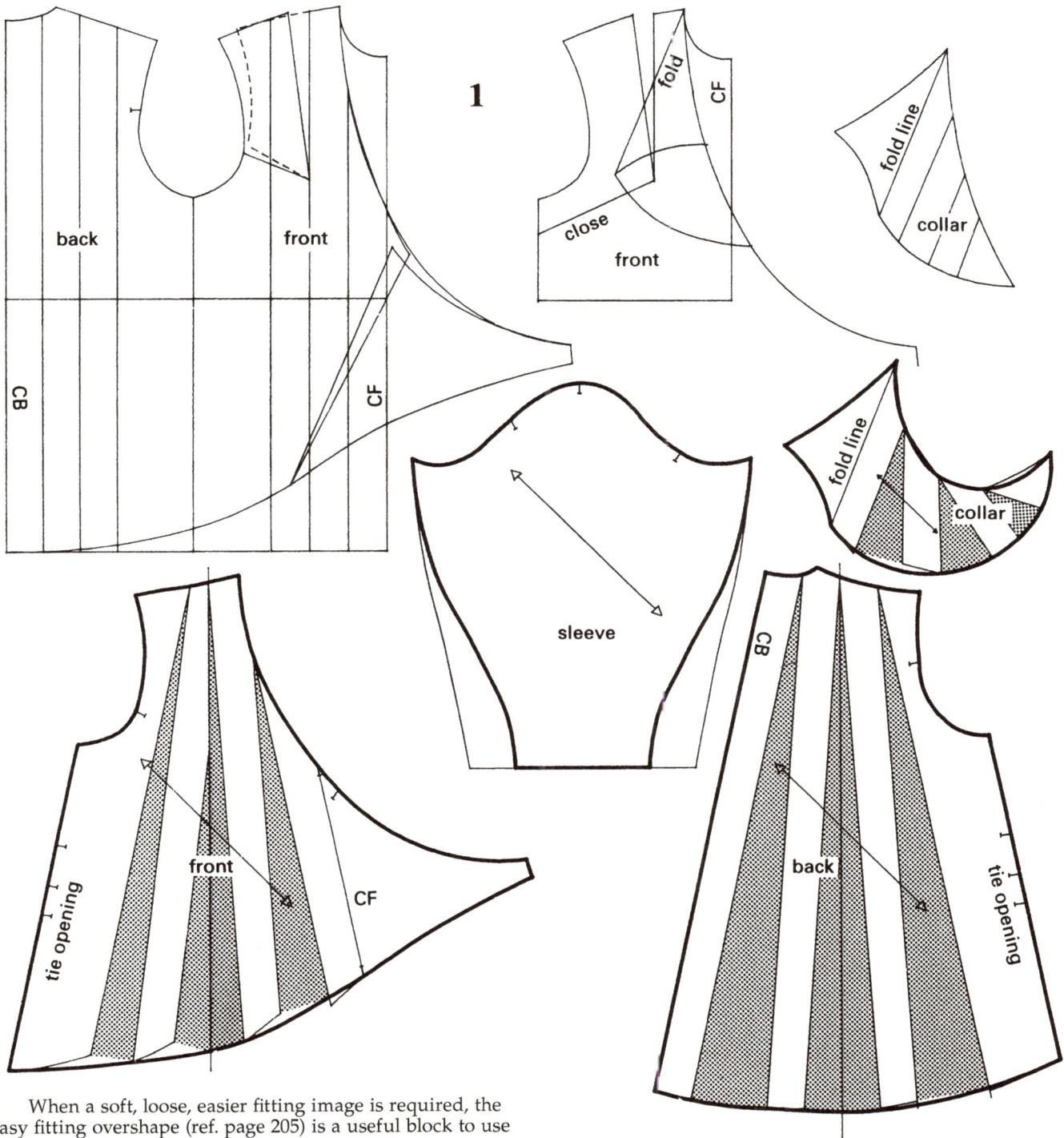

1

back   front

CB   CF

fold   CF

close   front

fold line   collar

fold line   collar

sleeve

front   CF

tie opening

CB   back   tie opening

When a soft, loose, easier fitting image is required, the easy fitting overshape (ref. page 205) is a useful block to use with crossway cutting.

1 Easier fitting shape

Body sections Trace round front block. Extend the length.
Place back and front sections together.
Swing the bust dart temporarily to the armhole line.
Divide the back and front vertically as shown.
Swing the bust dart to the centre vertical line.
Draw neckline; extend it the full width of right front to below waistline.
Draw in new curved hemline
Overlap front neckline to prevent 'sag' (approx. 4cm).

Redraw the front neckline with a good curve.
Draw in the basic collar shape as shown.
Trace off the pattern sections. Cut up sections.
'Cut and spread' the front and back the required amount.
Sleeve Trace round the sleeve block.
Shape in the underarm seams with smooth curves.
(If there is no opening at the bottom of the sleeve, the wrist meas. should allow the hand to pass through.)
Collar Trace off collar; divide into sections.
Cut up sections; 'cut and spread' sections required amount.
Tie Construct tie: width = width of right side seam tie opening; length = approx. 2.5 metres.

Crossway cutting and draped sections

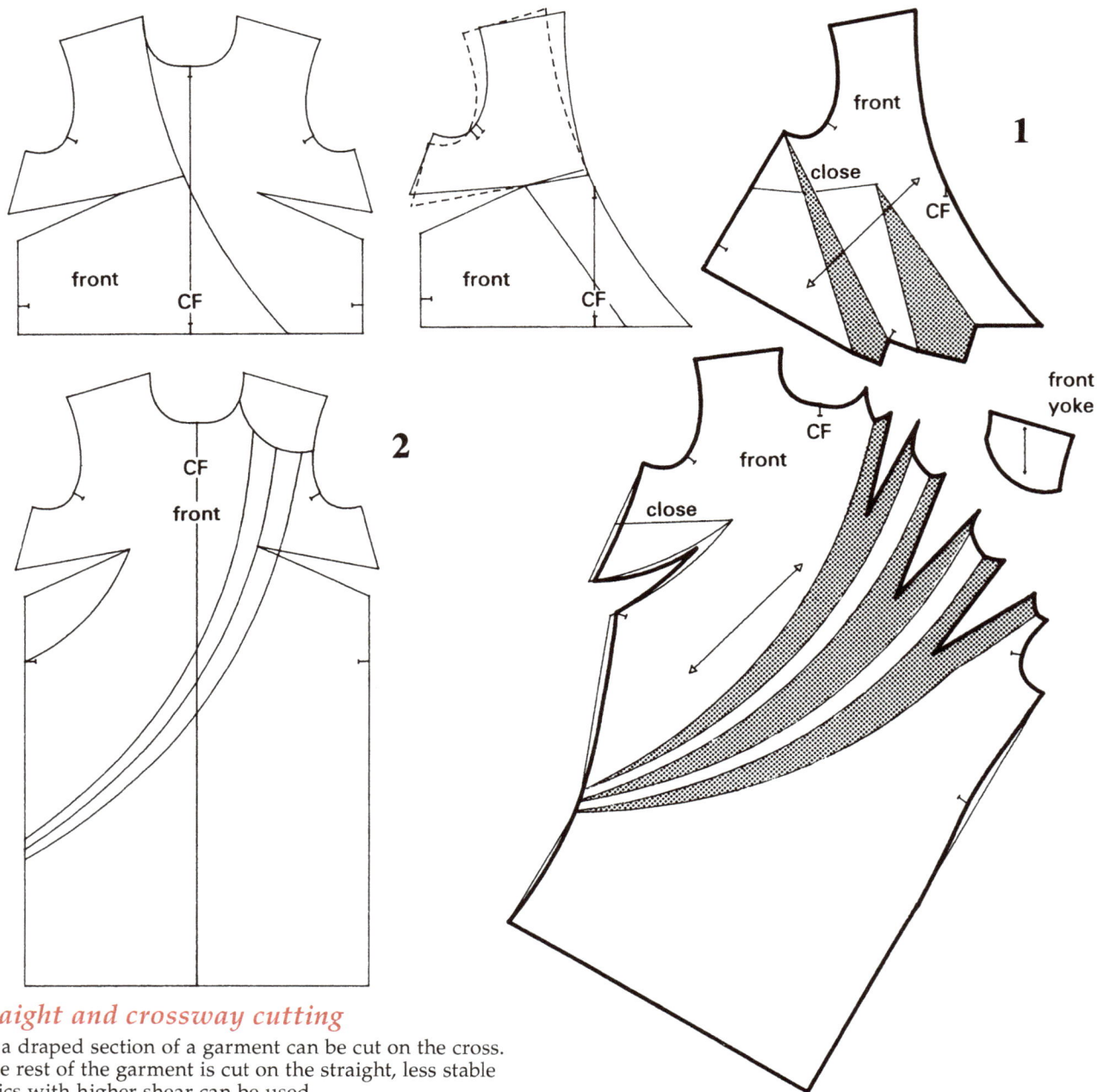

1

front

close

CF

front
yoke

2

CF
front

front

CF

close

Straight and crossway cutting

Just a draped section of a garment can be cut on the cross.
If the rest of the garment is cut on the straight, less stable
fabrics with higher shear can be used.

The first stages of a draped design can be made by
flat pattern cutting, and then the draped section can be
refined on the dress stand. The pattern shape without the
drape adaptation can be used as a mounting to hold the
drape folds in place. If deep draped folds are made, some
fabrics will require some of the bulk to be cut away.

The designs were cut from the close fitting bodice
(dress) block (ref. page 208). Both adaptations are shown
as if the patterns are laid on the right side of the fabric.

1   Draped top front bodice section

Only the front bodice section to be cut on the cross.
Right front body section Trace round the front bodice
block to the length required.
Mirror the block. Draw in the neckline.
Draw a line from the front bust point to the neck edge; cut
and overlap approx 1.5cm to reduce neck 'sag'.
Draw a line from the bust point to the waistline.

Cut up line; close the dart to create the first drape fold.
Draw a line from the armhole to the waistline.
Cut up the line; 'cut and spread' the second drape fold.
Left front section The left bodice is a reverse of the front
pattern before the 'cut and spread' adaptation.

2   Draped front bodice section

Only the front bodice section to be cut on the cross.
Front body section Trace round a mirrored block to the
length required. Draw in the yoke line.
Draw in a curved line from right waist to bust point.
Cut up line. Swing bust dart to new line; shorten the dart.
Draw in the drape folds from yoke to side seam.
Trace off the front pattern section.
Cut and spread the drape lines to create folds, closing the
left side dart to swing the shaping into the folds.
Shape the side seams slightly to give smooth lines.
Front yoke Trace off yoke; cut this on the straight grain.

1

Crossway cutting and mixing the fabric grains

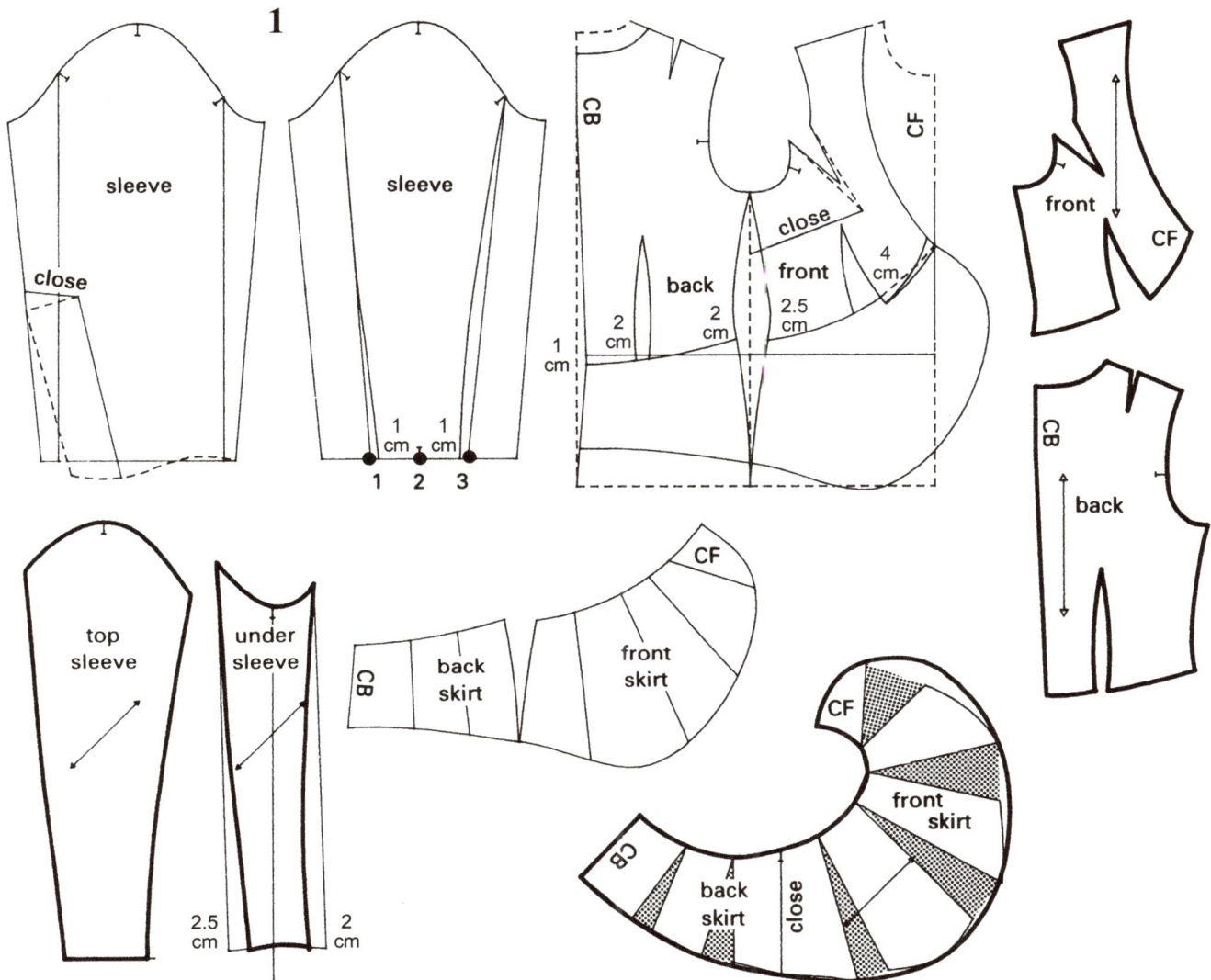

1

sleeve

close

sleeve

1 cm 1 cm

1 **2** **3**

CB

back

2 cm

close

front

2 cm

2.5 cm

1 cm

CF

4 cm

front

CF

CB

back

top sleeve

under sleeve

2.5 cm

2 cm

CB

back skirt

CF

front skirt

CF

front skirt

CB

back skirt

close

Straight and crossway cutting

The design illustrated demonstrates how crossway cut pattern sections can be stabilised, if the main bodice sections are cut on the straight. Crossway cutting of tight fitting sleeves ensures a close comfortable fit, and crossway cutting of the peplum enhances the drape.

The design is cut from the close fitting bodice (dress) block (ref. page 208).

1 Straight and crossway design

Body sections Trace round block to the length required.
Swing the bust dart to the armhole; shorten dart.
Lower the waist at the centre back approx. 2cm.
Draw in the neckline and waistline.
Shape in the centre back seam as shown.
Shape in side seam with curves to give a high waist.
Draw in curved waist darting on bodice front and back.
Take a 1cm shaping from the waist seam at the front neck edge to reduce neck 'sag'.
Trace off the pattern sections.

Peplum Divide back and front peplums into sections as shown.
Place back and front sections together.
'Cut and spread' as shown, giving more spread at the front of the skirt. (The peplum is slightly gathered onto the bodice.)
Sleeves Draw a line from the elbow dart to the base of the sleeve. Cut up the line and close the dart.
Divide bottom line into four sections. Mark points 1, 2, 3.
Draw lines from sleeve balance points to points 1 and 3.
Shape in the top sleeve back seam 1cm from the elbow.
Hollow the top sleeve forearm line 1cm as shown.
Top sleeve Trace off top sleeve pattern.
Under sleeve Trace off under sleeve pattern sections.
Place the underarm seams together.
Shape the outer lines of the under sleeve with smooth curves, hollowing the forearm slightly as shown.
The amount that is taken out will vary, according to the amount of stretch in the fabric.

PART THREE: FABRICS AND THE BODY FORM
Chapter 8 Stretch fabrics and the body form

Stretch fabrics

If fabrics have a high percentage of stretch, blocks without darts can be used and the garment will still fit the body shape. Fabrics with high stretch levels are usually knitted. The stretch characteristic in woven fabrics is mainly used for a 'comfort' fit or a closer fit whilst using basic blocks. Simple blocks with little or no 3D body shaping can be used for closer fitting garments; the natural stretch will accommodate the body shape. Close body-fitting garments require a consideration of the amount of stretch and other important factors because the measurements of some blocks have to be less than the body measurements.

Working with stretch fabrics can be confusing. In narrow fields of design, such as swimwear and some sportswear, complex calculations of stretch and other properties will be required. However, most design using stretch fabrics is not like that; different considerations have to be applied and block shapes change quite dramatically in different groups. An important consideration is the amount that the fabric stretches before it begins to distort unpleasantly, the *'visual stretch'* measurement.

This chapter offers some extra block instructions to supplement the blocks available in Chapter 14, and some basic guidelines to follow.

Note: If you wish to use percentages in any calculation, see a simple calculation method on page 21.

Selecting the block

The selection of a block will depend on the following factors:

(1)   the thickness of the fabrics;

(2)   the fabric should still look appealing **(visual stretch)** when it is stretched to fit the body;

(3)   the fabric should still look acceptable **(visual stretch)** when under stress from body actions;

(4)   fabrics with horizontal stretch and bi-stretch will generally reduce in length when under tension, requiring the adjustment of some vertical measurements;

(5)   if the fabric does not recover well after stretching, a block with more ease will be required.

Further modifications may still be needed depending on the fabric's structure. This usually takes place after the first fitting, when the appearance of the fabric on the body can be seen.

Stretch fabrics – knitted
Very close fitting blocks (knitted fabrics)

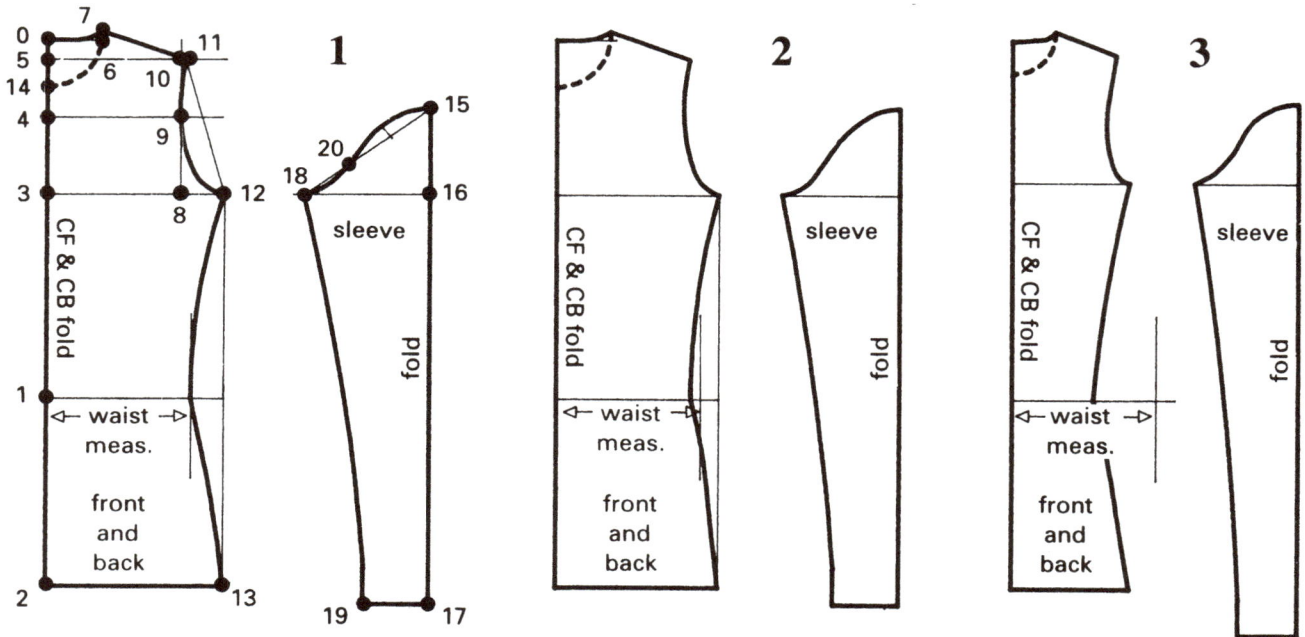

These three blocks are for close body-fitting designs in which the pattern's horizontal measurements are smaller than the body measurements. The block choice should be based on a consideration of factors listed on page 121 and the percentage **visual stretch** of the fabric; see page 21.

The images on the opposite page list and illustrate the factors that influenced the block selection for the garment.

1, 2 & 3 Very close fitting bodice blocks
Measurements required to draft the block
(example size 10) (refer to the size chart page 194)

bust	82 cm
nape to waist	39.5 cm
armscye depth	20.5 cm
neck size	35.6 cm
back width	33 cm
sleeve length	51.3 cm (jersey)
wrist	15.5 cm

Body sections Square down and across from 0.
0–1 neck to waist plus 1 cm; square across.
0–2 finished length; square across.
0–3 armscye depth minus 2.5 cm (3 cm) (5 cm); square across.

0–4 ½ the measurement 0–3; square across.
0–5 ⅓ the measurement 0–4; square across.
0–6 ⅙ neck size (–0.5 cm) (–1.5 cm); square up.
6–7 1.3 cm; draw in neck curve.
3–8 ½ back width minus 2 cm (–2.5 cm) (–6 cm); square up to 9 and 10.
10–11 1 cm; join 7–11.
3–12 ¼ bust measurement minus 1.5 cm (–3 cm) (–8 cm); square down to 13 on hemline.
Draw in the armhole curve, from 11 cm through 9 to 12.
0–14 ⅙ neck size minus 1 cm (–1 cm) (–1.5 cm); draw in front neck curve.
Shape in at the waist 3.5 cm (3 cm) (4 cm).

Sleeve Square down from 15.
15–16 ½ the measurement 0–3 plus 1 cm.
15–17 jersey sleeve length plus 3 cm (3 cm) (6 cm); square across.
15–18 the measurement of the diagonal line from 11–12 on the body section plus 1 cm (0.5 cm) (no ease).
17–19 ½ wrist (–0.5 cm) (–1.5 cm); join 18–19 with a curve.
Divide 15–18 into three sections. Mark point 20.
Draw in sleeve head.
18–20 hollow the curve 0.6 cm.
20–15 raise the curve 2 cm.

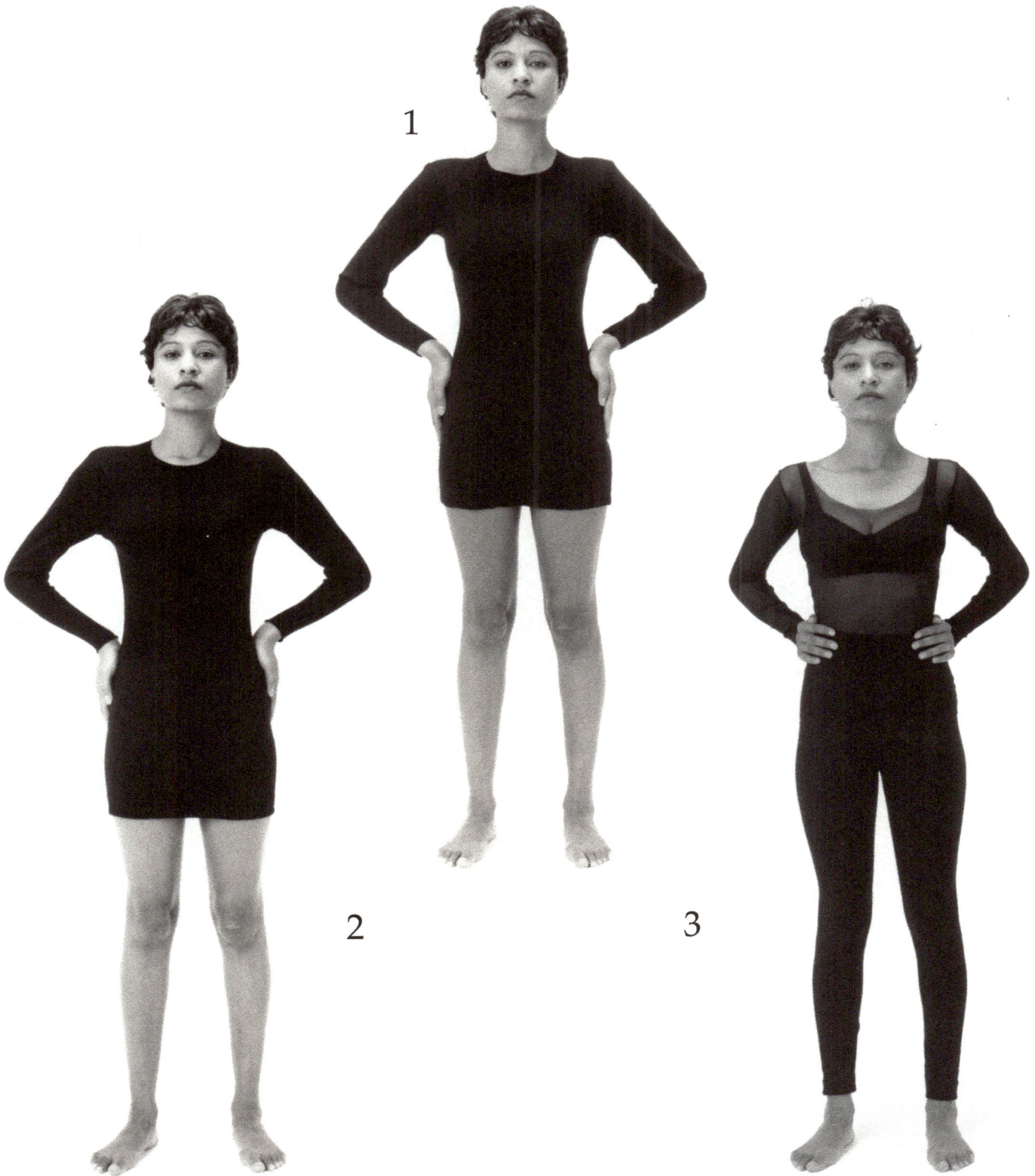

1

2

3

Fabric

1   Cotton/elastane (bi-stretch)
Medium stretch (15.5%): thick – low recovery.
2   Wool/elastane (bi-stretch)
Medium stretch (19%): medium thickness – high recovery.
3   Cotton/elastane (bi-stretch)
High stretch (66%): thin – high recovery.

Pattern cutting – selection

Block choice 1   The selection was based on the fabric thickness and the low recovery.
Block choice 2   The selection was based on the fabric thickness and stretch; the high recovery is a good extra factor. Many knitted fabrics are in this group.
Block choice 3   This block is very close fitting and the fabric needs to rate high on all factors.

1

3

2

Fabric

1 *Wool jersey (low bi-stretch)*
Medium stretch (12.5%): medium thickness – medium recovery.

2 *Wool/polyamide (low bi-stretch knit)*
Medium stretch (15.5%): thick – low recovery.

3 *Wool (warp knit)*
Low stretch (5.5%): medium thickness – low recovery. The fabric was used for an example only.

Pattern cutting – design choices

Block choice 1 The technical choice was overridden by the design choice for a less body-fitting garment.
Block choice 2 The technical choice was overridden by the design choice for a less body-fitting garment.
Block choice 3 Skirt block (ref. page 207).
The diagram (opposite page) shows an example of a modification for knitted fabric.

Close fitting blocks (knitted fabrics)

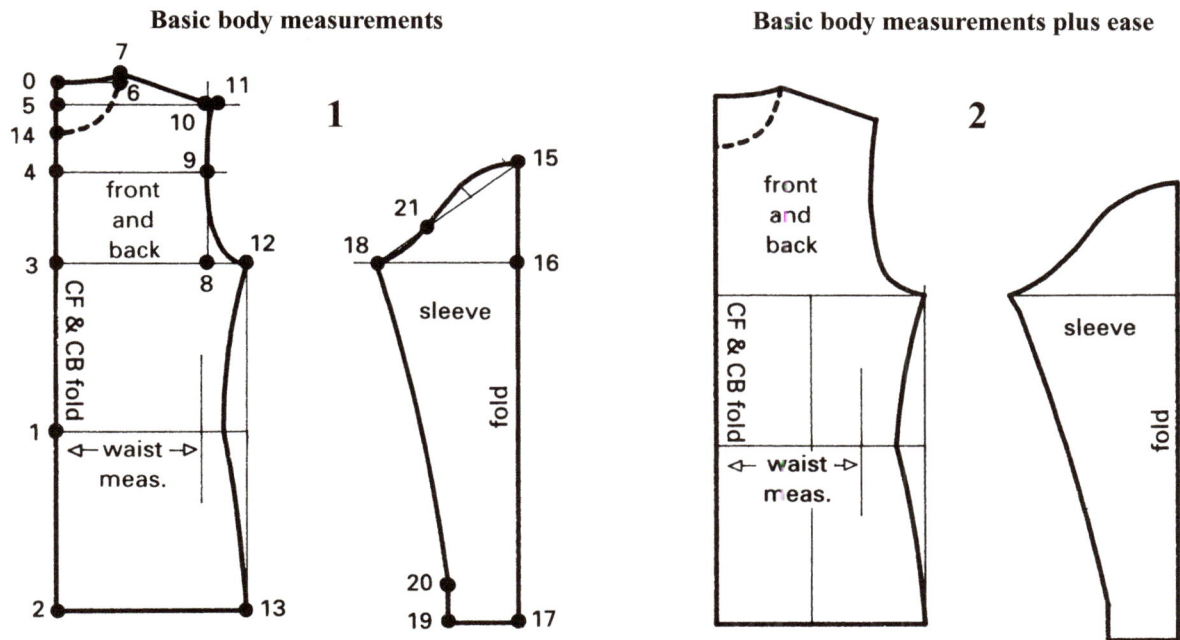

Basic body measurements

Basic body measurements plus ease

1 & 2 Close fitting bodice blocks (knitted fabric)

Measurements required to draft the block
(example size 10) (refer to size chart page 194)

bust	82 cm	neck size	35.6 cm
nape to waist	39.5 cm	sleeve length	51.3 cm
armscye depth	20.5 cm	(jersey)	
back width	33 cm	wrist	15.5 cm

Body sections Square down and across from 0.
0–1 neck to waist; square down.
0–2 finished length; square across.
0–3 armscye depth basic measurement (+1 cm) square across.
0–4 ½ the measurement 0–3; square across.
0–5 ¼ the measurement 0-4; square across.
0–6 ⅕ neck size; square up.
6–7 1 cm; draw in neck curve.
3–8 ½ back width basic measurement (+0.5 cm); square up 9 and 10.
10–11 1 cm; join 7–11.
3–12 ¼ bust basic measurement (+2 cm); square down to 13 on hemline.
Draw in the armhole curve, from 11 through 9–12.
0–14 ⅙ neck size minus 1.5 cm; draw in front neck curve.
Shape waist if required 2.5 cm (3.5 cm).
Added waist shaping can be achieved by waist darts.

Sleeve Square down from 15.
15–16 ½ the measurement 0–3 plus 1 cm.
15–17 jersey sleeve length plus 2 cm; square across.
15–18 the measurement of the diagonal line from 11–12 on the body section plus 1.5 cm (2 cm).
17–19 ½ wrist (+0.5 cm); square up to 6 cm to 20. Join 18–20 with a curve.
Divide 15–18 into three sections. Mark point 21.
Draw in sleeve head.
18–21 hollow the curve 0.6 cm.
21–15 raise the curve 2 cm.

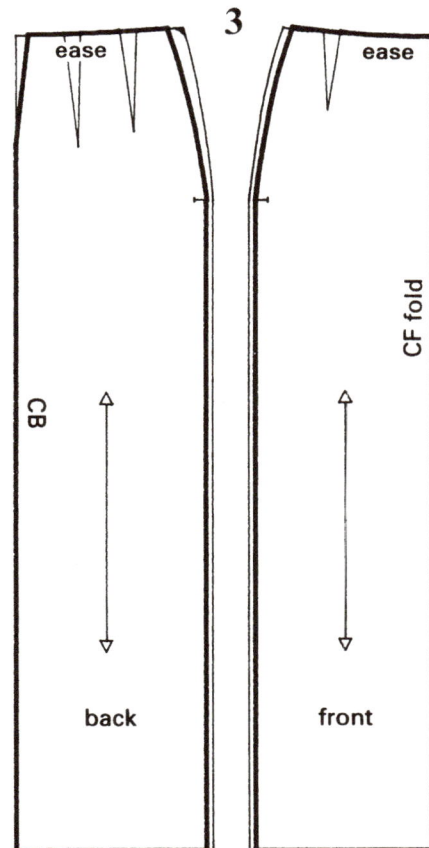

3 Close fitting skirts (knitted fabric)

Using the skirt block as a guide
The diagram and image show the pattern reduced to basic body measurements (see page 130 for further calculations). Transfer some dart shaping to side and back seams. The remainder can be left as ease, and the waist elasticated.

Cutting with dart and seam shaping (knitted fabrics)

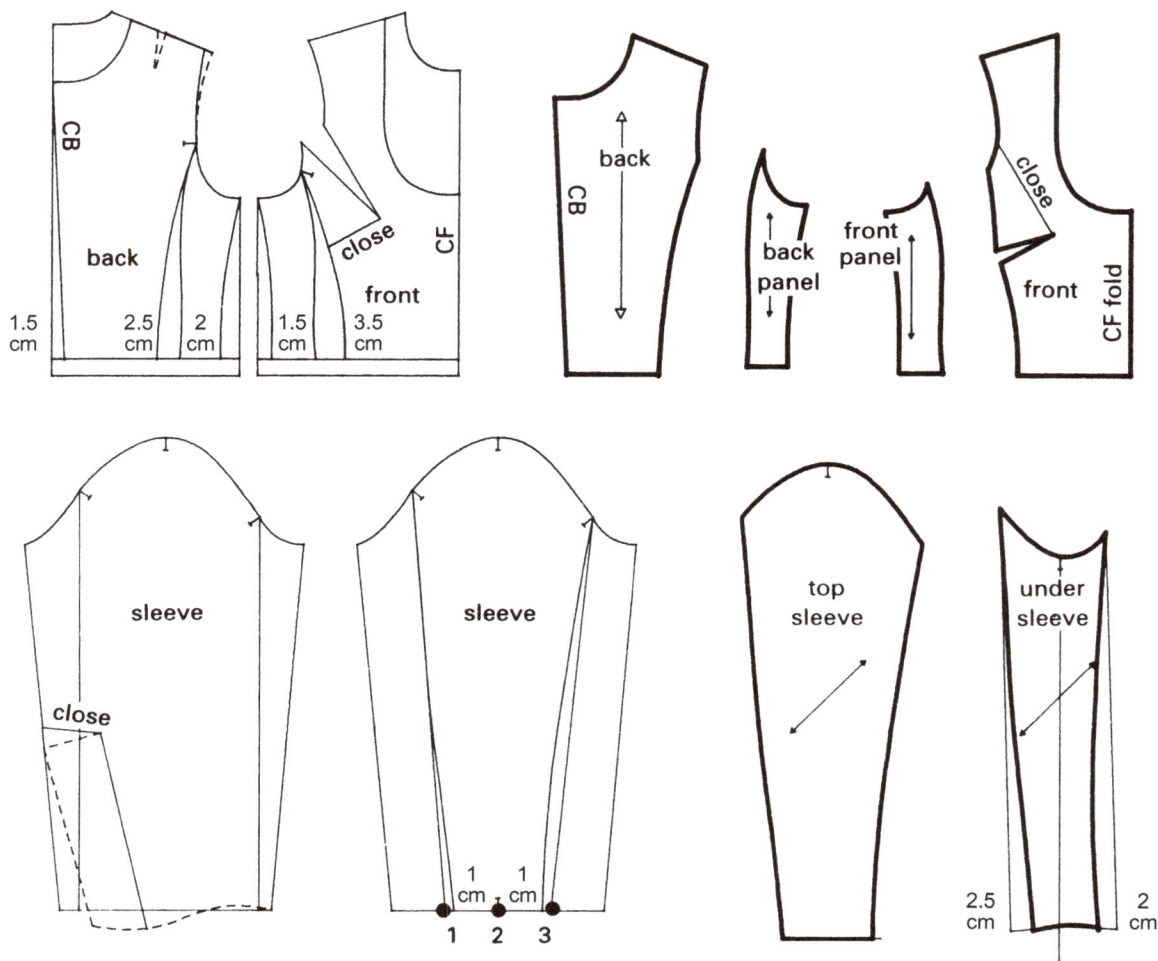

If a close fitting 'curvy' seamed style is required, woven fabric blocks with darting can be used with knitted fabrics. The fabric should be stable with low shear and drape, but could have low or medium stretch.

1 Styled overgarment

Body sections Trace round the close fitting bodice block (ref. page 208).
Remove the amount of back darting from the shoulder edge.
Transfer the bust dart to the armhole.
Draw in required back and front neckline.
Raise the waist level by approx. 2 cm.
Shape in centre back seam waistline 1.5 cm.
Shape in the side seams with curved seam lines as shown.
Draw in curved bodice seams from the sleeve pitch points.
Create waist shaping with curved bodice lines; draw in with the amount of waist shaping shown.
Draw a line from front bodice seam line to the bust point.
Trace off the bodice sections.
Close armhole bust dart on front bodice.
Sleeves Draw a line from the elbow dart to the base of the sleeve. Cut up the line and close the dart.
Divide bottom line into four sections. Mark points 1, 2, 3.
Draw lines from sleeve balance points to points 1 and 3.
Shape in the top sleeve back seam 1 cm from the elbow.
Hollow the top sleeve forearm line 1 cm as shown.
Top sleeve Trace off top sleeve pattern.
Under sleeve Trace off under sleeve pattern sections
Place the underarm seams together.
Shape the outer lines of the under sleeve with smooth curves, hollowing the forearm slightly as shown.
The amount that is taken out will vary according to the amount of stretch in the fabric.
Skirt Construct a gathered skirt (ref. page 62).

1

Fabric

1 Dress bodice – wool bouclé
A heavy fabric of medium thickness, low drape and shear, and medium stretch.

1 Dress skirt – mohair (weft knit)
A fabric of medium weight, thickness, drape, shear and stretch.

Pattern cutting

Using a close fitting bodice block with shaped seams prevents the fabric from distorting over the bust shape; it also allows the bulky fabric to be removed from the waistline. The stretch in the fabric allows the sleeve shaping to be cut close to the wrist.

The stable bodice anchors the less stable skirt fabric.

1

2

Fabric

1   *Wool bouclé (bi-stretch)*
A lightweight thin fabric, with high drape shear. It has medium stretch but low recovery.
2   *Wool worsted/elastane (bi-stretch)*
A fabric of medium weight and thickness with medium drape, shear and stretch.

Pattern cutting

Block choice 1 (ref. 1 page 125).
A basic body fit was required. There also had to be little strain because of the fabric's low recovery.
Block choice 2 (close fitting jacket block page 203).
A basic body fit was required; the elastane in the fabric was used to give a 'comfort' fit.

Stretch fabrics – woven
Close fitting bodice shaping (woven/stretch fabrics)

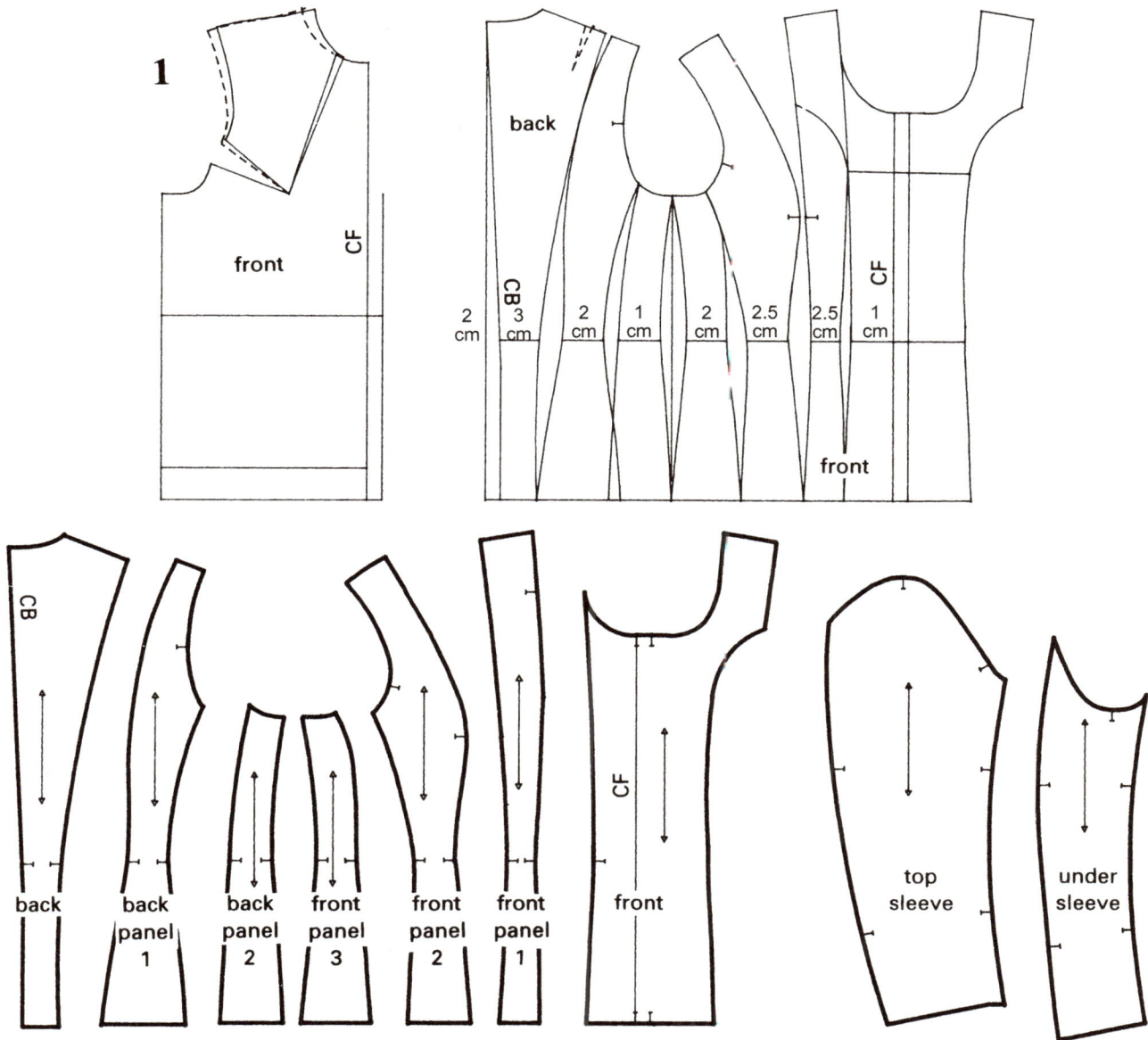

1

front

CF

back

CB 3 cm

2 cm

2 cm

1 cm

2 cm

2.5 cm

2.5 cm

1 cm

CF

front

CB

back

back panel 1

back panel 2

front panel 3

front panel 2

front panel 1

CF

front

top sleeve

under sleeve

1   Close fitting tee shirt: (woven/natural stretch fabric)

Because the close fitting knitwear block (ref. 1 page 125) was selected for this example, no diagram is shown.

Many woven fabrics have some natural degree of stretch; this will depend on the fibre as well as the structure. Some woven fabrics with a high degree of stretch can be treated as knitted fabrics. Most woven fabrics have a low recovery rate, so the very close fitting knitwear blocks on page 122 are not useful. The other criteria on page 121 also need to be considered. The close fitting tee shirt is treated in this way.

2   Close fitting jacket: (woven/elastane fabric – comfort fit)

Most worsted/elastane suitings have medium to low **visual stretch** characteristics, but have good recovery and stability. Many designs, such as the jacket example, are cut conventionally with close fitting seaming, and use the elastane as a 'comfort' fit. This example uses the elastane content to allow extra darting for a very close fit.

Body sections Trace off the close fitting jacket block to required length (ref. page 203).
Transfer bust dart to armhole.
Reduce neck curve (ref. page 96).
Place back and front sections together at the side seams.
Draw in curved seam lines with the 16 cm waist shaping evenly spread as shown.
Draw in new neckline as required.
Add button stand and extended facing.
Trace off bodice and pattern sections.
Sleeve Trace off basic sleeve pattern.

Close fitting skirt shaping (woven/stretch fabrics)

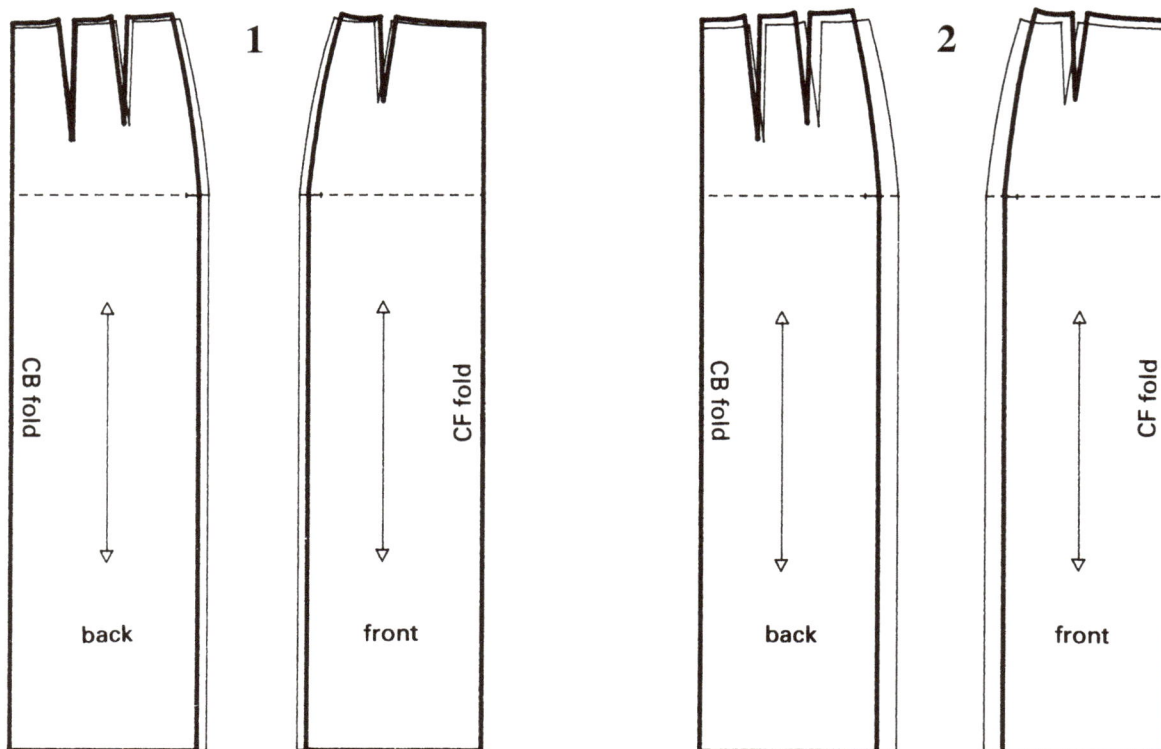

Cutting patterns for woven fabric with elastane

Many woven fabrics have natural stretch; using elastane in woven fabrics offers stretch and also good recovery. Fabrics in a narrow product range can have a set of criteria specially developed for them. The diagrams show how the mathematical procedures of cutting these fabrics with varying amounts of stretch, can control and retain the complex shape of a skirt block pattern. The diagrams show the changing shape as the percentage reduction is increased, and how it is necessary to distribute it evenly between all the block construction drafting points.

The skirt diagrams above were produced on a CAD system, which is the best way of obtaining accurate results. Most large companies have CAD systems that can automatically extend and decrease patterns horizontally and vertically. If fabrics are stretched horizontally, they often require extra vertical allowances.

General percentage reduction guide
(To refer to the calculation for percentages, see page 21.)
Reduce the pattern 5% in all horizontal measurements for every 10% visual stretch measurement.

Increase the vertical measure by 2% for every 5% where the fabric is under tension.

Ideally, this should be done at block construction by computer to reduce the pattern evenly. If the pattern has to be adjusted manually, by cutting and overlapping the pattern, the overlaps must take place proportionally in each section of the pattern, for example:

on a skirt	hip, dart positions altered;
on a bodice or jacket	neck width, back width, bust.

1 Skirt block pattern reduced slightly
The garment had the horizontal measurements reduced by 5% and the vertical measurements of the areas under stress increased by 2%, as shown in the diagram.

2 Skirt block pattern reduced further
The garment had the horizontal measurements reduced by 10% and the vertical measurements of the areas under stress increased by 5%, as shown in the diagram.

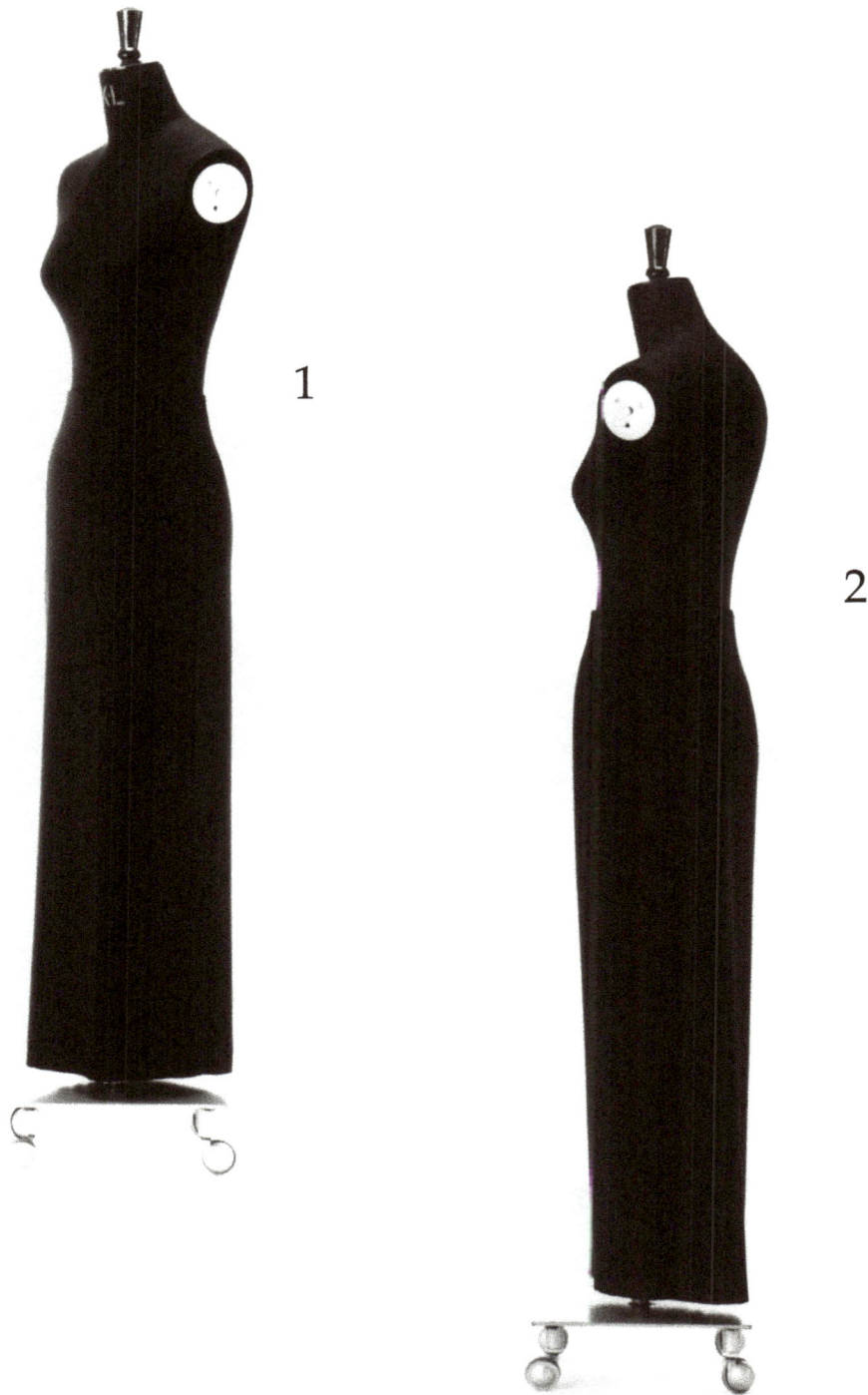

1

2

Fabric

1   *Wool/elastane (bi-stretch)*
A fabric of medium weight, thickness, drape and shear.
Medium stretch and low recovery.
2   *Wool/elastane (bi-stretch)*
A fabric of medium weight, thickness, drape and shear.
Medium stretch and recovery.

Pattern cutting

The skirt block (ref. page 207) was used to demonstrate the reductions that can be given with reference to the fabric stretch.

The tighter fit achieved, with a greater reduction of the block pattern, is shown in image 2.

2

1

Fabric

1 *Polyester/elastane*
A fabric of medium weight and thickness; low drape and shear; medium stretch and recovery.
2 *Wool/polyamide/elastane*
A thick fabric of medium weight, drape and shear. High stretch and medium recovery.

Pattern cutting

The design decision, which appears to contradict the technical data, was made for the following reasons. In image (1), the close body-hugging fit enhances the 'slick' quality of the fabric as it stretches over the body. In image (2), the thicker textured, ribbon weave fabric has medium shear that can be easily distorted. The design also aimed for a less formal, easier fitting shape.

Simple coat shape – comparisons of fabric stretch (woven/stretch fabrics)

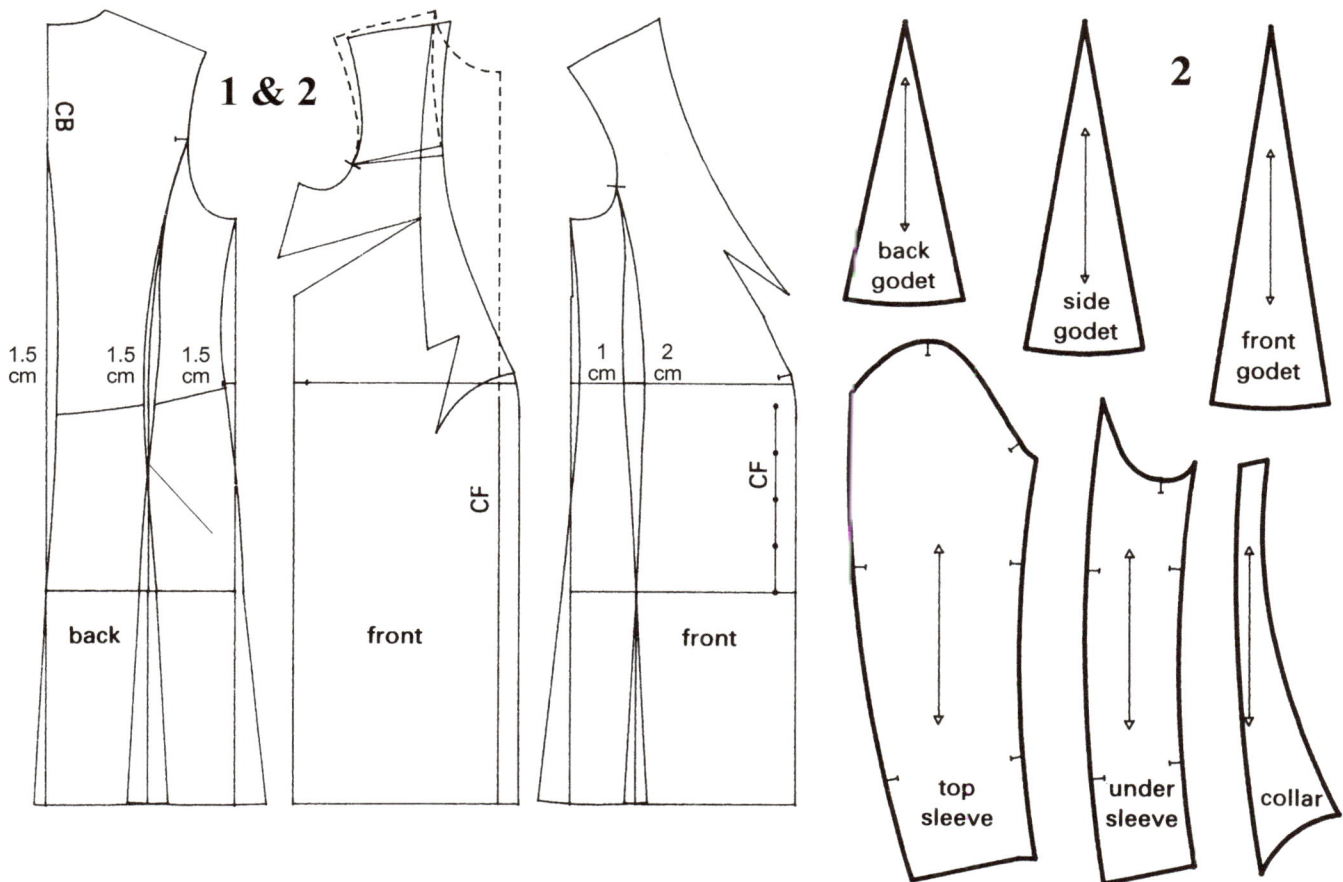

Comparisons of fabric stretch

The same basic pattern was used for both garments, except that the second image had godets inserted in the skirt seams. The close fitting jacket block (ref. page 203) was used for the examples. The design illustrates that more than just the stretch calculation has to be considered when creating a garment. Because the fabric in **Image 2** has a higher stretch rating than **Image 1**, you would expect that the second garment pattern should be reduced more than the first. However, the same pattern was used because an easier fitting design was required.

1 & 2 Close fitting coat – fabric stretch

Body sections Trace off the close fitting jacket block (ref. page 203). Remove rever shape.
Extend centre front line; draw temporary high neckline.
Add buttonstand.
Draw new low curved neckline.
Cut across to the armhole and overlap neckline 1.5 cm to prevent neckline 'sag'.
Draw in collar shape; trace off collar shape.
Swing bust dart to neckline.
Draw in panel lines with smooth curves and semi-fitting waist shaping as shown.
Add flare to the hemline on each of the panels.
Trace off all pattern pieces.
Sleeve Trace off basic sleeve.
Godets Simple triangular godets were inserted into the seams of **Image 2**.

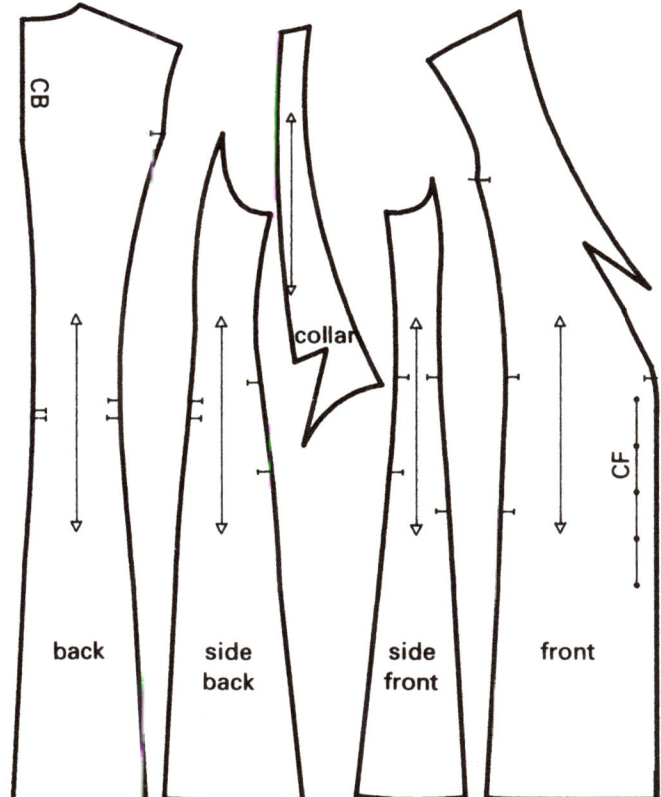

PART FOUR: FABRICS AND COMPLEX CUTTING

Chapter 9 Complex 'flat' cutting

Complex 'flat' pattern cutting

'Flat' pattern cutting gives the designer an opportunity to work with complex geometric shapes. The basic flat grid shapes can be developed into very complex 3D shaped garments. This is not a body-fitting look, although garments may fit closely to the body in places. A geometric shape is useful for exploring new elements of shape rather than being *driven* by the body shape. It is a different relationship between body and fabric. When using fabrics with high drape or shear, interesting folds can form around the body. Alternatively, working with structured fabrics can produce designs that are often described as architectural; they use the moving body to display and change the shape. A 'flat' pattern shape can have little resemblance to the shape of garment it produces. A crucial part of its transition to garment is the part played by the fabric's characteristics.

A 'flat' envelope shape has to be large enough to allow for movement; this factor particularly affects trousers. Patterns developed from geometric shapes have to provide gussets or increased fabric in the most stressed area of the garment. The envelope shape can be comfortable, if it is large enough, if the fabric will stretch enough, or if gussets allow for movement.

All the blocks in this chapter are 'flat' blocks. They are: a knitwear block, the basic grid and the shirt block. All the blocks are constructed wider than the body and have no bust darting.

Knitted fabric

'Flat' pattern cutting provides the base for most of the garments made from knitted fabrics. Some structured knitted fabrics can be cut using the same principles as woven fabrics, but also exploiting the unique characteristics of high drape and high stretch inherent in most light or medium weight knitted fabrics. Knitted fabrics have distinct characteristics. Most knitted fabrics have a low-shear rating, but loose tension or coarse gauge fabrics can distort when they are cut and seamed across the wales; or they can bow outwards when under strain, if they have a low recovery from stretch.

Complex 'flat' cutting – knitted fabrics

Complex 'flat' cutting: coat (knitted fabrics)

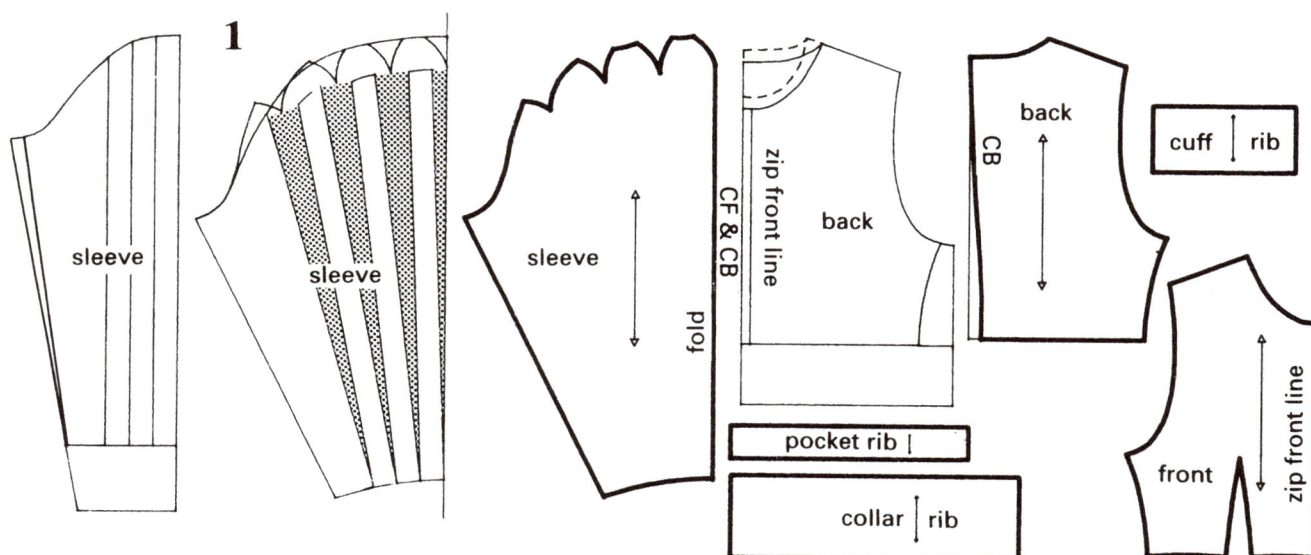

The 'flat' knitwear blocks

Close fitting knitwear blocks can be found in Chapter 8.
The easy fitting knitted fabric body shape (page 201) is a good basic shape for knitted fabric overgarments. It can be used for a wide range of designs in casual wear. It can also be used for complex garments.

1 Knitted coat

Body sections Trace round the easy fitting knitted fabric body shape (ref. page 201).
Mark in the high waistline, front zip line, lowered neckline.
Shape in side seam with a curved line; shape 4 cm at waist, 2 cm at the underarm.
Trace off front and back bodices.
Shape in back the seam 1 cm.
Construct a 2 cm front waist dart.
Sleeve Reduce the sleeve width at the armhole, the same amount as bodice armhole.
Reduce the sleeve by the cuff depth – 6 cm.
Divide the sleeve into sections, 'cut and spread' as shown.
Raise the sleeve head approx. 4 cm for extra fullness.
Construct convex darts to make the sleeve head the same measurement as the armhole.
Skirt Construct three skirt panels: length = length required; width of the three panels to total 3 x the measurement of the full bodice waist.
Divide the waist fullness into concave darts.
Collar, pocket and cuff These are constructed from a firm ribbed fabric.

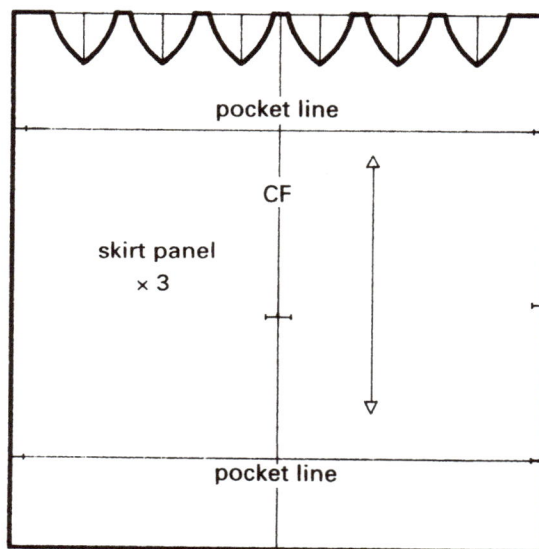

1

Fabric

1 Wool/viscose (weft knit)
A thick, heavy fabric with low drape and shear, and medium stretch. Loose or unstable fabrics are unsuitable for this type of cutting. Fleece or double jersey fabrics are more successful.

Pattern cutting

Knitted ribs can control and force different outlines and hold necklines on knitted shapes.
Darts can be used where the fabric is too thick for making gathers.

1

Fabric

1   *Linen (weft knit)*
A medium weight, light fabric with high drape and medium shear and stretch. Many light to medium weight fabrics will drape beautifully when cut on the straight grain.

Pattern cutting

The bodice, cut in a raglan shape, requires taping to hold the raglan seam. The skirt was constructed by draping the fabric directly on the stand. This is usually the most successful method.

Complex 'flat' cutting: dress (knitted fabrics)

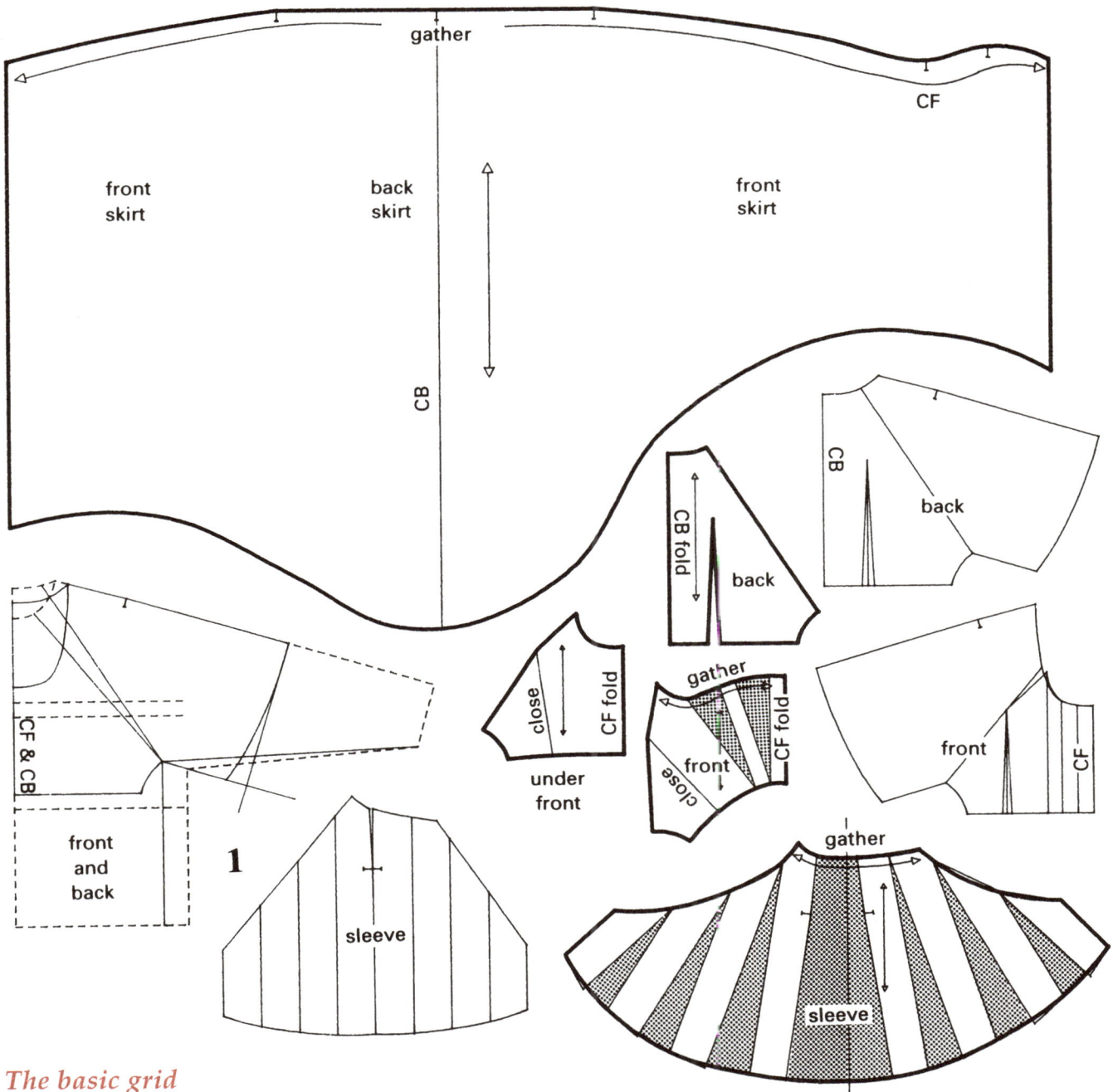

Diagram labels:

gather — CF — front skirt — back skirt — front skirt — CB — CF & CB — front and back — **1** — sleeve — close — CF fold — under front — gather — close — front — CF fold — CB — back — back — front — CF — gather — sleeve

The basic grid

The basic grid (ref. page 195) is a basic block draft that provides a simple but effective way of cutting both knitted and woven fabrics.

1   Draped knitted dress

Back and front sections Trace round the easy basic grid draft with angled sleeve line. Reduce side seam by 4cm.
Draw in high waistline.
Draw an inside sleeve line parallel to the outer sleeve line.
Draw in sleeve length; shape up at the underarm.
Draw in a curved side seam; shape in 3cm at waist.
Draw in the back and front raglan lines.
Draw in lowered neckline.
Trace off front and back bodices.
Construct 1.5cm waist darts.

Take a 1.5cm dart out of the front neck to prevent 'sag'.
Cut off the sleeve sections.
Front Divide the front neckline into three sections.
'Cut and spread' the neckline as shown.
The original front pattern remains as an under bodice.
Sleeve Draw a vertical line. Place sleeve sections together at the line, a small shoulder dart will remain.
Divide sleeve pattern into sections as shown.
Trace off the pattern sections. 'Cut and spread' the sections; leave a gap at the centre for gathers.
Skirt A proportionate pattern is shown of the skirt section; this was draped on the dress stand.

Geometric 'flat' cutting: trousers (knitted fabrics)

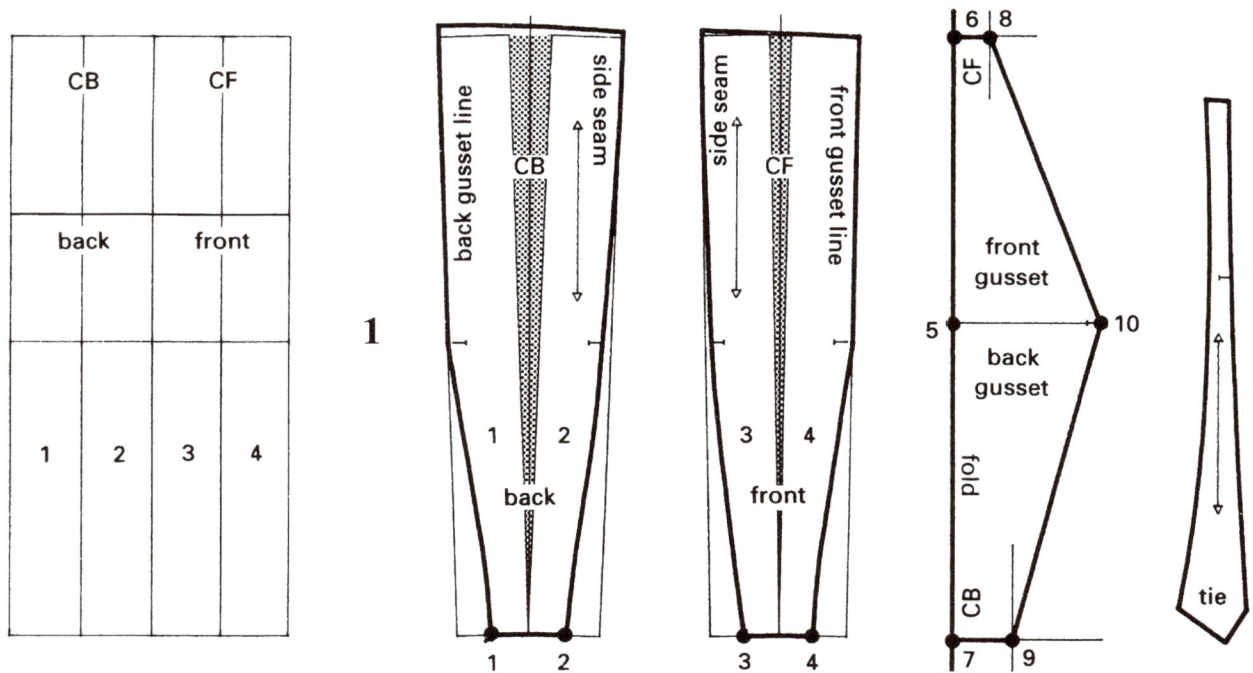

Geometric cutting

Geometric cutting offers an infinite number of shapes to clothe the body. This example is influenced by historical reference. Studies of historical costume and the work of Japanese designers illustrate the creative possibilities of geometric cutting.

1   Trousers – geometric cutting

Main sections Construct a rectangle: length = required length; width = ½ hip width plus 5 cm.
Draw a line approx. 30 cm from the top edge.
Draw a low crutch line 50 cm from the top edge.
Divide into two; make back section 1 cm larger than front section.

Divide back and front into two sections.
Cut out the sections.
'Cut and spread' the waistline, opening more at the back than the front.
Mark points 1, 2, 3, 4, approx. 4–5 cm in from outer edge.
Draw curved lines at side seam from hip point to hem.
Draw curved lines at inside leg from crutch point to hem.
Gusset Square up and across from point 5.
5–6 = 4 cm; 5–7 = 4 cm; 6–8 = 6 cm; 7–9 = 10 cm.
5–10 = 24 cm.
Join all outer points of the shape.
Tie Construct a tie the required length and shape.

1

Fabric

1   Viscose flocked polyester (weft knit)
The fabric is of medium weight, thickness and shear, giving some structure to the trousers. Its most important characteristics of high drape and stretch allow the fabric to drape around the figure.

Pattern cutting

A simple geometric base can create many different trouser shapes. Studies of historical costume books show how cutting trousers developed. They also provide a source for exploring many methods of geometric cutting.

1

Fabric

1 Lambskin with fleece
The fabric is of heavy weight and thickness, low drape shear and stretch. This type of fabric will create its own structure that can be exploited.

Pattern cutting

Designs influenced by folk costume can become complex shapes with asymmetrical style lines. The shape of the lambskins determined some of the outer edges of the pattern sections.

Complex 'flat' cutting – woven and leather fabrics
Complex 'flat' cutting: coat – lambskin

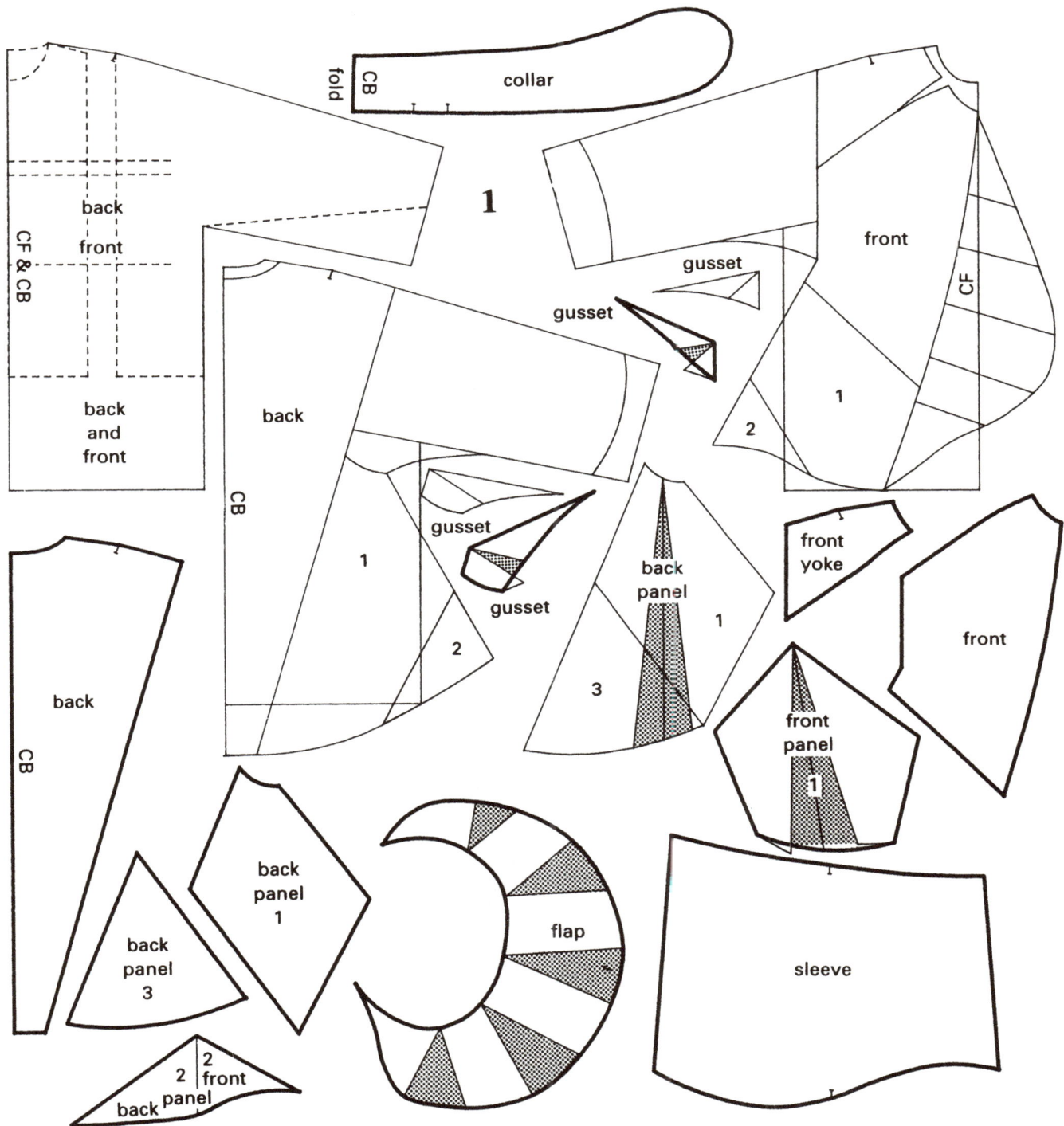

The basic grid – angled sleeve

The basic grid (ref. page 195) gives freedom to experiment with complex shapes. Irregular shapes can be drawn on the block, divided into sections, and further adapted.

1   Lambskin coat – asymmetrical cutting

Body sections Trace off block to length required.
Widen body section of basic grid (approx. 5 cm).
Draw in new sleeve line parallel to outer line.
Draw in lower edge of sleeve and shaped hemline.

Draw in style lines and flap. Draw in 1 cm neck dart.
Draw in a shaped gusset section at the underarm.
Trace off the pattern sections. No grain lines are required.
Skirt panels Join back and front panels 2 at side seam.
'Cut and spread' back and front skirt panels 1.
Divide back panel 1 to create back panel 3.
Sleeve Join sleeves; draw a slight curve at sleeve head.
Collar Construct a simple collar to the shape required.
Flap 'Cut and spread' the flap to the shape required.
Gusset Divide gusset through centre: open approx. 4 cm.

Complex 'flat' cutting: jacket (woven fabrics)

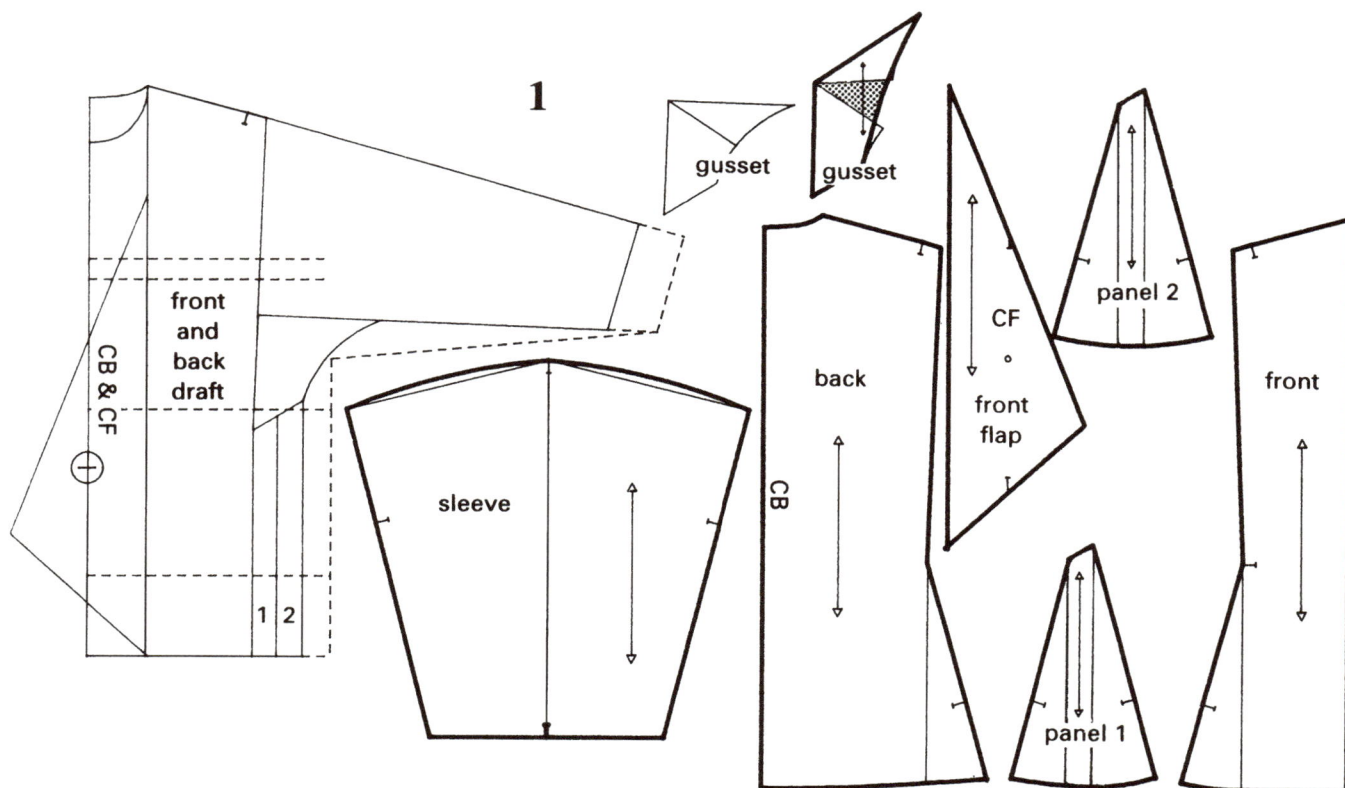

1

The basic grid – angled sleeve

The basic grid with the angled sleeve (ref. page 195) is again used to give a further example of creating a complex shape; it also adds gusset ease within a panel.

1 Jacket

Body sections Trace off block to length required.
Reduce the body section of the basic grid (approx. 3 cm).
Reduce the sleeve length and underarm seam, creating a new curve to the side seam.
Draw in style lines; create a gusset shape and two skirt panels from the base of the gusset.
Square down from neck shoulder point to hem.

Draw in front flap.
Trace off the body pattern sections.
Back and front Add approx. 5 cm flare to the skirt from the gusset point.
Panels 1 and 2 Add approx. 5 cm flare to each side of the panels.
Gusset Divide gusset through the centre; open approx. 4 cm.
Flap Trace off the front flap.
This pattern section could also be 'cut and spread' to create a fluted effect.
Sleeve Trace off the sleeve sections.
Place back and front sleeves together; make a smooth curve at the sleeve head

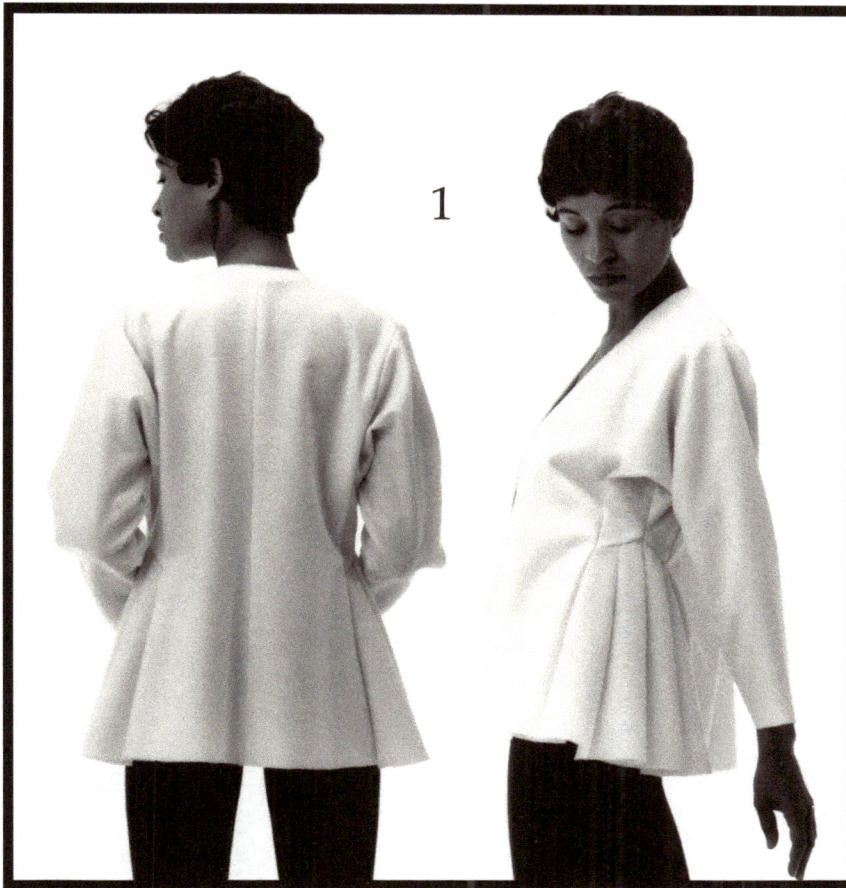

1

Fabric

1   Wool

The fabric is of medium weight, thickness, shear and drape, but low stretch. The fabric has stability, but its fibre gives it the ability to drape in soft structured folds.

Pattern cutting

This is a great fabric for experimenting with shape. The stability of the fabric allows the style lines to be distinct, and the extra style lines create more complex shapes.

146

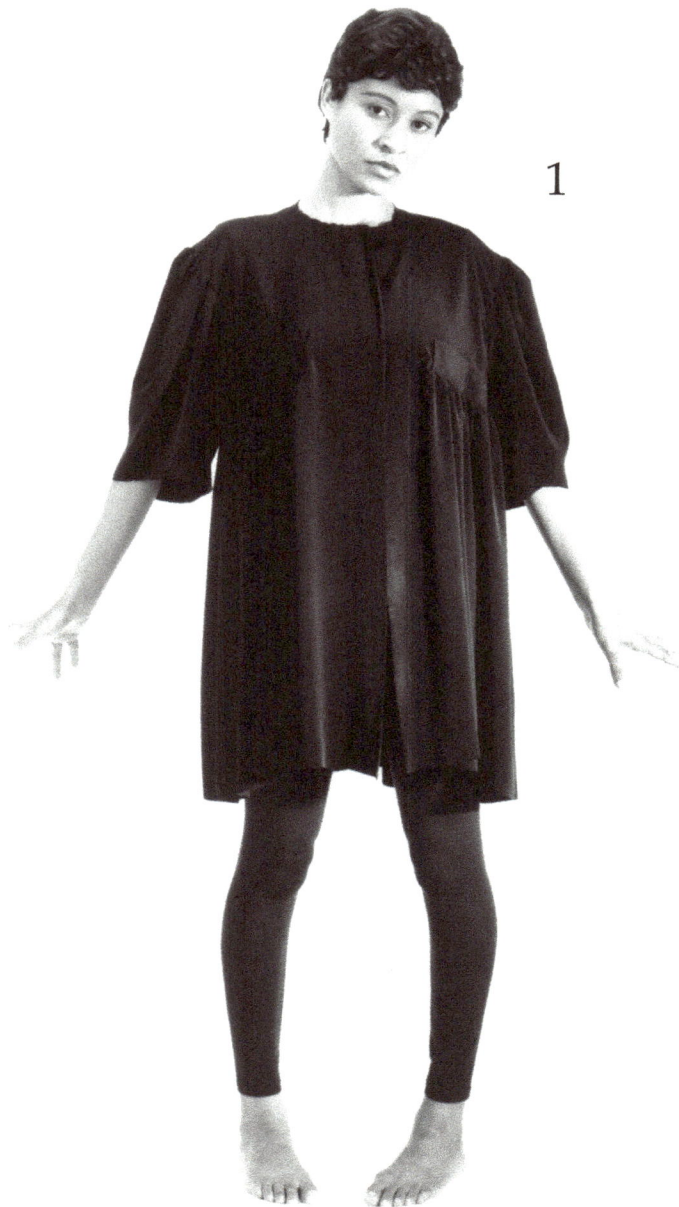

Fabric

1   Polyester (micro-fibre)
The fabric is of light weight and thickness, high shear and drape, but low stretch.

2   Polyamide
The fabric is of light weight and thickness, low shear, drape and stretch.

Pattern cutting

Two fabrics, whose only difference is their shear and drape, create quite different outlines.

Complex cutting can be a marrying of concept with a precision of cut and selection of fabric.
The shirt block is a great basic shape that is rarely used in this way.

Complex 'flat' cutting: using the shirt block (woven fabrics)

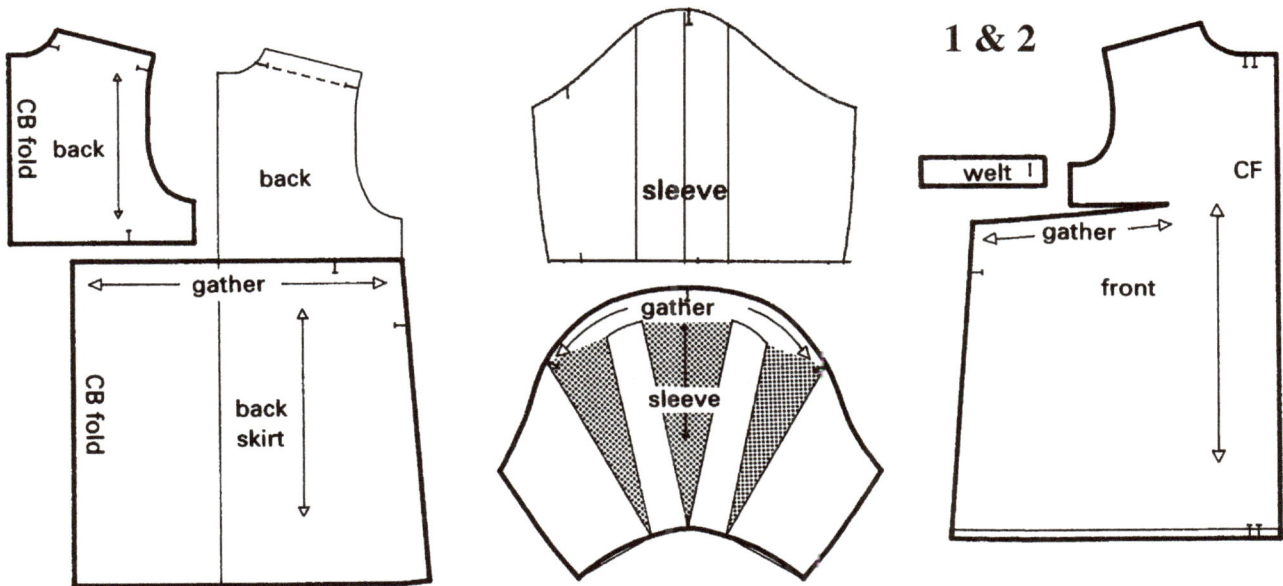

1 & 2

Shirt block

The shirt block (ref. age 198) has no bust darting and can be classed as a 'flat' block. However, if you try to lay the garment flat you will find it will rise slightly under the arms, showing that a form of hidden gusseting exists within the shape. The block in this book is an easy fitting women's shirt block; it can be used for all types of garments, from formal to casual wear, and in virtually all woven fabrics and all lengths. Knitted fabrics with a very stable structure could also be used with this block.

1 & 2   Adapted shirt styling

Back sections Trace round back shirt block. Extend to the length required. Draw in back yoke line.

Back yoke Trace off back yoke.
Back skirt Extend the back skirt the required amount for gathers.
Front Trace round front shirt block. Extend to the length required. Extend the length a further 2 cm.
Construct a dart at front gather line: length = 7 cm; width = 2 cm.
Extend the front skirt the required amount for gathers.
Sleeve Trace round sleeve to required length.
Draw three vertical lines at the centre of the sleeve.
Cut up lines; 'cut and spread' the sleeve head as shown.
Raise the sleeve head as shown.
Trace round the pattern.

Creating a 'flat' body map for cutting

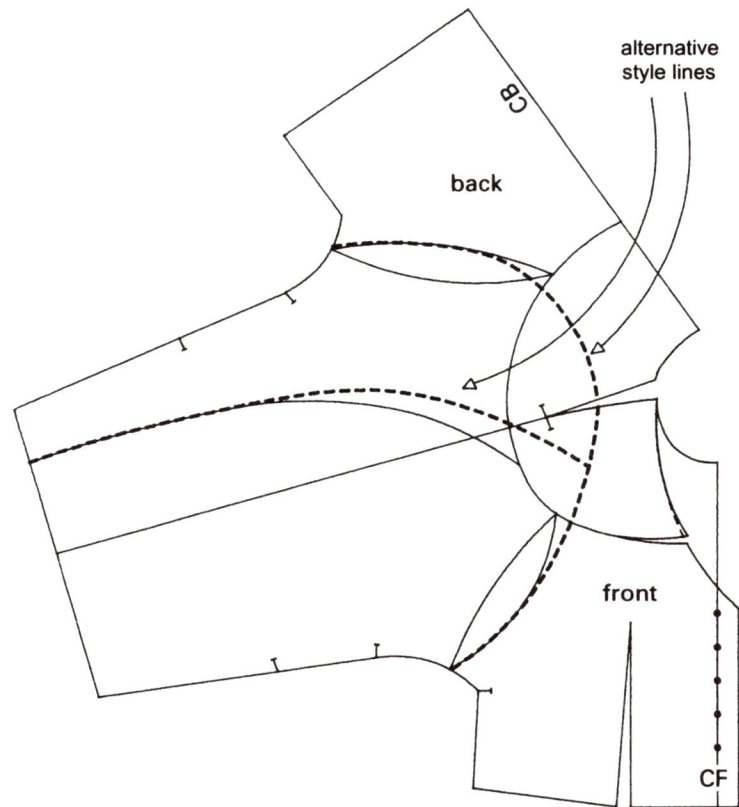

alternative
style lines

CB

back

front

CF

Creating a body map – using a kimono shape from the basic grid or the shaped kimono block

A simple body map can be created using the simple kimono block from the basic grid (ref. page 195) or the shaped kimono block (ref. page 197).

Example: using the shaped kimono block

Body section Trace round back and front blocks.

Place the outer sleeve seams together. A small dart will appear at the neckline.

Many different style lines can be then drawn on the new block shape; they can extend from the front to the back of the design, as shown above.

The sections can be separated and further adaptations can be made to the pieces to create different outlines.

PART FOUR: FABRICS AND COMPLEX CUTTING

Chapter 10 Supporting fabrics

Structure

Fabrics with structure can be cut to create their own form, see pages 136, 142 and 146 in the previous chapter. However, garments cut away from the body often have some structure added to the fabric to control the shape. Added structure also may be needed to create exaggerated or sculptured shapes that a fabric cannot create alone. Shapes may be required for theatrical or performance garments that are not practical in the general sense. Standard techniques are often of little help and great ingenuity is required to build many of these constructions.

The handle of fabrics, or the shape of a garment can be subtly or dramatically changed by the type of interlining. Interlinings are used in many garments; it may only be a small amount to strengthen certain areas such as collars, cuffs and waistbands or may cover large areas. In some cases, such as mounting, it may completely back the fabric. A garment may require substantial areas to have a different handle yet have the same surface appearance. A great deal of research has been focused on providing fusible and non-fusible interlinings that are sympathetic to fabrics and will wear, launder or dry clean without distorting them. They can be expensive. Couturiers will use silk and cashmere to give delicate fabrics support yet retain a light and high drape handle. Almost any fabric, woven knitted or bonded, can be used to support another. However, most interlining and mounting fabrics have a close structure, are light in weight, and are black, grey, beige or white. These fabrics can be sew-in or fusible. The majority of interlinings today are non-woven.

Interlining and mounting fabrics

Techniques for using sew-in interlinings can require some skill. Conventional basic plan weave fabrics in natural fibres are still used as sew-in interfacings, particularly in couture and bespoke tailoring.

Non-woven and knitted interlinings are used as sew-in interlinings; however, the amount is decreasing. Fabrics must be pre-shrunk by laundering or steaming.

Fusible interlinings

Fusible interlinings had some strange effects on the outer appearance of garments when they first became available in the 1950s. Fabrics shrank, bubbles appeared, 'board-like' sharp revers on jackets signalled their use. Today, most manufacturers use fusibles very successfully; the range is enormous in knitted, woven and bonded structures. They are used in all types of garments, from fine semi-transparent designs to heavy tailored or padded overgarments.

The fusible interlining consists of the base fabric and its coating (in scatter, paste or powder dot form), which heat-sets the interlining to the garment. Natural fibres are still used in many interlinings for tailoring, and graduated 'canvases' are available to give different thickness over the chest areas. However, man-made fibres dominate the fusible interlining market (mainly polyamide, polyester, viscose and polypropylene). Warp-knitted fabrics are gaining popularity as a base fabric; although there can be problems of handling the fabric, they have a sympathetic handle, particularly when used on jersey fabrics. Competition for knitted fusibles may come from the new developments in woven-stretch interlinings which are taking place. They are being developed to complement many of the new stretch and micro-fibre fabrics.

Non-woven interlinings

The fibres are bonded together by a variety of means; by entangling the fibres, stitch-bonding, or binding by chemical or heat processes. Many of the early problems of stiffness or disintegration of the lighter weights have been solved. Their greatest advantage is their stability in mass-production.

Supporting fabrics

Structure: fitting the body

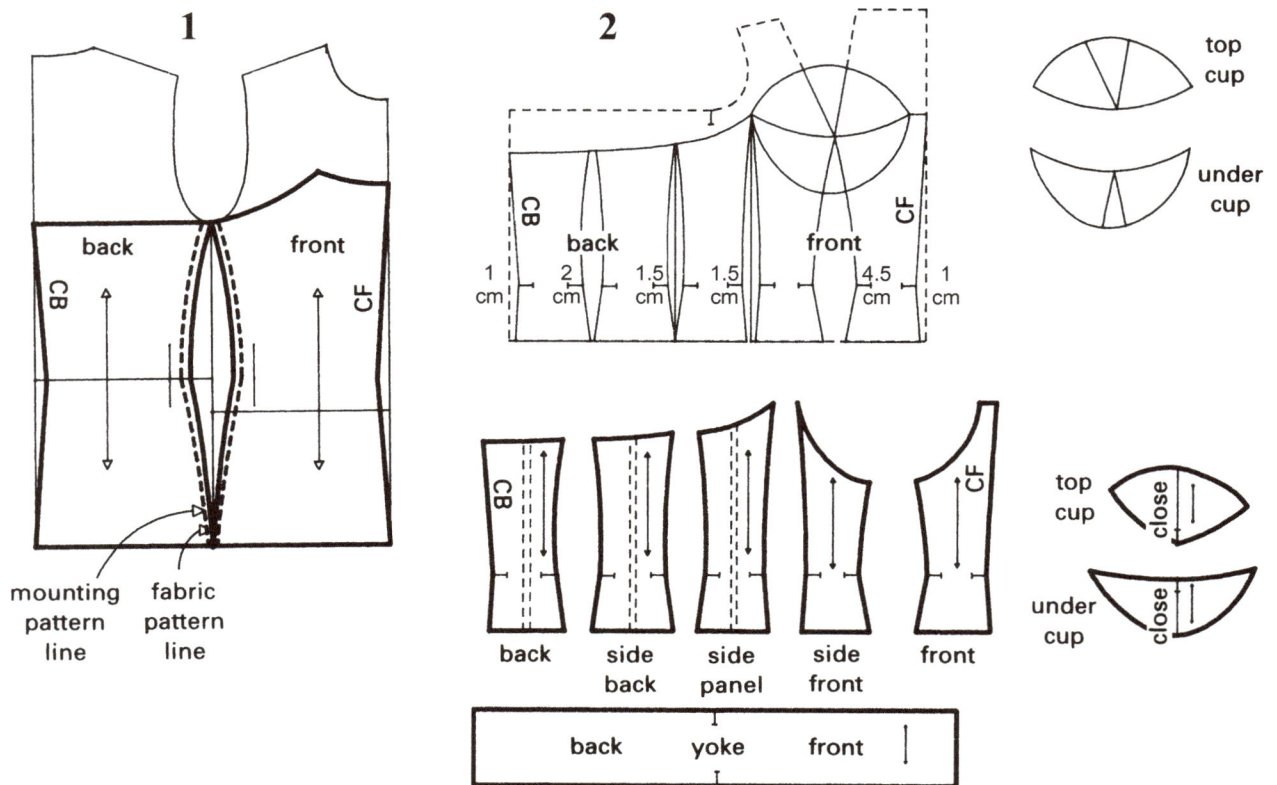

1

back   front

CB   CF

mounting   fabric
pattern   pattern
line   line

2

CB   back   front   CF

1   2   1.5   1.5   4.5   1
cm   cm   cm   cm   cm   cm

top
cup

under
cup

CB   back   side   side   side   front   CF
        back   panel   front

back   yoke   front

top
cup   close

under   close
cup

1 Flexible structure – natural shaping

Body fitting garments in fabrics with high shear can be stabilised; any distortion can be contained by a slightly smaller underbody made from a stretch fabric, particularly knitted elastane.
Body sections Construct the body sections of a knitwear block (ref. 1 page 125).
Mirror the front section.
Shape in the back seam 1.5 cm.
Draw in curved side seams, shaping the waist 3 cm.
Reduce the under body pattern 1 cm at the side seam.
Skirt A simple gathered skirt is shown on the image. The width is 3 x the measurement of the total base of the bodice pattern.

2 Classic boned bodice – constructed shaping

Permull (known as body stiffening) provides a good base for strapless designs or corset shapes. It will mould into shape with steaming, and boning will retain the structure where required. The fabric used for the cups is interlined with a fusible jersey fabric.

Body sections Trace off the lingerie block which has wide bust dart shaping (ref. page 209).
Place back and front sections together.
Draw in the bust cup shape.
Draw in body panels, re-distributing the waist shaping as shown.
Trace off the body panels.
Close the darts in the upper and lower cups.
Suggested positions for boning are shown.
Skirts They can be cut in any dramatic width or shape. Underskirts of paper nylon and layers of net achieve the exaggerated bell shape on the model stand. Underskirts for this type of design should always hang from skirt yokes to lessen the bulk at the waist.
The thickness of the fabric will determine the amount of fullness that can be gathered onto a tight bodice.

Note: Wiring can be used to control the shape around cups or to give distorted shaping to fullness in any area of the garment. The model shows a hem twisted and buckled using wiring.

Fabric

1 *Cotton lace – main fabric*
   Wool/elastane (weft-knit) – underbody
The main fabric is of medium weight, thickness, drape and stretch and high shear.

2 *Silk/lurex – main bodice*
   Silk/linen/viscose – bodice cups and skirt
The main bodice fabric is of medium weight, thickness, shear and stretch, but low drape. The remaining fabric used in the design is a light, thin fabric with high drape and shear, but low stretch.

Pattern cutting

Image (1) The underbody has low shear and high stretch. This means that the lace fabric is contained by the elastane underbody, and this retains and controls the natural body fitting shape of the lace.

Image (2) Structured body shapes work best if fabrics have some shear and stretch so that the bodice can be moulded with the permull interlining. Fabrics with high shear have to be more firmly interlined; for example, the bodice cups.

Fabric

1 Polyester

The main fabric is of light weight and thickness, high drape and shear, but low stretch.

2 Polyamide/elastane – main fabric
Polyester – padding and lining

The basic fabric is of light weight and thickness with medium drape, shear and stretch. The process of padding and quilting the fabric changes its thickness, drape and shear very dramatically.

Pattern cutting

Image (1) is a simple 'A' line jacket in polyester chiffon. Interesting contrasts can be made by using very light-weight fabrics in transparent fullness together with a padded section, the collar.

Image (2), contrast its shape with image (1). The same pattern shape (totally padded), with slightly more flare inserted, creates a totally different outline.

Notes: The fabric should be padded before cutting out. Closer fitting shapes have to be cut with extra ease.

Structure: padding

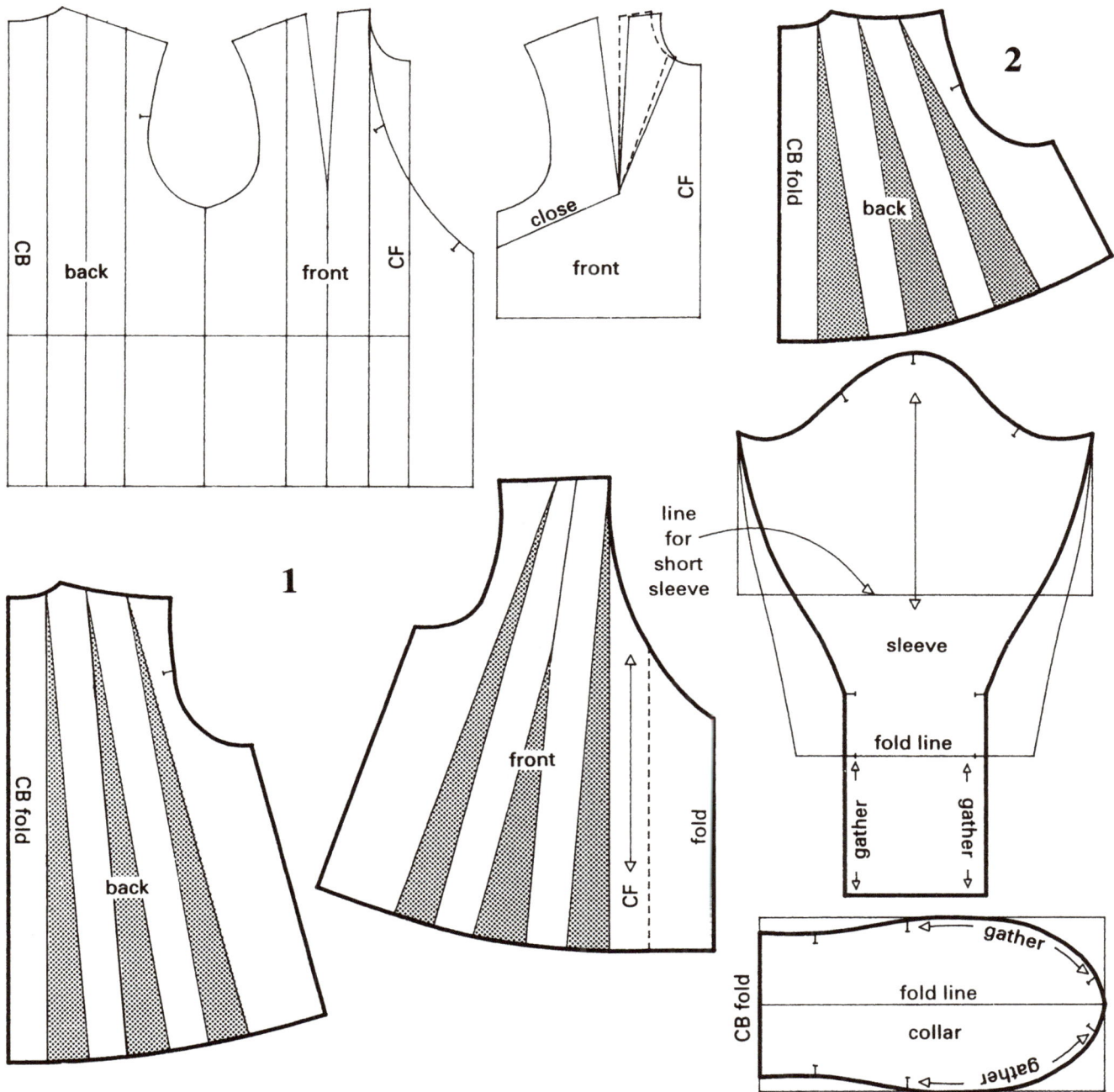

1 Wide overshape – padded collar

Body sections Trace round the easy fitting overshape block (ref. page 205) to the required length.
Swing bust dart to the shoulder.
Overlap neck (ref. page 96).
Draw in a wide buttonstand; draw in a low neckline.
Divide block into sections; drop a line from the bust dart.
Trace off pattern sections.
'Cut and spread' the hemline, closing the bust dart.
The front and back are cut in double fabric.
Sleeve Shape in the sleeve as shown; extend the cuff section at least twice the length.

Collar Draft a rectangle; the length is the neck measurement, extend it by the amount of gathering required. Draw in collar shape.

2 Quilted overshape – total padding

The adaptation uses padded and quilted fabric.
Body sections Trace round the block to the required length. Continue as adaptation 1, with extra flare.
Sleeve Square down from armhole points to short sleeve length. 'Cut and spread' the sleeve hem.

Structure: mounting

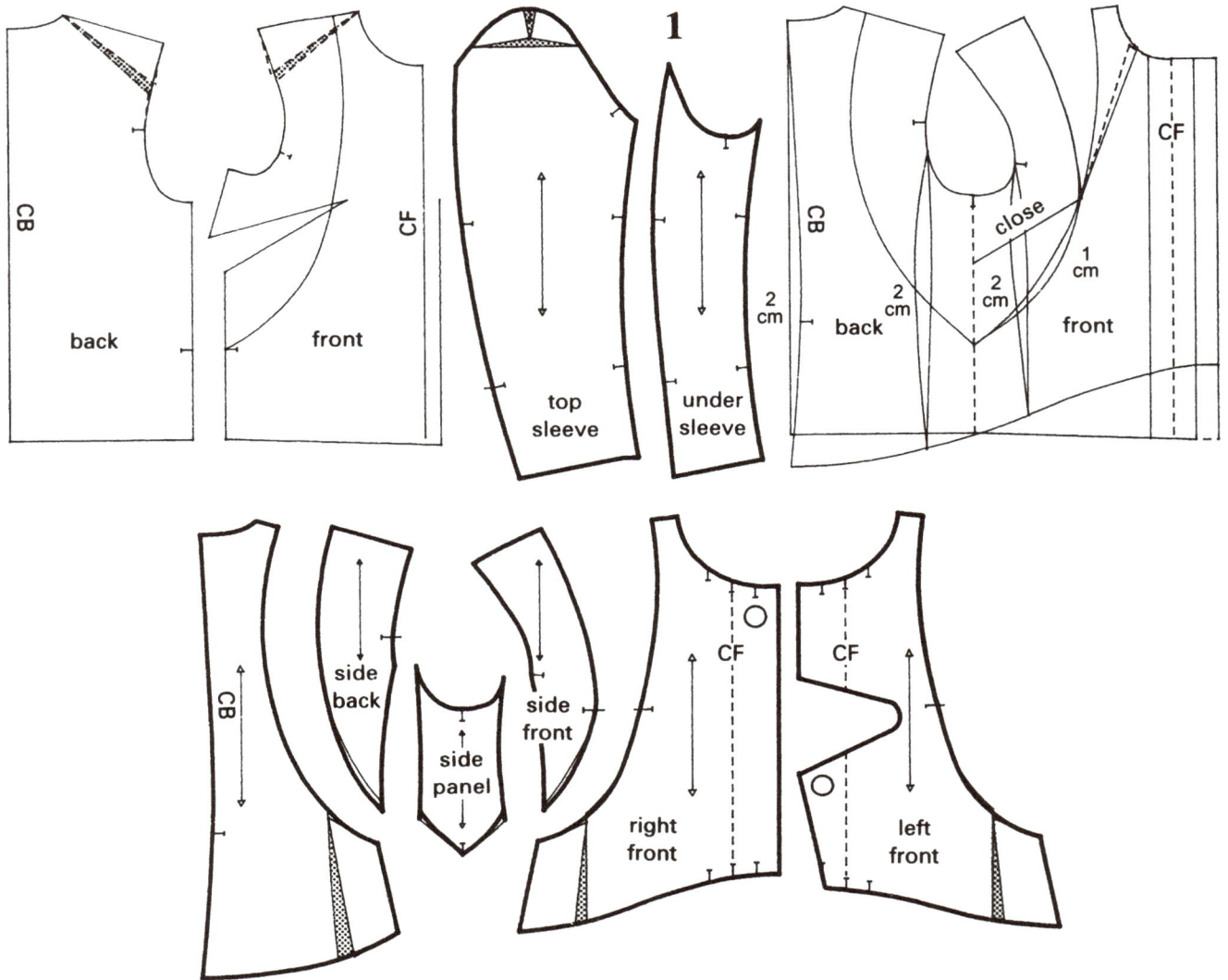

Mounting

Mounting is a technique used (mainly in couture houses) to give particular strength or stability to high shear or delicate fabrics. All the pattern pieces are cut out in both fabrics, basted together and made up as one. Mass-production companies are more likely to use fabrics bonded together synthetically. The linen jacket was developed from the close fitting jacket block (ref. page 203). It is mounted on a fine strong black cotton.

1 Jacket shape: classic mounting

Body sections Trace round the block to required length. The jacket block includes ease for a light shoulder pad. If a higher shoulder pad is to be used, cut and open armhole line; raise shoulder the depth of shoulder pad. Cut across sleeve head and raise the same amount. Draw in front style line.

Swing bust dart to the shoulder.
Overlap neck (ref. page 96).
Place back and front together in order to draw in the back curved style line.
Lower back waist approx. 2 cm.
Draw back seam line and side panel lines with curved lines shaping the waist the amounts shown.
Mark two button lines 3.5 cm each side of centre front line.
Add 3.5 cm buttonstand.
Draw in shaped hemline.
Trace off the pattern sections. Mirror fronts.
Draw in, and cut-away overlap as shown.
Mark in button positions.
On main bodice sections, close waist darts to flare hem.

Note: The pattern is shown as if placed on the right side of the fabric.

1

Fabric

1 *Linen – main fabric*
   Cotton – mounting fabric

The main fabric is of medium weight, thickness and
shear, but with low drape and stretch.

The cotton mounting fabric is of lighter weight and
thickness, but its low drape, shear and stretch gives
added stability without bulk.

Pattern cutting

Mounting is used to hold a shape that the fabric cannot
sustain alone. It is very important that the right fabrics
are used. Neither fabric must shrink or expand during
wear, laundering or dry-cleaning. The fabrics are made
up as one and stitched into the seams; therefore, they
are most successful in designs with many seams.

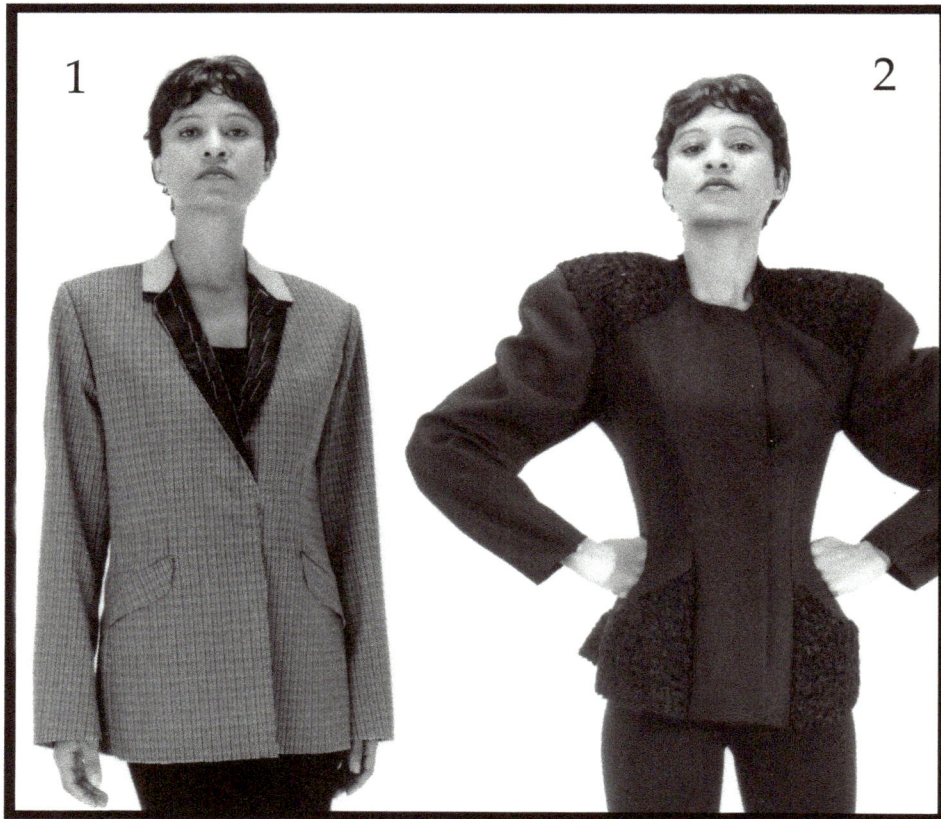

Fabric

1   Wool worsted
The main fabric is of medium weight, thickness, drape, shear and stretch.

2   Polyester suiting – main fabric
Polyester Astrakhan – trimming
The basic fabric is of medium weight and thickness with low drape, shear and stretch.
The Astrakhan is heavy and thick with low drape, shear and stretch.

Pattern cutting

Tailoring is a skill that moulds an underlying structure and fabric to create a conventional shape, image (1). Fusible interlinings, that can mould with the main fabric under steam or heat pressure, are now used in 'High Street' tailoring.

Interlinings and trimmings can be used to exaggerate a fabric's strong, stable structure, and create sculptural shapes that do not fit the body contour, image (2).

Structure: classic and exaggerated shapes

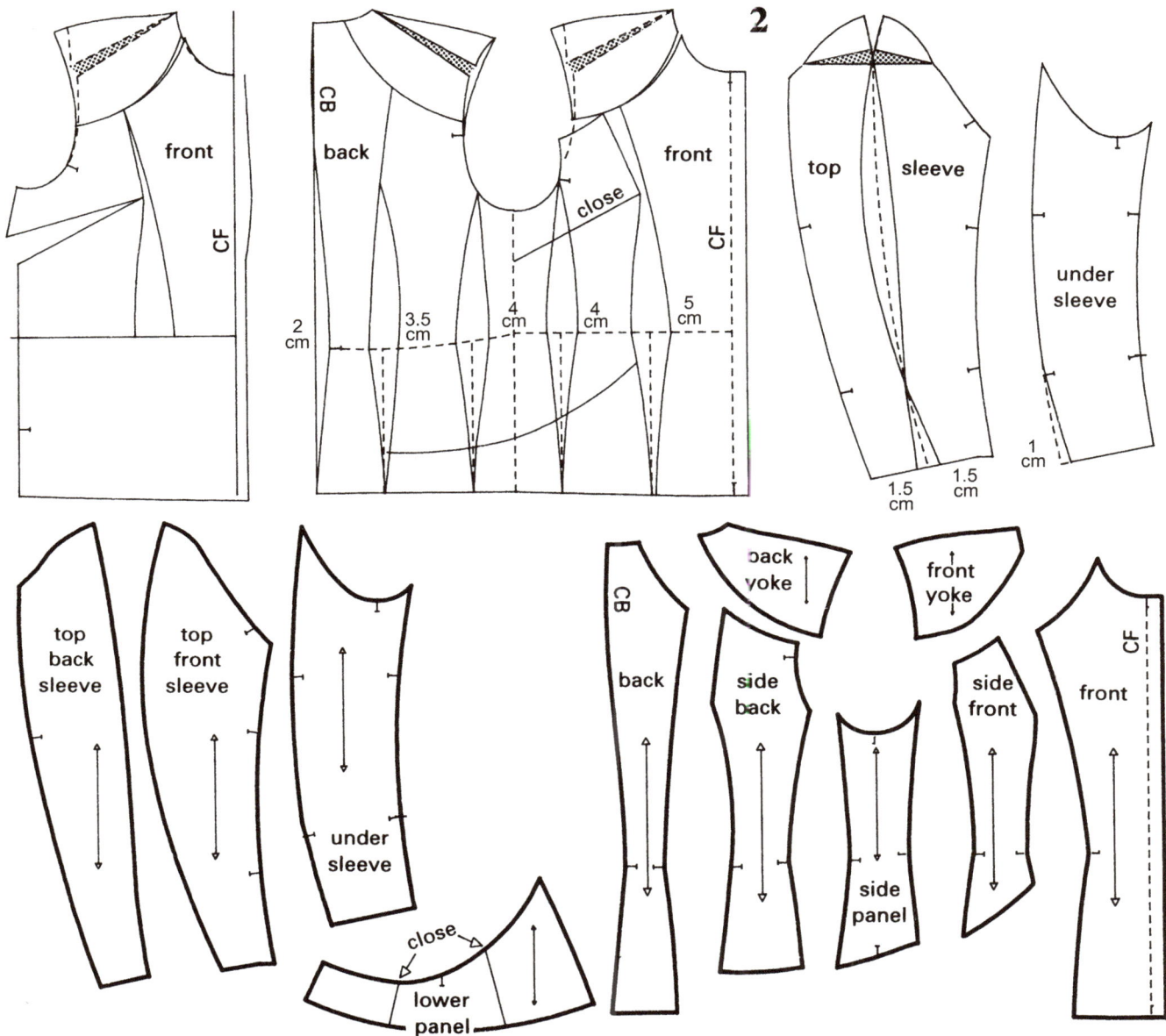

2

front

CF

back

CB

close

front

CF

2 cm

3.5 cm

4 cm

4 cm

5 cm

top sleeve

under sleeve

1.5 cm

1.5 cm

1 cm

top back sleeve

top front sleeve

under sleeve

close

lower panel

back yoke

front yoke

back

CB

side back

side panel

side front

front

CF

1 Classic tailored jacket

The easy fitting jacket block (*no diagram shown*, see ref. page 204 for diagram). Image 1 (opposite) is constructed in a wool worsted fabric. It is interlined traditionally with non-fusible wool/hair canvas, chest canvas, felt and linen. Compare the jacket with the same block, constructed in different fabrics, minus interlinings on page 105.

2 Exaggerated shape

The easy fitting jacket block (ref. page 204) is used with widened shoulders and very fitted waist. Firm, fusible interlining, large shoulder and hip padding is used to hold the shape. Synthetic fur (Astrakhan) on the shoulders and pockets emphasise the design.
Body sections Trace round the block to the required length. Add straight buttonstand.
Cut and open armhole line, raise shoulder the depth of shoulder pad.
Re-draw armhole line.
Draw in yokes and front panel line.
Draw in 1 cm shaping at front neck in yoke line.
Swing the bust dart to front panel line; join side seams.
Lower back waist approx. 2 cm.
Draw in back and side panel lines with smooth curves; shape the waist line as shown in diagram.
Trace off pattern sections.
Hip yoke Close panel seams.
Sleeve Cut across sleeve head; raise the sleeve head the same amount that the shoulder is raised.
Split the top sleeve, shaping outwards at top arm and shaping in at the wrist.
Shape under sleeve slightly in at back.

PART FOUR: FABRICS AND COMPLEX CUTTING

Chapter 11 Combining fabrics

Combining fabrics

This chapter shows examples of combining and using new fabrics to visualise the different shapes that they can form. Considerations of how they may distort each other in manufacture or wear have to be considered. It can also mean that traditional cutting processes and manufacturing techniques have to be adapted or new ones created.

Combining fabrics

Combining fabrics: simple insertions

1

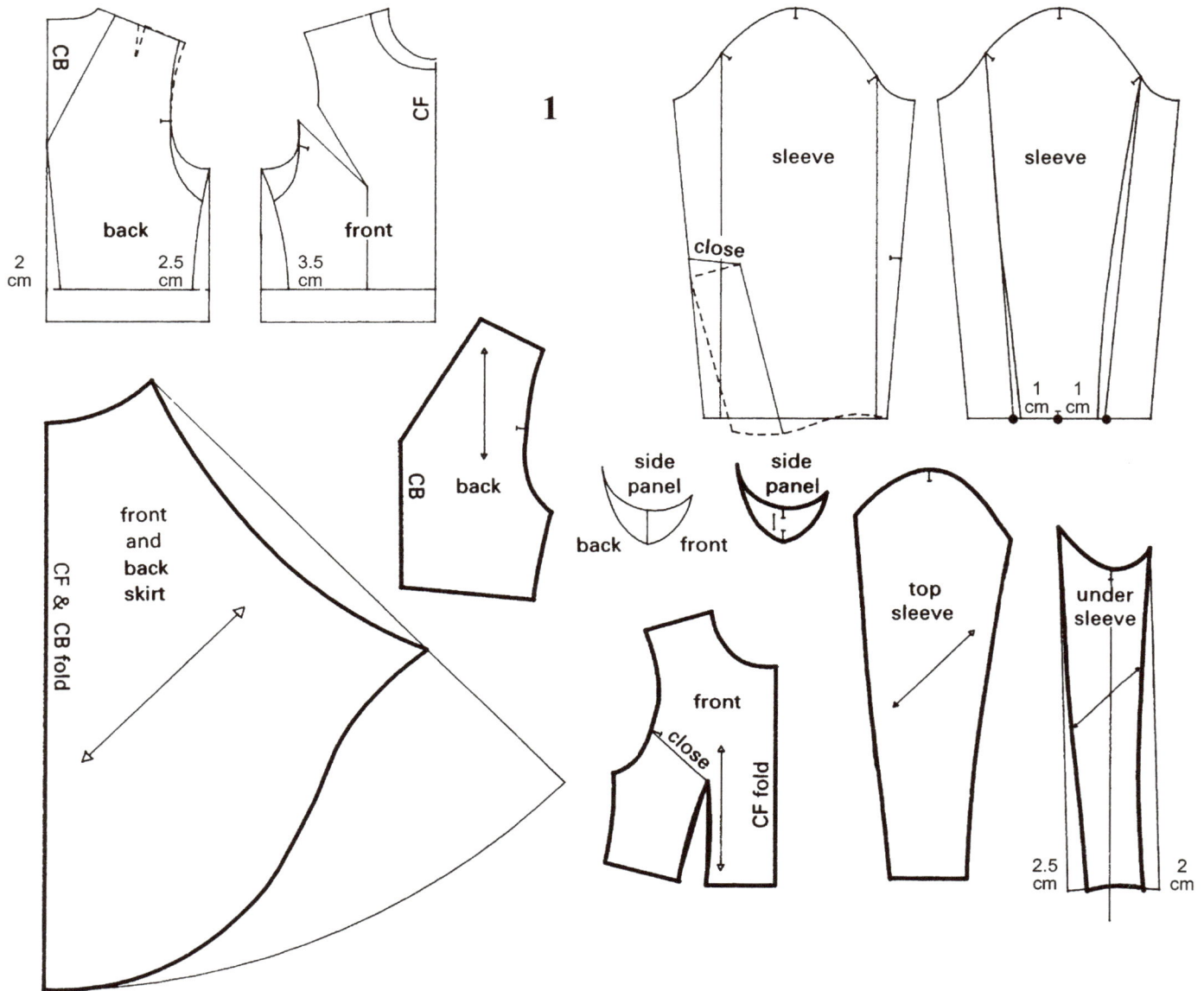

Simple sympathetic fabrics

Different fabrics are often combined in the same garment. Few problems arise if these fabrics are 'sympathetic', sharing a common or similar fibre source and a compatible structure. A stronger fabric can give a weaker one support, and the position of the grain of the fabric is important. The close fitting bodice (dress) block (ref. page 208) is used for this example.

1   Simple fabric insertion

Body sections Trace round block.
Mark in the high waistline.

Draw in the neckline.
Remove back dart allowance from the armhole edge.
Transfer bust dart to the armhole.
Shape in at the centre back and side seams as shown.
Draw in the shape of the underarm panels.
Trace off the pattern sections.
Join the two panels at the underarm.
Sleeve Construct a close fitting shaped sleeve (ref. page 119).
Skirt Construct a quarter circle panel (ref. page 11) to a measurement twice the high waist measurement.
Divide the panel in half.
Draw in a skirt shape as required.

1

Fabric

1 *Acetate crepe – main fabric*
   Acrylic/acetate (warp knit) – insertion
The main fabric is of medium weight, thickness and
shear, but with high drape and low stretch.
The ribbon knit insertion is of medium weight,
thickness and stretch, low drape, but high shear.

Pattern cutting

Although the crepe is cut on the crossway to emphasise
the draping qualities in the skirt and to give a close
fitting sleeve, the ribbon bodice (cut on the straight) is
stable enough to support it. However, its high shear
characteristic requires a crepe insert panel where there
is strain at the underarm.

1

Fabric

1   *Wool/elastane (weft knit) – main fabric*
     Cotton lace – insertion
The main fabric is of light weight and thickness,
medium drape, low shear and high stretch.
The lace fabric is of medium weight and thickness, high
shear, low drape and stretch.

Pattern cutting

Fabrics with elastane give a designer some flexibility
around the body shape. Many stretch warp knit fabrics
are used with lace in 'lingerie' type designs.

   The design took the motif around the body; the high
shear flexibility made this possible; otherwise, motifs
have to be inserted in shaped pattern pieces.

Combining fabrics: complex insertions

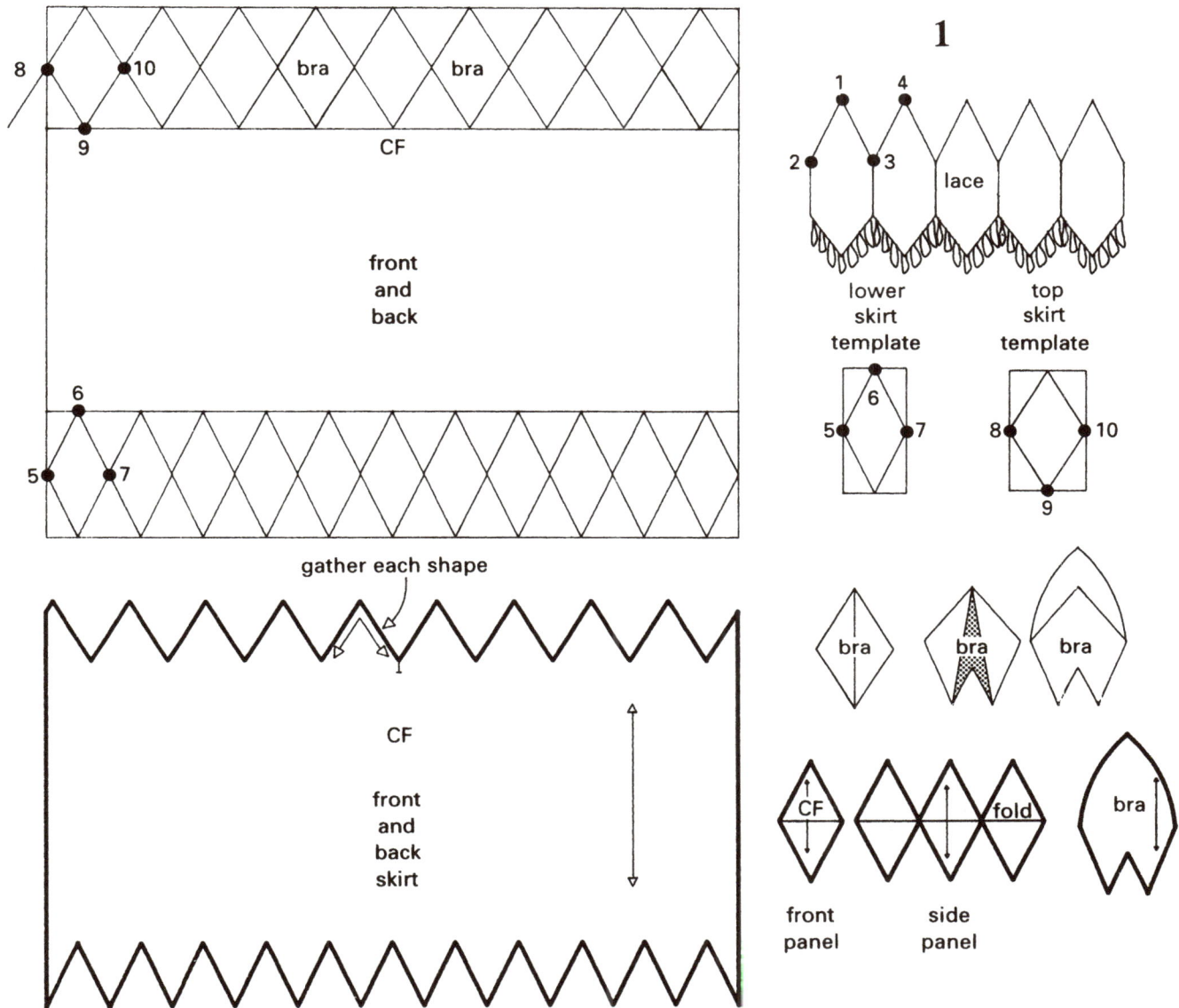

Complex insertions

Designs which are created around a feature fabric (in this case the lace), or dominated by a fabric motif, are often mathematically constructed. This type of design, where the motif determines the cut of the pattern, is usually constructed by direct measurement.

1 Geometric design

Create a rectangle the required length.
Balance the width between the measurement of the hips and the lace repeat.

Calculate the number of motifs required to fit the hip measurement.
Mark out the 11 diamond shaped motifs along the base of the skirt.
A balance between the widest point of the garment and the lace repeat is made.
Calculate the measurement around the rib cage.
Calculate the number if the 9 motifs are required. Stretch the motif shape 120% to fit the rectangle.
Extend two diamond shapes into a bra shape as shown.
Cut folded diamond shaped top to make a stable edge for the top of the garment.

Combination of fabrics and techniques

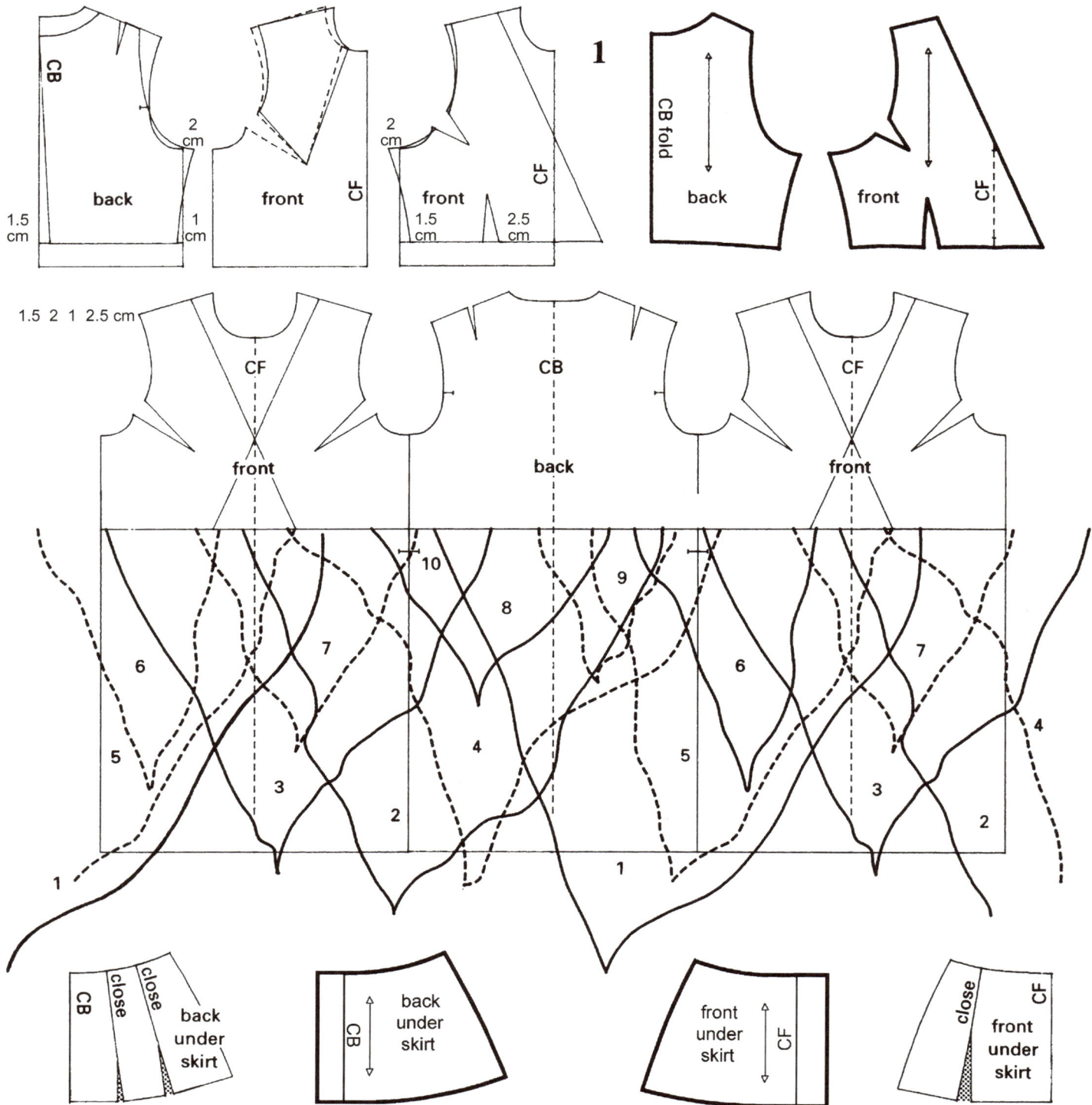

Combining fabrics and techniques

Image (1) is taken to a first stage by flat pattern cutting methods to create a 'map'. The skirt sections then have their shapes refined on the stand.

1 Combining 'flat' cutting and modelling on the stand

Body sections Trace off the close fitting bodice (dress) block (ref. page 208) to the required length.
Mark in the high waistline. Draw in the front overlap.
Mirror the back and front. Trace off an extra front.

Place side seams together to create a 'map'.
Draw in the random skirt pieces; match the overlap.
Bodice Trace off the bodice pattern sections.
Shape in bodice at centre back, side seam and with a dart on the front bodice as shown.
Skirt Trace off skirt sections. Widen to give gathered fullness. Further modify skirt pieces on the stand.
Skirt under yoke Trace skirt block (ref. page 207). Close darts as shown to create a shaped yoke.
Extend centre back and centre front lines to ensure that the waist meas. of the yoke equals the bodice waist meas.

1

Fabric

1 *Wool/cotton – bodice section*
   Cotton lawn and calico – skirt

The bodice fabric is of medium weight, thickness and shear, but with low drape and stretch.

The lawn skirt fabric is of light weight and thickness, with medium drape, shear and stretch.

The calico skirt fabric is of medium weight and thickness, with medium drape and shear, but low stretch.

Pattern cutting

The bodice is made in a double layered fabric of wool flannel and cotton lawn. The cotton lawn is cut away in random shapes.

The skirt pattern shapes (first planned on the pattern draft) follow the same theme. Pre-washed, shrunk calico and cotton lawn layers are used to give the same effect as the main fabric.

Note: The skirt can be draped solely on the stand.

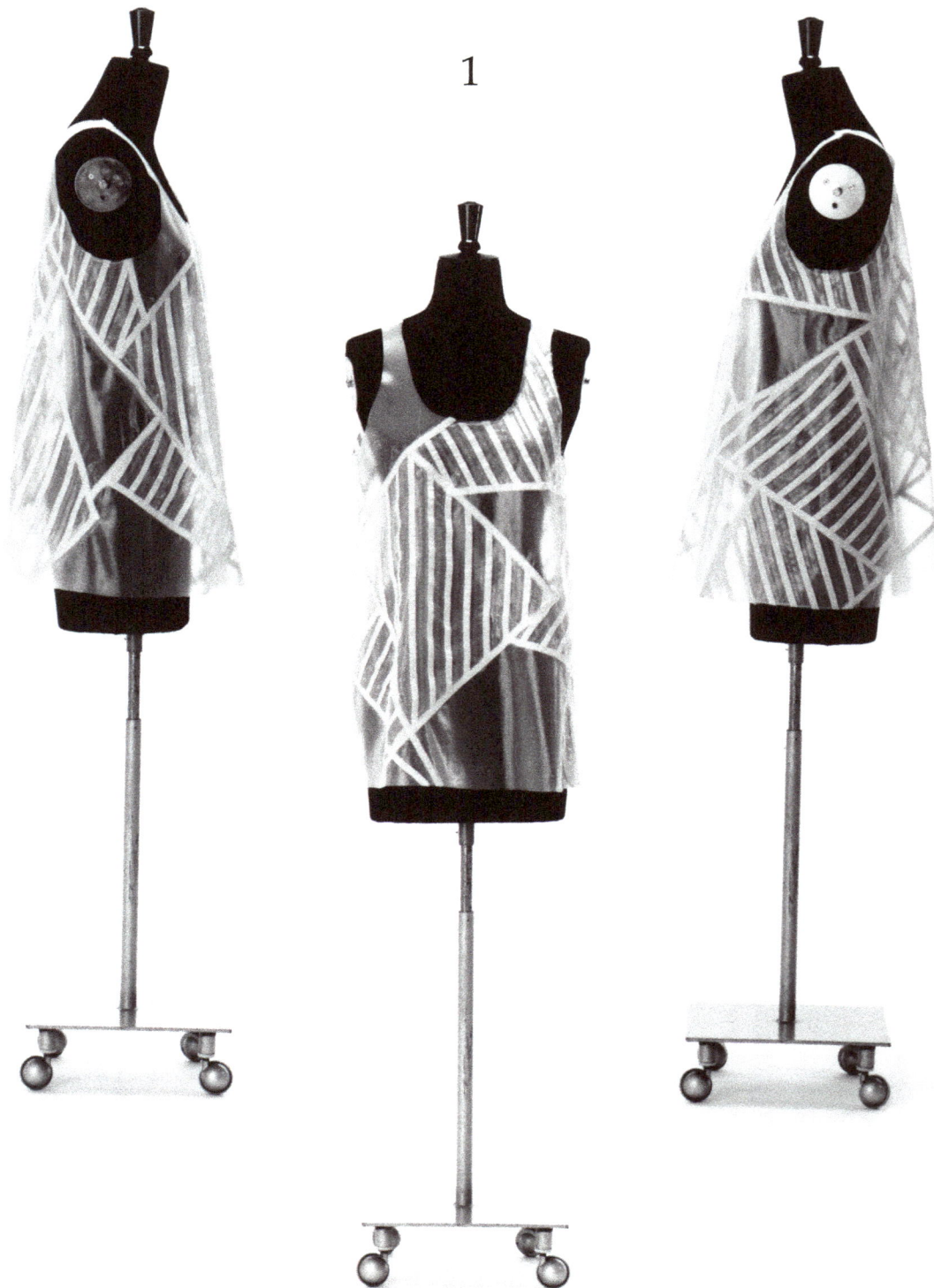

1

Fabric

1 *Nylon/polyurethene net – main fabric*
   Cotton/nylon – appliqué
The main fabric is of light weight and thickness,
medium drape, with low shear and stretch.
The appliquéd fabric is of medium weight, thickness
and drape, with low shear and stretch.

Pattern cutting

Using large areas of fabric as appliquéd panels can give
new dimensions to structure. The patchwork of panels
is designed to retain but re-emphasise the basic shape.
A patchwork of different panels on the same garment
can create unique shapes that a single fabric cannot
achieve.

Combining fabrics: appliqué

1

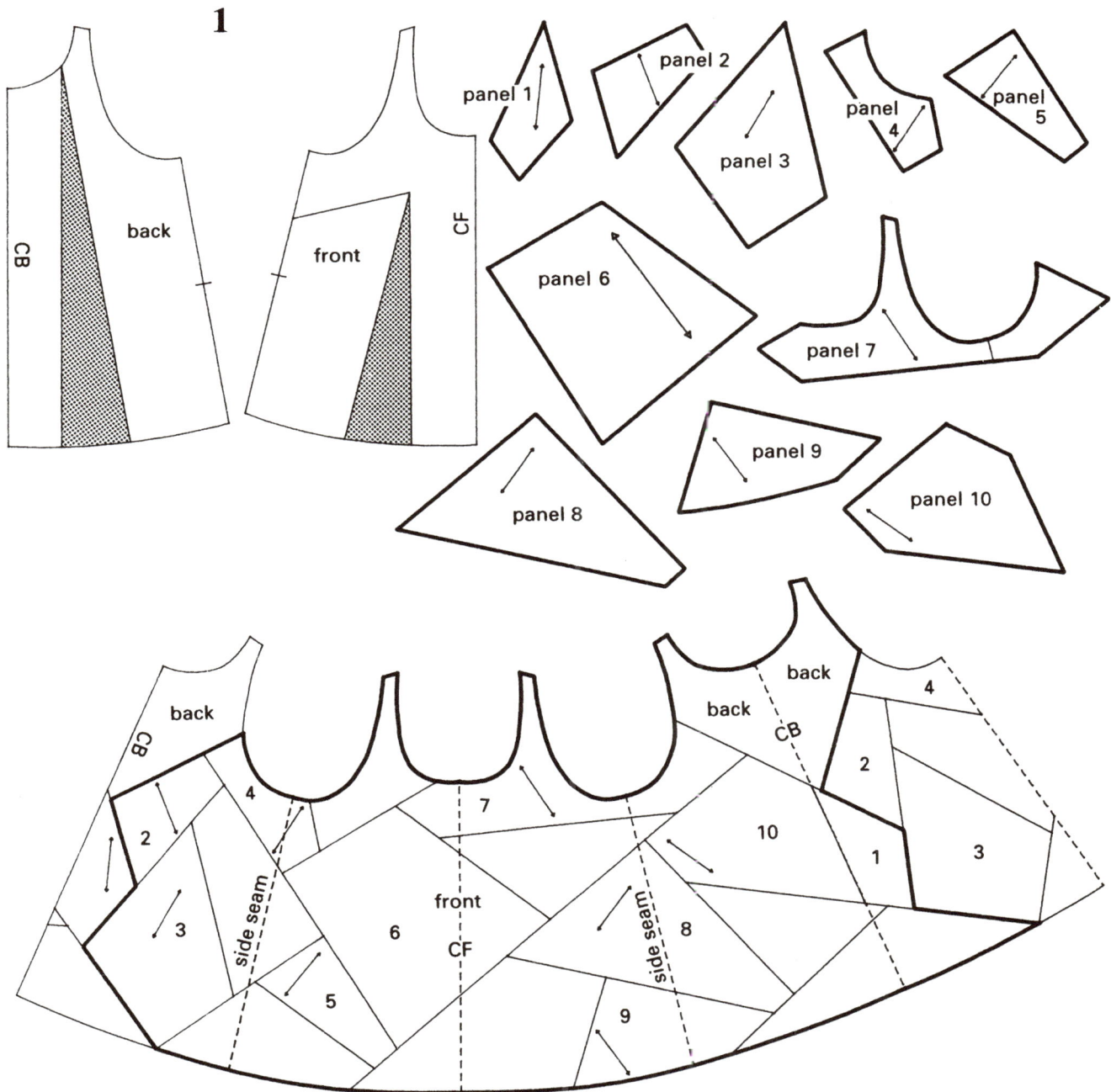

Appliquéd fabrics

Unique fabrics can be created by many surface decoration methods: machine embroidery, appliqué, decoupé, pulled threads and interwoven threads, ribbons and braids. These techniques can change a fabric's structural shape.

Lengths of fabric can be appliquéd before the garment pieces are cut out; or garment pieces can be cut out and then appliquéd as shown above. Image (1) is constructed by an appliqué of nylon/cotton stripe fabric onto a polyurethene coated net.

1 Appliquéd 'A' line shape

Body sections Trace off the block required.

Draw in the neckline and armhole shape.
Draw a vertical line from the back neckline; draw a vertical line from the bust dart point.
Trace off the divided sections.
Cut up the vertical lines and spread at the hem; the bust dart should close.
Draw hemline with a smooth curve.
Join the paper pattern pieces; overlap an extra section (the half back) so that the design can be integrated.
Draw in any appliqué design.
Image (1) is divided geometrically.
Trace off the appliqué pattern shapes from the main pattern shape; mark the grain required.

Combining fabrics: framing fabrics

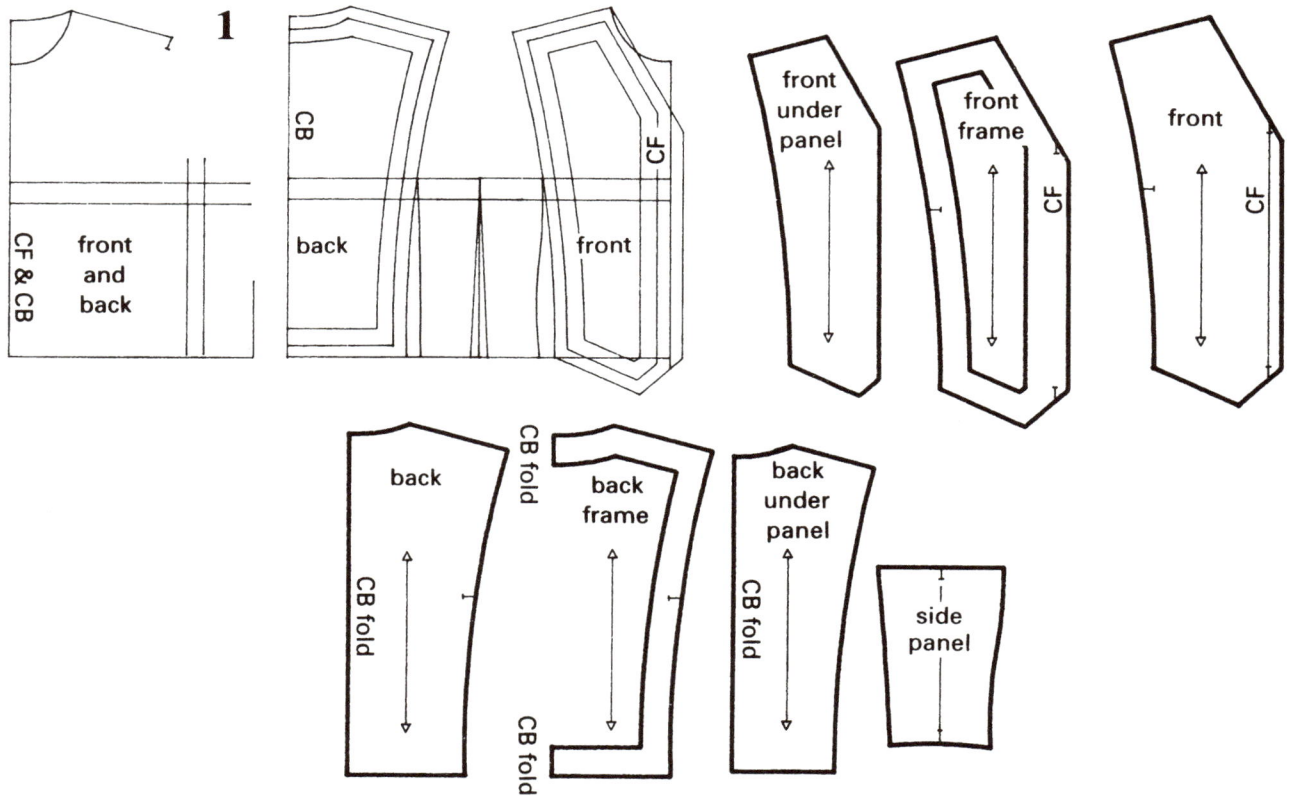

Framing

Small sections or whole body sections can be framed. The fabric can be totally enclosed. Any section of a garment can be framed to highlight very decorative fabric pieces. More delicate panels with high shear may need to be mounted onto a backing fabric.

To avoid distortion, it is important that both fabrics complement and are 'sympathetic' to each other.

1   Major framing: simple shape

Body sections Construct a basic body shape from the basic grid (ref. page 195).

Mirror the front. Place the side seams together.
Draw in side panel lines with a slight curve.
Draw in 1.5cm waist shaping on back panel line; 2cm on front panel line.
Draw 2cm waist dart at the side seam.
Square across at the armhole depth.
Add buttonstand.
Draw in frame lines (approx. 5cm) around back and front sections.
Draw in the decorative under panel lines 1.5cm from the pattern edge.
Trace off all the pattern sections.
Close side seam dart.

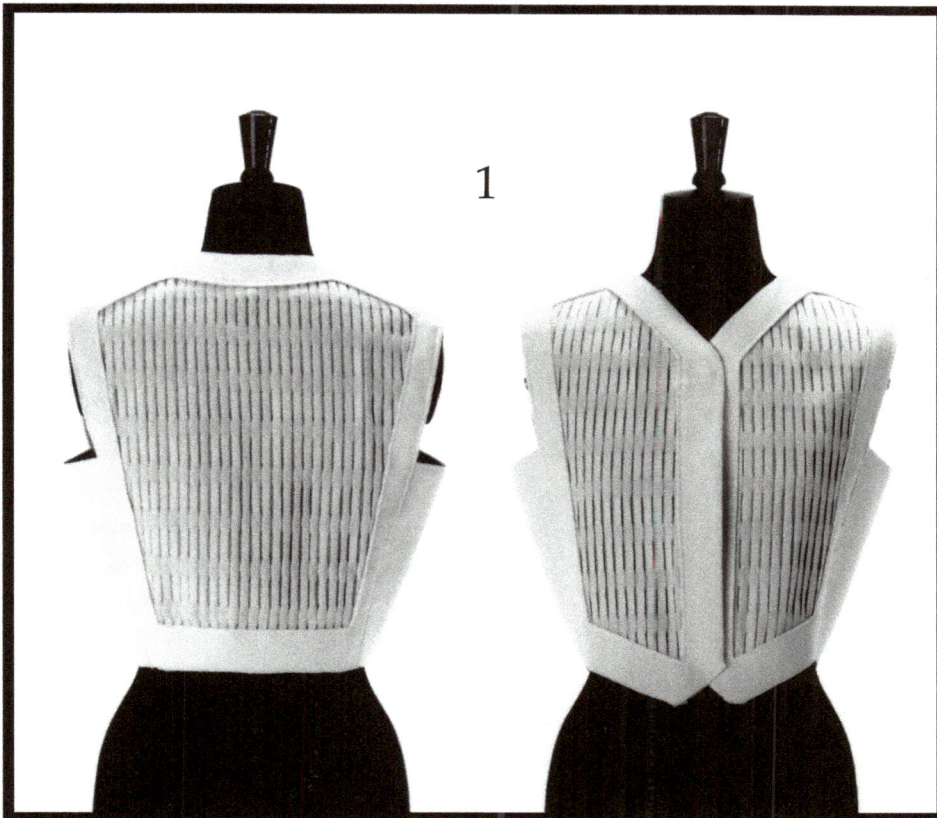

1

Fabric

1   *Wool – main framing fabric*
    Wool – interior fabric

The main bodice fabric is of medium weight, thickness, shear, stretch and drape.

The decorative fabric is of heavy weight and medium thickness and shear, and has low drape and stretch.

Pattern cutting

The fabric panel in the image is too bulky to insert into a seam, so framing is a useful technique. This is often the case with decorative panels, particularly highly embroidered or beaded ones. More delicate panels with high shear may need to be mounted onto a backing fabric.

PART FIVE: BASIC TEXTILE TECHNOLOGY

Chapter 12 Basic textile technology

Basic textile technology

Basic garment fabric technology

For the designer or pattern cutter the 'handle' of the fabric is crucial in the creation of a style. This chapter helps students to understand the underlying technologies that contribute to this characteristic. The 'handle' of a finished fabric is determined by the fibre, the character of the yarn, the structure of the fabric and the finishing process. Therefore, this chapter includes separate sections covering these basic elements of fabric production. The chapter also includes a section on ecological concerns.

Fibres

Although a garment fabric does not have to begin with a fibre, for example, leather or plastic sheeting, the vast majority of fabrics used for making garments have been made from yarns produced from fibres. The characteristics of the original fibre are usually carried through into the finished fabric. They can, of course, be suppressed or enhanced by the chemical finishes of the yarn or fabric and the structure of the fabric. So it is important to understand the characteristics of the basic fibres and how they are modified and changed.

A fibre is long compared to its diameter; this enables it to be twisted with other fibres to create a yarn. A finer fibre of the same type will usually reduce in strength and increase its bending capacity. Halving a fibre's thickness reduces its breaking strength by a factor of four, making it fragile.

Fibres can be divided into two main groups, natural and man-made. But fibres from most groups can be blended to gain the properties of each component fibre. A description of the source and use of the major fibres, e.g. cotton, silk, viscose, polyester etc., is given in Chapter 3 of *Selecting fabrics*. Some minor man-made synthetic fibres have been added to the classification table (Fig 11), so a brief description of these fibres is given at the end of the next section.

The classification of fibres

Natural fibres

The major natural fibres are *cotton, flax (linen), silk, wool*. Natural fibres can be divided into two groups, vegetable and animal. These can be sub-divided again to form the generic groups by which the fibres are labelled (see the fibre classification table opposite).

Although frequently blended or woven together, many garments are made entirely from the main fibres: **silk, wool, cotton and flax (linen).** Other minor natural fibres such as *hemp, bamboo, angora, cashmere* are usually mixed with the main fibres to add practical characteristics or aesthetic interest to the fabric. When characteristics are added or suppressed by chemical processes and breeding, the structure of the fibres are not changed. Advances in present gene research are beginning to alter this position. Fabrics made from natural fibres, especially cotton, still hold a strong position in the market, despite the fact that they can be more expensive than a product made from man-made fibres. This may alter as the price of oil continues to increase. Natural fibres are comfortable to wear because of their natural absorbency, and there is great aesthetic appeal in their textures, their dye affinities and their handle.

All the natural fibres, except cultivated silk, have relatively short fibres (staple) which are combed and twisted to form yarn that is strong enough for use in the manufacture of the fabric. However, cultivated silk which is unwound from the silk moth's cocoon can be 2,000 metres long and is therefore considered as continuous or a filament fibre.

Man-made fibres

The major man-made fibres used in clothing production are *viscose, acetate, polyamide, polyester, acrylic, elastane.* They are produced from chemical solutions that are manufactured into fibres. For example, a chemical liquid can be forced through minute holes and then solidified by chemical (wet spun) processes or in air (dry or melt spun). They are used as filament fibres or cut to form staple fibres. A fibre can be produced from a solution that has a natural source, a solely chemical or mineral source, or from a natural source that is chemically changed. The fibres classified in Figure 11 are edited so that they relate to garment production.

Man-made fibres can be divided into two main sub-groups, regenerated fibres and synthetic fibres. Regenerated fibres originate from natural living sources and are reconstituted by converting natural products, such as wood pulp and cotton, into a liquid form for spinning. Most synthetic fibres have a chemical source; many are petroleum based. However, new generic synthetic fibres, such as *polyactide (PLA)* and *polyamide 11* originate from natural sources and are difficult to classify.

Man-made fibres began by copying the characteristics of natural fibres. Originally, man-made fibre lengths were matched to those of existing natural fibres because natural fibres were successful and the new fibres could be processed on existing machinery. These regenerated cellulosic fibres, a chemical reduction of a natural source (wood pulp), created the first man-made fibre (rayon viscose) known as 'artificial silk'. Acetate followed, and more recently the fibre **lyocell** has been produced. The manufacture of synthetic fibres for the garment industry has now overtaken the production of all natural fibres. Nylon, polyester and acrylic originally displayed unique characteristics that were easy to identify. Until quite recently it was fairly easy to place the fibres of a fabric within a generic group and make certain assumptions about their properties; now, recognition is more difficult.

Minor synthetic fibres and coatings

Polyactide (PLA): is manufactured by producing polyactic acid that is derived from carbon and other elements in the sugars of corn or sugar beet.

Polyamide 11: is a new nylon fibre produced using two polymers derived from the castor oil plant.

The fibres listed on page 174 are only a small part of

Natural fibres

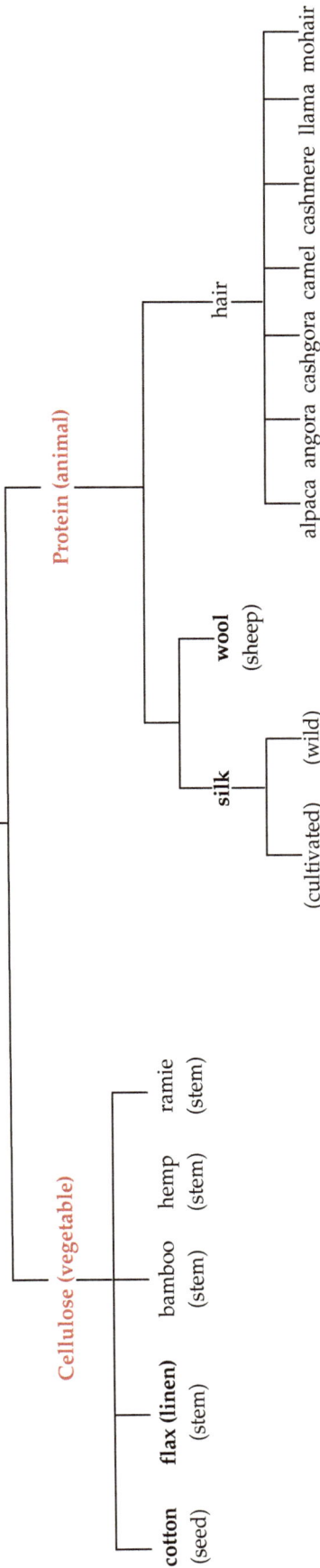

Cellulose (vegetable)
- **cotton** (seed)
- **flax (linen)** (stem)
- bamboo (stem)
- hemp (stem)
- ramie (stem)

Protein (animal)
- **silk**
  - (cultivated)
  - (wild)
- **wool** (sheep)
- hair
  - alpaca angora cashgora camel cashmere llama mohair

Man-made

Natural polymer
- animal (casein)
- vegetable (cellulose)
  - **viscose** modal cupro lyocell
- crustacean (shell)
- alginate (seaweed)
- cellulose-ester
  - **acetate** diacetate triacetate

New natural polymers
- Polyamide 11 (castor oil seeds)
- Polyactide PLA (tapioca soya)

Synthetic polymers
- aramid
- **polyamide** (nylon)
- **polyester**
- polyurethene
  - **elastane**
- polyvinyl
  - **acrylic** modacrylic chlorofibre
  - polyvinyl chloride (PVC)
- polyolefin

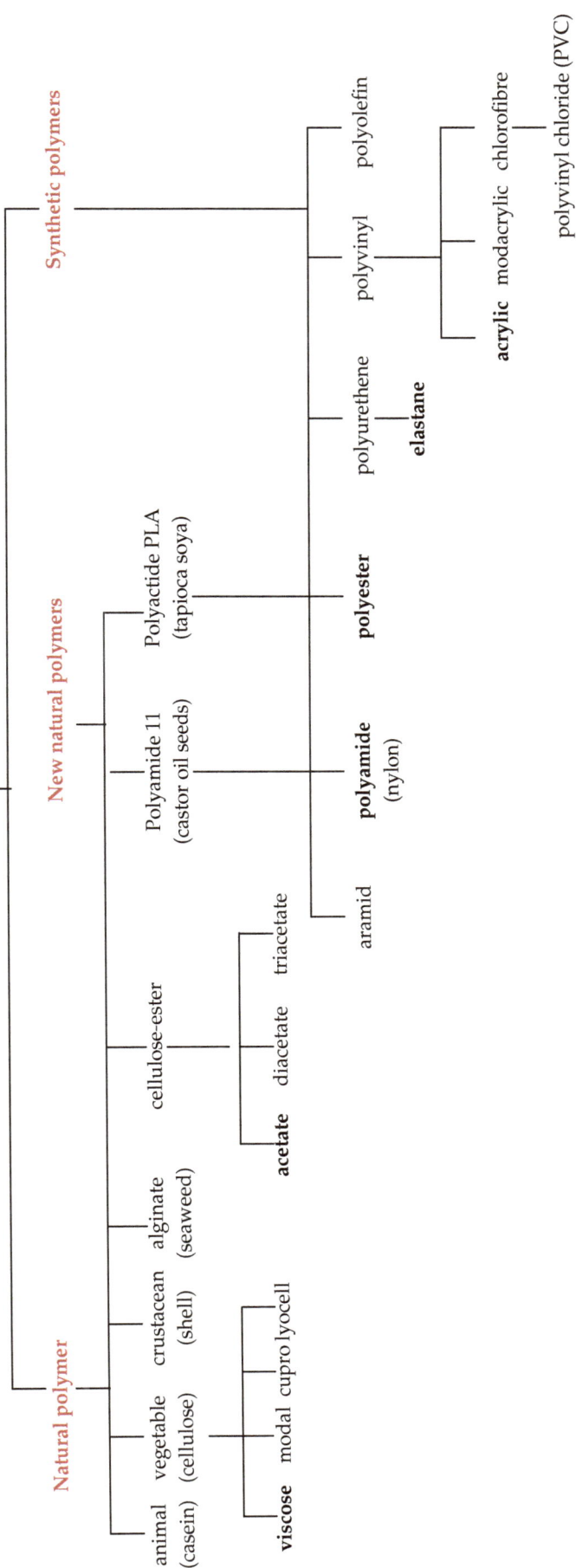

Figure 11 A classification of fibres used in the garment industry – generic terms. The dominant fibres used for clothing are shown in a **bold typeface**.

garment fibre production. Many of the blends and laminates are being explored by designers for new practical and aesthetic end uses. A number of new finishes are based on micro-encapsulation and nano-technology; these coatings are only 3–5 mm thick and have no effect on the drape or permeability of the fabrics.

Polyurethene, polyvinylchloride: Many coated and laminated fabrics are created by spraying or bonding plasticised coatings onto fabric backings. Most are impermeable to water and air. Metal foils sandwiched in plastic film (Lurex) are used in many decorative fabrics. Chlorofibres, from polyvinylchloride, are inert to chemicals and mainly used for thermal underwear, sportswear.

Polyethelene: The source is ethylene; the melt-spun fibres are produced in filament form. Its shiny hard surface can produce interesting surfaces in knitwear, particularly in mixtures of contrasting textures.

Polypropylene: The most common plastic, its first commercial production began in 1960. The yarn is slit from wider extruded film. Very durable, light and quick drying, it is used mainly for high performance garments. Designers are beginning to use its aesthetic qualities for special hard shiny effects.

Polyoxamide: A new generic name given to one of the first hydrophillic man-made fibres. Its main property is the absorption and transmission of moisture.

Fibre characteristics

The appearance, handle and comfort of a fabric are affected by the structure of the fibres. Whilst the length and external surface of the fibre is important, the internal structure also determines the basic properties of a particular fibre. The shape of the fibre can determine the lustre; for example, the filaments of silk are prism shaped and reflect light. The cross-sections of fibres can be changed by varying the holes on the spinneret to match the shape of natural fibres or experiment with new shapes. These can be round,

cross-like, triangular, Y-shaped or bean-shaped. The structural shapes of fibres also determine more mechanical properties such as bulk, stiffness and absorbency; for example, circular shaped fibres tend to resist bending, Y-shaped fibres give resilience, hollow fibres are light in relation to their bulk. However, the yarn construction, fabric structure and finish have to be combined intelligently to satisfy aesthetic and practical market demands.

Today man-made fibres are increasingly difficult for the designer to categorise from a chemical perspective. Bi-component fibres combine polymers at very early stages in the production of the fibres and new blends with regenerated fibres have created new 'families' of fabrics more closely related to the product. Designers are becoming less concerned with a fabric's origin than its proven qualities in use and appearance. New technological processes in fibre and yarn construction can be used to create fabrics as varied as gabardine and synthetic fur to silk-like jerseys from one fibre source (for example, polyester). The proliferation of fibre brand names can obscure knowledge of the chemical source of the fabric and can extend the confusion.

Micro-fibres

The name micro-fibre is not a generic term, but there is general agreement amongst producers that it describes a fibre of 1 decitex or less. Silk is the only natural fibre that approaches this degree of fineness and it is the Japanese who have specialised in creating silk-like fabrics with high drape qualities. The exploitation amongst European and American producers has been aimed at underwear fabrics (lightweight but 'full and soft') and weatherwear (light and dense); therefore wind and weatherproof but allowing the escape of perspiration. Most micro-fibres are produced from polyamide and polyester fibres. Many more micro-fibres can be used in a given size of yarn; they offer good draping qualities and a lightweight bulk unmatched by other fibres.

Yarns

The fineness of yarn or filament (count) is measured by weight/length. The measurement of the fineness of the yarn is expressed by Denier (grams per 9,000 metres) or more usually Decitex (grams per 10,000 metres). Most fibres for clothing are usually in the range 5–15 decitex; micro-fibres are defined as fibres with a maximum count of 1 decitex.

Staple fibres are short in length and must be twisted to form yarns; they are known as spun yarns and they are usually more soft and textured than those from filaments (continuous fibres). The direction and the amount of twist inserted in the yarn will affect the characteristics of the finished fabric. The fibres are often encouraged to lay in all directions to increase the bulk and texture of the yarn. Complex yarns can be constructed where yarns of varying thickness, crimp and fibre source are spun together. Introducing effects into the yarn such as loops, knots, pile (chenille) or metallic filaments produces fancy yarns.

Filament fibres have a continuity of length and are usually spun with the filaments lying parallel; this makes the yarn more compact and will enhance the

fibre's natural lustre and smoothness. Fibres that are destined for smooth fabrics are combed after carding to ensure the fibres lay parallel.

Man-made fibres are chemically created; their reaction to heat and other chemicals offers the opportunity to produce yarns that can be enhanced or textured in ways that are not possible with natural fibres. The use of elastane fibres has given woven fabrics some of the stretch and stability characteristics that could only be achieved by knitted constructions. Corespun yarns have a fibrous sheath twisted around a core filament thread; for example, elastane yarns have a core thread of elastane covered with the main fibre. New methods of electrospinning blend fibres in electro-spin laced mat layers that can be combined with coatings.

Yarns can be single, folded (2 or 3 yarns twisted) or cabled (folded yarns twisted). The direction of twist can be a Z or an S twist. Different twists can be found in the same yarn and are used in different warps and wefts to create different fabric appearances.

Fabric construction

Yarns and fibres are woven, knitted, interlaced or pressed into a fabric form. In most situations it is the fabric which the designer faces when realising the design range. The first aesthetic reactions will be a major part of the criteria that determines the purchase.

Fabric construction can enhance or subdue the characteristics of a yarn. The complex forms that can be produced from the major means of manufacture (weaving and knitting) now offer bewildering choices; textile designers have to balance the visual and textural qualities with its stability and its 'fitness for purpose'. It can require a close examination of some fabrics to distinguish which manufacturing process has been used. The bonding of fabrics of different manufacture can confuse simple categorisations.

The scale of world production of woven and knitted fabrics has changed. During the last two decades, knitted fabric production has increased at the expense of woven fabric production.

Fabric structures

The principal methods of creating fabric are knitting and weaving. The minor methods, interlaced, embroidered and braided, are used in many luxury or hand-crafted fabrics (see Figure 8). Non-woven fabrics are: felt, many types of interlinings, PVC sheets and some pile fabrics fused onto PVC backing.

Woven fabric

A fabric is considered to be woven if horizontal threads (the weft) are interlaced with vertical threads (the warp). Garments are usually made up with the warp threads running down a garment, and the weft threads running across or at an accurate 45° angle (which is known as the bias or crossway) to give increased stretch and draping qualities. Pattern pieces are always marked with a grain line to ensure the garment is cut correctly.

The yarns can be interlaced in many different ways to create weaves. Classic weaves become easily recognised: plain weaves give horizontal, vertical and chequered effects; twill weaves give diagonal or herringbone structures; jacquard weaves create complex patterns; satin weaves give smooth surfaces and lustre. Different yarns inserted in the warp and weft can give three dimensional rib effects. In pile constructions, yarns in the warp (velvet) or weft (velveteen) give different effects. Many unusual weaves can be created by combining different weaves, or by creating double or double-face fabrics; for example, cloqué is produced by one set of threads shrinking at a different rate and producing blistering. Matellasse has extra warp threads inserted which produce a quilted effect. When yarn types and colour and print are added to weave constructions, combinations become almost limitless.

The rate of woven cloth production has been increased by the rapier looms which fire (by air or water jet) a number of weft threads across the loom instead of the old shuttle method. Other methods (multiphase or triaxial weaving) have been developed; they offer faster as well as different production methods.

Knitted fabric – weft-knit

Weft-knitted fabric is made on machines where the yarn is held by latch needles that move up and down to create rows of interlocking loop stitches across the fabric. Some machines produce flat fabrics, others circular or tubular fabrics. The structure of the fabric is flexible and varies with the gauge (how closely the needles are positioned) of the machine, the type of yarn, and the tension that the yarn is being held whilst it is knitted. Some machines knit shaped garment parts on fully fashioned knitting machines, but most of the production is produced on flat or circular machines. A proportion of the production is in 'body blank' form; the fabric is knitted to the width and length of the body pieces, but minor shaping (necks and armholes) are cut later. The remainder of the fabric production is sold as piece lengths; garment shapes are arranged into lay plans and are cut in a similar manner to cutting woven fabrics. The major problem is that loosely knitted structures can unravel, ladder or distort in handling.

Variations of stitch and patterning, ribbing, inlays, interlock, intarsia and jacquard, create an incredible range of options for the knitwear designer. Weft-knitting can respond to short orders; the machines do not have the complicated setting up of warp threads that is required for woven or warp-knitted fabrics. A thriving craft industry of small knitwear businesses, that is design led, has had a strong influence on mass-market design. 'Influence' should not infer copying; copyright battles of the 'David and Goliath' kind have been more successful recently. Designs, which have been bought to be copied in the Far East and then sold cheaply in High-street stores, have had to be withdrawn from sale.

Fully fashioned machines create finished individual garment shapes that are then seamed. Designers can also create exciting 3D shaping using some fully fashioned knitting machinery and an increasing amount of sportswear is being knitted in one-piece garment form.

Knitted fabric – warp-knit

Warp-knitting machines create vertical interlocking loop chains. Two yarns are often used together to give the fabric stability. There has been a great increase in warp-knitting; the machines are very fast and produce a large amount of fabric from man-made fine filament yarns. The fabrics are particularly suitable for lingerie; openwork and net effects which can be produced on the machines. Raschel machines are taking the place of traditional lace machinery, particularly Leavers lace. Raschel machines can knit complex patterns, but these patterns are limited by the machinery; for example, the width of the guide bars that swing the threads across the warp. The use of micro-fibres, particularly TACTEL blended with LYCRA on Raschel machines, produces extremely fine, strong, soft, stretch fabrics for lingerie. The names of warp-knit fabrics can be confusing, particularly the pile fabrics; the most common are fleece (brushed velour), terry cloth, velvet, corduroy, loop and pile fabrics. Warp-knit fabrics also provide the backing structure for many laminate and flocked pile fabrics. Depending on its use or its aesthetic effect, the pile side may be used on the face or the back of the fabric.

Other developments on Raschel machines have been the 'laying in' of warp or weft threads during the knitting process. Soft staple yarns are used; complex patterning and rigidity in the structure can give a 'woven fabric' look to the fabric which still retains a specified amount of stretch.

Interlaced and embroidered fabrics

Lace machines (for example, Leavers or Schiffli) can be compared with embroidery machines where the pattern is laid on a net background. Traditional machine lace-making is reducing, and therefore the skills required to use some of the older machinery are no longer available.

Many laces are known by the region where the original handmade lace was made; for example, Alençon, Cluny, Chantilly. Pillow lace was constructed over a pillow with many bobbin threads interlaced to form the fabric. Many types of lace designs are now copied on a Raschel machine. Luxury effects are now added to many laces by machine embroidery, ribboning and beading. Crochet and tatting effects can also be copied. However, hand-worked embroidered laces from the Far East often compete on price, choice and availability.

Guipure lace is embroidery made with multi-head embroidery machines. Embroidered fabrics can be made up of 90% surface decoration and 10% backing. Complex structures can be built up incorporating many processes; this makes it difficult to categorise the fabric under a single group, unless under the heading 'constructed textile'.

Barmen machines create a braided heavy lace mainly used in furnishings but the lace appears in fashion ranges when the mood is 'natural'.

Although embroidery and lace making is seen as separate, some advanced knitting machinery can create 'mock lace' and some weaving machines can integrate embroidery into the weaving process.

Fabrics of different structures

Pressing the fibres of fabrics together would seem to be a simple way of making fabric, but until man-made fibres were produced, only wool had the properties that allowed the fibres to felt together to form a mass. This group of fabrics, often referred to as 'non-woven', is used mainly in the garment industry for interlinings. These fabrics often have adhesive backings for fusing to garments. To prevent the pressed web from breaking up, a number of techniques are employed: interlacing the fibres, adhesives, thermal bonding, stitch-bonding and punching. Improvements in laminating techniques have improved the handle of bonded fabrics. Fibres can be held together by chemical binders by heat-setting one of the fibres. Unexpected handle can be achieved; satin that is bonded onto a felt-like backing can give designers new opportunities for shapes. New waterproof, breathable membranes have been produced for weatherwear.

Leather and fur are natural non-woven fabrics. Leather can vary from delicate light suede fabrics with soft drape to heavy dense skins (horse). Stretch leather is achieved by bonding a sliver of suede onto a stretch jersey backing.

Simulated suedes and leathers are mainly produced on a warp-knitted backing. PVC is usually considered a non-woven fabric, but in many cases some form of plastic material is sprayed onto a fine web or knitted backing.

Fabric finishes

All fabrics are finished, the simplest form is simply washing, shrinking and pressing, but most fabrics have some form of extra finish, many of which are complex and may be a completion of an earlier process of manufacture (for example, crepe or stretch fabrics). The finish may be added to improve the aesthetic and tactile quality of a fabric, to enhance or suppress its natural properties, or to add some specific or novel quality. The finish can be permanent or temporary. Many new developments in fabric production are centred on finishing processes.

White dyed or printed fabrics produced from cellulose fibres have to be bleached. Fabrics made from fibres that have a rough texture can be smoothed by cropping and singeing, by chemical finishes (for example, mercerising and biopolishing), or by calendering, glazing and engraving. They can have their rough appearance enhanced; the surface is raised by brushing or plucking. Many of these fabrics then have a pile or 'nap' that is usually cut one way with the fibres laying towards the bottom of the garment; however, interesting effects can be created by cutting up and down a napped fabric. Thicker and softer yarns woven on the back of a fabric can be brushed to give an outer flat appearance and a warm fleecy back. Stripe effects can be made by pile finishes on groups of warp yarns.

Fabrics made from filament yarns are usually smooth and lustrous, and many of those made from man-made fibres imitated silk. However, experiments with combinations of fibre and yarn structures and finishes have created a large explosion of new fabrics which respond to unusual finishes and produce unique combinations of qualities.

Combinations of many of the above techniques, in certain areas or finishes targeted at particular yarns, can give uneven and sculptural effects to fabrics. Fabrics made from thermoplastic synthetic yarns can achieve similar effects by heat-setting. Coating or bonding fabrics usually produces dramatic change to any fabric; many of the coatings on bondings are thermoplastic and are heat-set.

Most of the processes discussed in this book are those that alter the characteristics that are of interest to the process of pattern cutting. However, many finishes are developed for garments that are used for particular purposes; for example, athletic wear requires high absorbency, weatherwear requires waterproofing, and some industrial wear requires chemical and flame proofing. The designer has to consider this kind of parameter when developing a range in a particular product field.

Some finishes (crease resistant, distressed and textured) are completed after the garment is made up. This means that quite complex shrink allowances are required during the development of the pattern, and tight controls are required on the finishing processes.

Fabric production

The production of textiles and garments is the fourth largest global industry. New developments and ecological changes are therefore of major importance. It is also a complex industry; the route between fibre and finished garment can be more complex than creating stable products such as buildings or artifacts. The long supply chain, the instability and variability of the material, and the fashion demands create huge challenges for all sectors.

During the last two decades, the growth in the use of man-made fibres has been spectacular. The Far East has increased its supply of low-cost, high quantity textiles. European producers' attitudes to fabric production therefore changed; they looked for higher value products rather than quantities. This has entailed the development of more sophisticated fibres and fabrics. It has also meant greater co-operation between industries: the fibre producers; the spinners; the weavers and knitters; the finishers and printers. There is less division between man-made fibres and natural fibres. Fibre marriages in blends can exploit the unique qualities of the natural fibres and the 'structural engineering' of the man-made fibres. Lightweight fabrics that offer good performance in warmth and wear are in demand and most natural fabrics have a limit to their degree of fineness.

The next decade may see changes of direction beginning to take place. As oil prices rise, we see a great deal of the new research affected by ecological issues. As commodities become scarce and budgets tighten, the customer may become more inclined to consider style, quality, wear and performance factors rather than 'throw away fashion'.

Fabric lengths and widths

Fabrics are produced in piece lengths which vary in length and width. The piece length of a roll of fabric for major production orders is decided by the weight and bulkiness of the fabric and the colourways ordered. Quite short lengths of fabric are produced for special orders of expensive fabrics.

Fabric widths will vary; from 72 cm (Harris Tweed) which is woven on narrow looms, to circular jersey fabric that can be as wide as 180 cm. Light weight fabrics have mainly been woven 90–114 cm in width; but companies, who produce large quantities, are demanding wider fabrics to gain greater efficiency in their garment lays. Woollen fabrics and tweeds are generally woven at 150 cm width. The width of the fabric is crucial to the garment designer. Costing negotiations frequently require modifications to a design. The final cut of the garment may be determined by the width of the fabric.

Fabric weights

Fabric weights are given in two ways; weight per running metre or weight per square metre. The latter is the most useful when comparing different qualities. Fabric swatches do not always state the type of weight, therefore the designer or technologist may have to re-weigh a sample piece. Very light weight fabrics have to be made from strong fibres or specially processed fibres; they tend to be more expensive than medium weight fabrics. Heavy weight fabrics are usually expensive because of the quantity of yarn used. Exceptions to these generalisations can be found and hard wear or strength may not be characteristics of principal concern for the designer.

Fabric thickness

The thickness of a fabric is dependent on a large number of variables: the fibre structure; the yarn structure and finish; the fabric structure and finish; surface decoration, fabric bonding or lamination. Double-faced fabrics can be made by interweaving two layers of woven cloth, or in knitting, using the front and back needles. A great improvement in bonding techniques has led to many combinations of fabrics being bonded: to give strength to a weak or flexible structure; to 'sandwich' insulating fabric to create reversible cloths; to bond weatherproof membranes; and to create a particular handle or three dimensional appearance.

Cutting fabric

The majority of fabric lays in mass-production are cut with the warp grain of the fabric running vertically through the garment. Although many fabric lays have the pattern laid up and down on the cloth, some fabrics can only be cut one way; for example, fabrics with a nap (raised surface finish), one-way printed designs, one-way woven checks and stripes, and many knitted fabrics. Cutting in one way can place restrictions on the shapes of the patterns. Angular shapes do not interlock easily and give a poor utilisation of the fabric. Cutting crossway across the fabric can also give poor utilisation figures, but the advantages of using this method for body clinging styles can override this problem.

Fabrics do not have to be cut with the warp hanging vertically. As fabrics are now available in widths of 160 cm or 180 cm, the length of the pattern could lay across the fabric. However, as warp threads are usually the strongest threads, it is sensible that these threads are where the fabric is likely to get the greatest strain. However, some woven fabrics have dominant weft stripes and they can be more flattering if they are cut down the garment.

The right side of the fabric is the one with the finished surface. But designers exploit all characteristics of fabrics, sometimes using the wrong side as well as the right side in one garment.

New developments in fabric processes

Fabric handle

There are so many new developments in fabric production that it is impossible to cover them in this book. This section includes some major new processes and focuses on those that are likely to affect the handle characteristics of the fabric. These processes also focus on fabric developments that are now available rather than experimental fibres and fabrics that are still at the research stage. More general developments for product sectors are shown in the table on page 179.

Natural fibres and yarns

Natural fibres have their own unique appearance and qualities that many man-made fibres attempted to copy whilst adding further qualities such as lightness, strength and washability. The competition from man-made fibre development has led to new efforts to 'improve' the qualities of natural fibres, by biological methods of breeding, by fibre engineering, and by the chemical treatment of fibres. For example:

cross-breeding and genetic engineering is producing new breeds of cotton with longer stronger fibres, and spider silk that has extreme strength;

Cashgora is a new natural fibre produced by crossing feral goats with angora bucks;

Tough Cotton has a 20% better tensile and tear strength yet preserves its drape and handle;

Cool Wool is an easy-care and super light weight fabric;

new soft fibres are being produced from bamboo.

Man-made fibres and yarns

Whilst the total fibre market volume has increased at a rate of more than 3% over the last twenty years, the largest increase has occurred in man-made fibre production, particularly the synthetics. This has accounted for 82% of the growth in fibre production during the last decade.

Although there may seem to be a bewildering number of new fabrics on the market, the cost of the research and development means that very few new generic fibres are developed. Many so-called new fibres are complex engineering of existing fibres; for example, micro-fibres and bi-component fibres (composites of two generic filament fibres, i.e. polyester and nylon). Researchers are also constantly attempting to increase or suppress basic characteristics of natural or man-made fibres in order to compete in the market. New synthetic generic fibres are being produced from sugars in crops such as corn or oil from the castor oil plant.

The growth of multi-nationals has provided the means to fund expensive synthetic fibre engineering that changes the structures of man-made fibres. Fibre structures are the source of many new visual effects and can be engineered to mimic natural fibres. New fibre structures have been realised from studies of the natural world, to copy and create new surfaces on fabrics, such as the structure of *Super Mi-croft*. But man-made fibres do not have to look like natural fibres; co-polymers with different characteristics and reactions to finishes create new textures with a different aesthetic appeal.

Whilst a micro-fibre is a fibre of 1 decitex or less, nano-fibres, produced by electro-spinning, are fundamentally different in scale (one nanometre is one billionth of a metre). They have a large surface area in comparison to their form. They are used in specialist areas, (see the table on page 179).

Regenerated fibres

Viscose: (which has the highest production), has a great disadvantage: it is weak when wet. However, modified rayons (**modal** and **cupro**) have reduced this problem. *Micro-Modal* yarns can be spun ultra-fine for delicate clothing; 10,000 metres of yarn weigh only a single gram.

Lyocell: which is sometimes labelled by a trade name *Tencel*, is a fairly new generic cellulosic fibre. At first seen as a luxury fibre, it is now in the collections of High Street fashion. Its drape qualities give a new handle to fabrics used in casual wear.

Semi-synthetic fibres

Acetate: is a fibre that is regarded as semi-synthetic because of its chemical production process. Because it is heat-set, it is the only cellulosic that is thermoplastic. This means that embossed, crinkled or pleated fabrics can be permanently heat-set.

Diacetate and triacetate: are fibres that demonstrate higher levels of these qualities and have a greater stability and crease resistance.

Synthetic fibres

Polyamide: new fibre structures and multi-filament yarns give polyamide fibres a soft luxury handle and high drape. The marketing for this new generation of fibres has had to overcome preconceived ideas about the unsympathetic nature of the fibre.

Polyester: micro-fibre fabrics are ultra-fine filaments packed in high density. They create unique light weight fabrics with soft handle, such as fine fleece fabrics with a velvety nap for comfort and performance. False twisted yarns create fabrics that resemble cotton; with added crimp they become both bulky and elastic. Air textured yarns can create loopy yarns with no open spaces. New stretch polyester fibres can expand to two-thirds the expansion function of elastane.

Acrylic: fibres originally had problems with pilling and static electricity. These problems have now been solved and although still popular as a substitute for wool, many new soft delicate fabrics with high absorbency are finding new markets.

New generic fibres

New competitors to the most used synthetic fabrics polyamide and polyester have emerged; they are based on natural sources.

PLA: the source of the new synthetic fibre PLA is corn and sugar beet. Polyactic acid is manufactured from the carbon and sugars that they contain. The fibres are heat-set. As pressure grows for the sustainability of natural resources in manufactured textile products, it is seen as a future strong competitor for polyester.

Polyamide 11: this fibre was developed from the crushed seeds of the castor oil plant. It is a new innovation that appears to be the first polyamide based on a natural source, reducing the dependence on oil products.

Fibre and fabric performance developments in particular product areas

Technology is adding value to garment fabrics which have to perform in different environments. It is many of the large multi-national companies that have the finance and expertise to drive these developments. *PremierVision*, the fabric show for buyers held twice yearly in Paris, has created 24 Performance Codes to add to fabric labels.

These enable exhibitors to highlight the specific properties or qualities of fabrics whether they are visible or not. For example: antibacterial, easy-care, thermal, windproof, organic. This emphasises how the buyers' interest, particularly in product areas, is focused on obtaining added qualities for their garment ranges.

A table describing some of the latest performance developments in particular product areas

SPORTSWEAR	Hollow fibres that speed up evaporation Fibres that warm muscles and react to body temperatures Nano-fibres incorporating minerals for de-odorising 'Second skin' fabrics for streamline racing Membranes that swell to absorb moisture Fabrics with de-odorising properties Engineered hollow fibres that trap pockets of air to give thermal and wicking properties Micro-polyester technology transfers moisture to the outside of the fabric TRANSDRY cotton yarns now transfer moisture to the outside of the fabric which dry quickly
WEATHERWEAR	Fibres can be encapsulated with silicone to make them waterproof Micro-pores and breathable wicking membranes for waterproof clothing Spacer fabrics with pockets between fabric layers for warmth Body heat stored between layers, released as the body cools Ceramic interlinings that store heat Hydrophobic emulsifiers not only soften leather but also offer waterproofing qualities A weatherproof polyester membrane with wicking that can be bonded to almost any fabric Sensory fabrics that respond to changes in the environment
PROTECTION	Micro-fibre ranges which include fibres with UVA and UVB protection Breathable nano-fibres that protect against fire and chemicals Chitosan fibres from insect skeletons and crab shells that are biologically inert Bio-engineering of nano-particles of metals, providing antimicrobial fibres and finishes Nano-coatings can give stain resistance
APPEARANCE	'Shape memory' finishes provide the retention of pleats and crinkles after washing Split filaments create mock suede and leather Thermachromatic fabrics can change colour on contact with body or external heat Neochrome fibre is dyed during the production of the fibre Rectangular fibre forms give added sheen to synthetic fibres
DECORATION	Soft flexible metals and transfers New coatings and laminates New fibres incorporating metals and gem stones Super bright polyester dope dyed yarns and bi-colour effects Cross-sectioned polyester yarn gives an opalescent appearance Chromatic materials that change colour in response to light, heat or pressure
ELECTRONICS	Sensors that measure performance or organ function Built in music and alarm systems Fibres that will recharge batteries
MISCELLANEOUS	New fibres are responding to the sensual demands of touch, sight, smell and hearing Nano-capsules containing perfumes

Blends and mixtures

Many new blends and mixtures are taking place in order to create fabrics with a different handle, such as cotton and cashmere or bamboo and cashmere. The latter offers the bright features of bamboo yet the soft delicacy of cashmere. Bouclé and chenille yarns are being spun with animal hair to give new surface appeal. A new cotton fibre with a wool core creates washable fabrics that are soft, smooth and warm, but also have great moisture absorption characteristics.

New textures and drape characteristics are being produced by blending natural fibres with man-made fibres; for example, pile structures and soft filling yarns on nylon or polyester bases.

Blending man-made fibres can also create high fashion yarns with new textures; for example, viscose is transformed when it is spun or mixed with micro-fibres to create 'natural' soft yarns that are exclusive.

Elastane: is always used with another fibre. Many new developments in elastane fibres have taken place, including an improvement in dimensional stability and the softness of the fibre. Blended with natural fibres it has given them stretch.

Fabric finishing

A range of finishes

Although wool promotes its unique features, it is also competing with man-made fibres by using finishes that improve washability. The handle and appearance of the wool can be given a soft, lustrous or 'vintage' finish.

Many of the new finishes are concentrated on fabric performance; for example, waterproofing can mean depositing polymers, hydrophobic silicones, coatings, waxes or membranes (see the table on page 179), and they can radically change the handle and drapability of the fabric.

However, other finishes are aimed at providing fabrics with a softer handle and improved drape that retain their quality when washed or worn. For example:

Process 2000: keeps garments wrinkle free or retains distressed finishes when washed;

'shape memory' finishes allow pleating to reappear after washing;

Biopolishing: gives the fabrics softness, smoothness and reduces pilling;

enzyme technology has improved the handle and finish of sheepskins and lambskins;

silicon finishes are creating softer handles.

The finishing of a fabric can lightly enhance the intrinsic quality and aesthetic of the fabric or it can become a highly specialised technical procedure.

An example of this is given on the label of a pair of denim jeans:

Yarn: Fibre content 98% cotton 2% elastane; ring spun yarn; filling cotton spandex corespun.

Finish: Cut into body pieces; washed with enzymes and stones; tumbled with plastic balls; sprayed with *Stabycryl Dshine.*

Other processes can include hand abrasion and bleach spraying.

Ecology

Introduction – the environment

Ecology is a branch of science that deals with human beings' relationship with their environment. For many decades textile and clothing technology has centred on the comfort and protection of the human body; but a greater concern is now emerging – that of the survival of the environment itself. This has had serious implications for the textile industry. The Kyoto Treaty signed in 1997 was the first serious attempt to curb the emission of greenhouse gases, but it is not the only environmental problem. The major threats to the environment and human life come from resource depletion, pollution and global warming. Textile and garment production increases the threats in the following ways:

Vegetable fibres (crop growth)	pesticides
Animal fibres/skins (cleaning)	pollution
Man-made fibres	resource depletion, energy use, pollution
All fibre/fabric/ garment production	energy use, pollution
Retailing	energy use, pollution
Discarding clothes	resource depletion/pollution

Design

There are an increasing number of young designers and fashion students who are specialising in eco-fashion. But, the overriding focus of many designers is still the visual aspect of design and not the eco-consequences of producing the fabric or the trims. There has to be a strong commitment by any company to pursue ideals, but there has also to be a demand from the public. A consistent eco-position may be hard to pursue economically. Fashion itself depends on the public discarding garments in favour of the new season's range. This concept pays scant acknowledgement to ecological concerns and frustrates the fabric technologists not familiar with transient fads. Short-lived fashion trends aimed at tempting the consumer can mask a serious long-term problem for the clothing industry as customers start looking for durability.

Designers may have to start taking into consideration the end-of-life process. This not only means using ecologically sourced fabrics that can be re-cycled, but the need to reject any means of manufacture that could prevent the process. Trimmings such as threads, zips and buttons have also to be considered.

A concern for the environment places designers as educators of society leading the customer into appreciating eco-friendly products and the aesthetic character of a fibre that has not been over-engineered or treated. They also already create household items and garments where sections of new fabrics are stitched to form the fabric or garment piece. They could become part of a revival of crafts that cut out sections of discarded garments for re-use.

Manufacturing

The greatest pollution in textile production or leather processing is produced from scouring, bleaching, dyeing, printing, finishing and tanning. Effluent has always been a particular problem for sizing, dyeing and finishing plants. New laws are now in place which affect all areas of the textile/garment production cycle. These differ from country to country. UK and EEC regulations and directives are increasing pressure and imposing costs in order to clean up the industry's pollution and emissions. Western European fibre producers have already spent vast amounts of money on meeting standards; they publicly support a 'green' image, but their concern is that their competitors in other areas of the world are not subject to the same controls. During the production process, the energy used and the carbon emissions produced are incurring increasing costs; they are therefore becoming a new focus of a company's attention. Company and farming associations are advising on ways of improving methods, attempting to adhere to these whilst remaining commercial.

The wearing of natural fibres can appear to be ecologically responsible, but much of the cotton grown uses large amounts of pesticides on the crops and the effluent from the chemicals used in its processing, finishing, bleaching and dyeing are pollutants. Ecologically sound 'green cotton' is only a very small percentage of total production. As waste disposal and recycling become critical, the advantages of natural fibres and synthetic sustainable fibres is that they are degradable. There is an increasing interest in fibres from sustainable sources such as soya bean or castor oil.

An increasing number of technical textiles are being produced. The fibres and finishes are designed to appeal to the customer's comfort, protection or aesthetic appreciation. They can become impossible to recycle. As natural and chemical resources become scarce it may become a matter of priority that fibres' research becomes increasingly focused on engineering fabrics for their end-of-life process.

Retailing

Although more supermarkets are seeing the success of offering organic produce or FAIRTRADE products, the shopper's enthusiasm does not appear to have spread yet to clothing. Many consumers may wish to be supportive of environmental issues but lack information.

The buyers for retailers have tremendous control over the design and manufacturing process which has been geared to continual changes of style to tempt the customer, and the company has to make a profit to survive against foreign competition. Some companies can see marketing advantages in appearing ecologically sound, and public relations and information are now crucial marketing strategies of the manufacturers and retailers. Some major retailers have launched organic cotton ranges or garments made from sustainable fibre sources; but these sales initiatives are only a tiny percentage of their total turnover.

Recycling

The landfill of products that cannot be recycled is an enormous problem, but it becomes critical in a small over-populated island such as the UK, and European directives will result in huge fines if the problem is not solved.

In the textile industry about half of clothing produced is re-used. It is sold through the charity shops and also exported overseas to poorer countries. This saves water, energy and pollution and is the easiest way of recycling. During the last decade, as new clothing prices reduced and people felt affluent, more clothing went to be recycled. It also became harder for recycling companies to make a profit and textiles got less support in this area than other sectors of industry. This may change as resources become scarcer or family budgets reduce. But recycling garments is not easy; few garments are made from one material and the fibres have to be identified. Most garments have to be stripped of trimmings and different areas separated. Processes such as gluing and laminating mean that some sections cannot be separated.

Clothing made from natural fibres can be broken down and re-spun, but most of the resulting fibres are grey and coarse. There can be a reluctance to use recycled fabrics for clothing unless they appeal aesthetically to the designer and the buyer. Therefore, they are used mainly for paper or household products. More successful has been the recycling of plastic bottles to make fleece fabrics.

PART SIX: MODEL FIGURES AND GARMENT BLOCKS
Chapter 13 Model stands and figures to reproduce

Model stands and figures

Many fashion drawings appear to have figures that are elongated or distorted. This type of illustration is usually part of the process of creating moods, ideas and stories for presentation. It is also a reflection of the designer's personal ideas and expression during the early stages of design development. However, pattern cutters require more proportionate drawings if they are going to interpret the design correctly. So it is useful for students to draw accurate designs before cutting a pattern. The following pages show images of the model and the stand used in the book illustrations. They can be photocopied up to A3 size. Detail paper can be placed over the stands or figures and style development drawings produced that will correspond to the block shapes.

The images are labelled A, B, C etc. to enable the front and back figures to be matched.

A

B

C

Front view

3/4 right view

Side right view

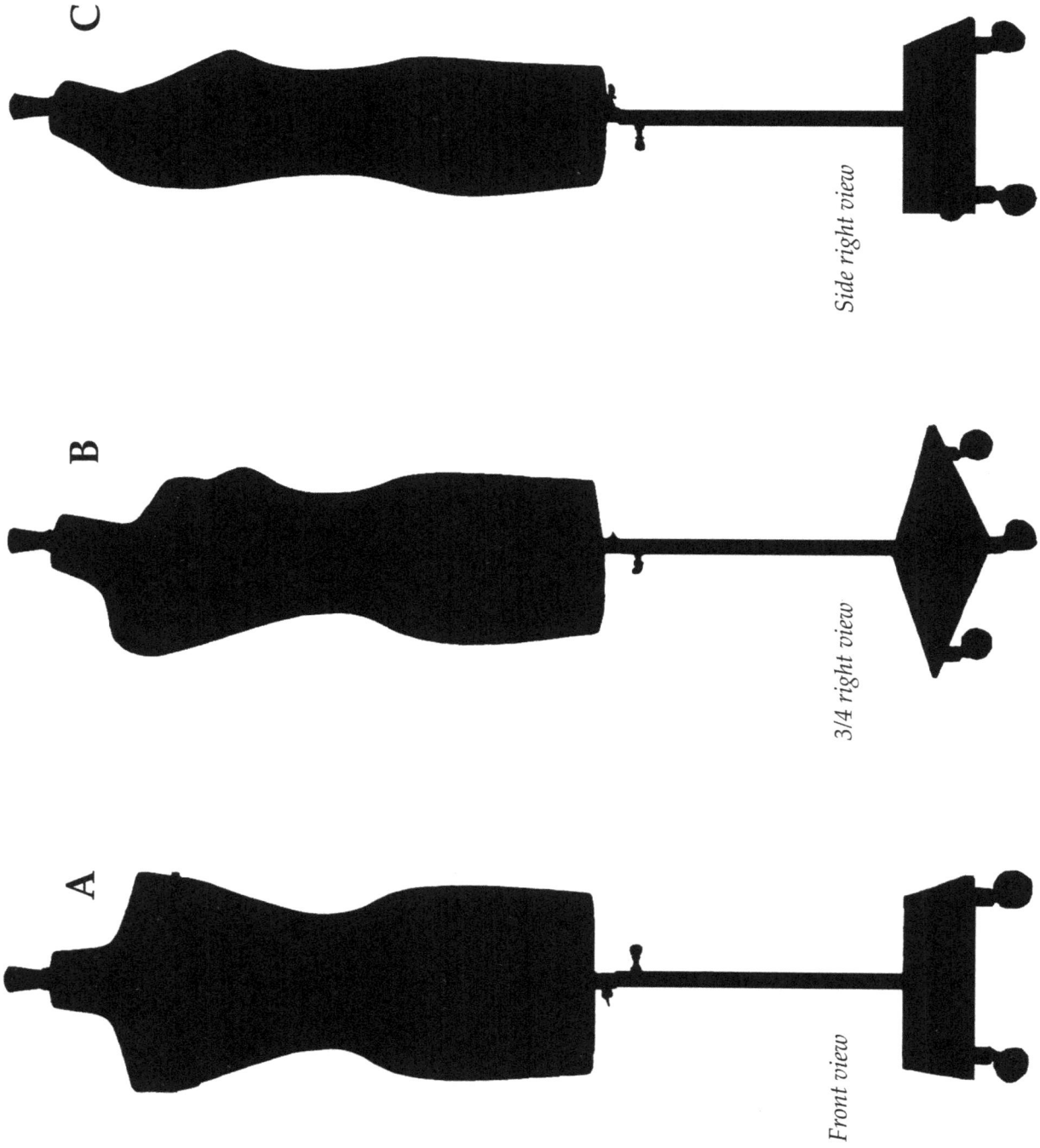

The model stands—front and right views

F

Back view

E

3/4 left view

D

Side right view

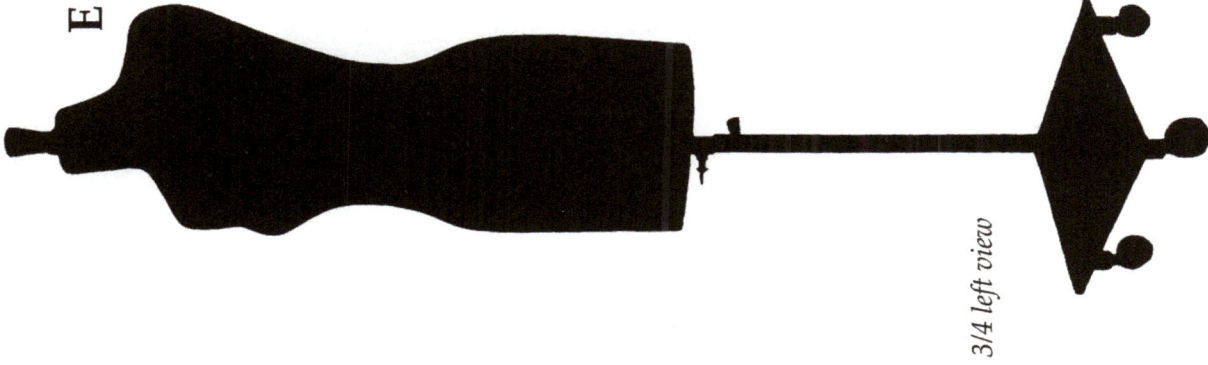

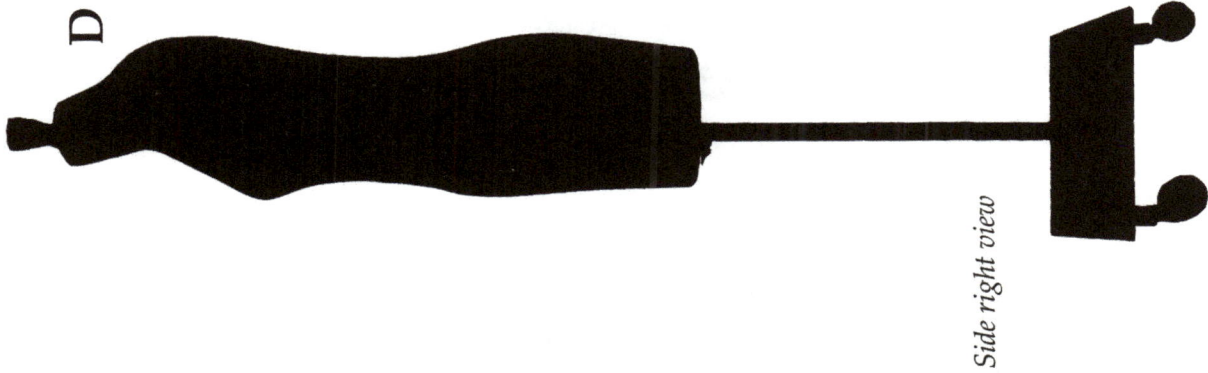

The model stands—back and left views

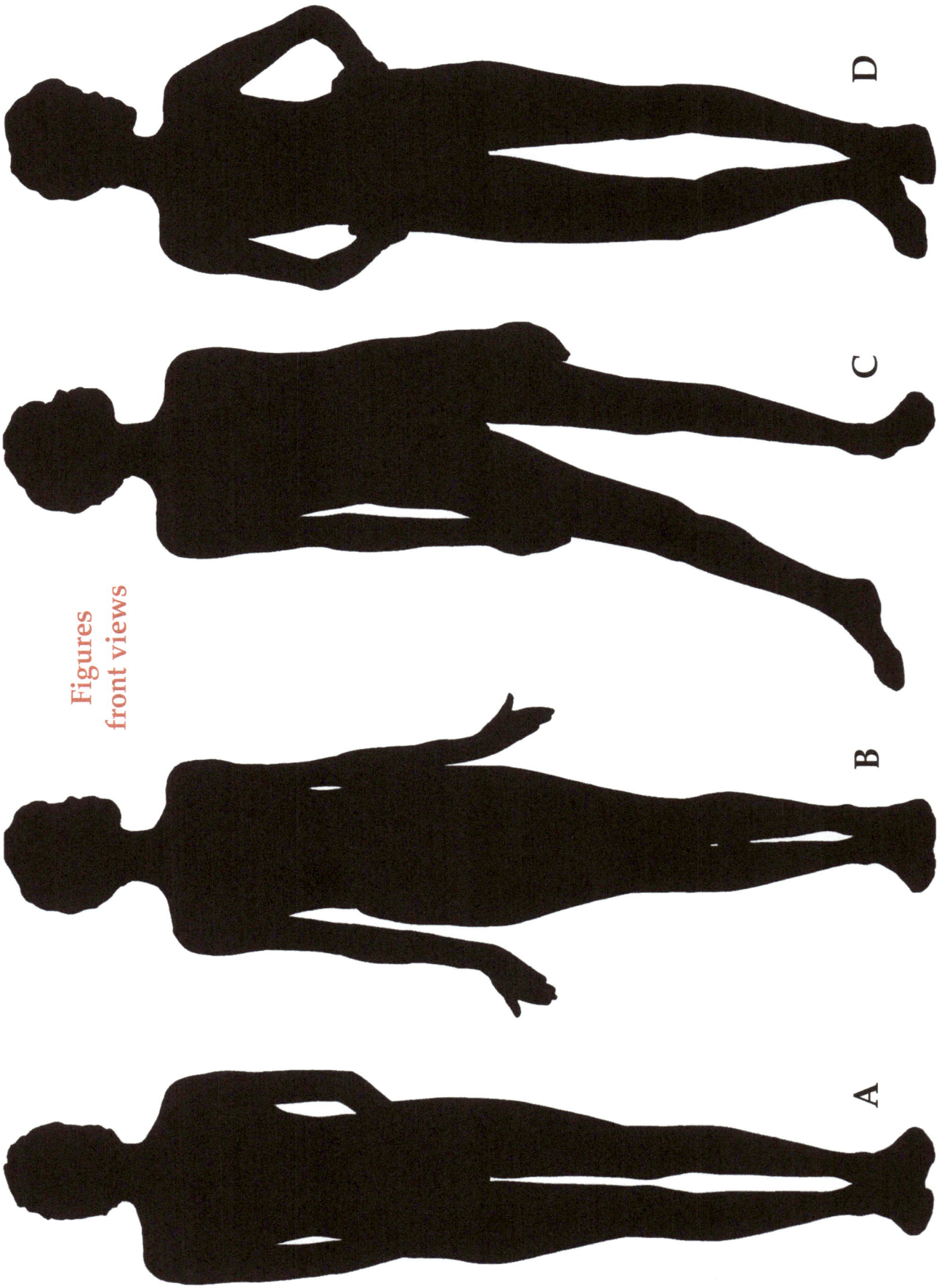

Figures
front views

D

C

B

A

187

G

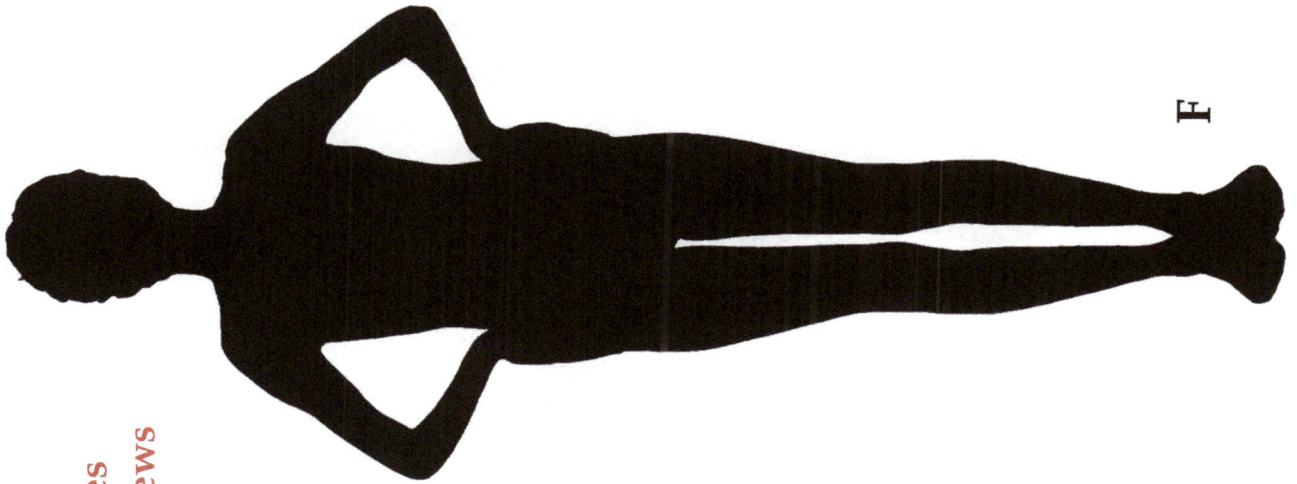

F

**Figures
front views**

E

Figures
back views

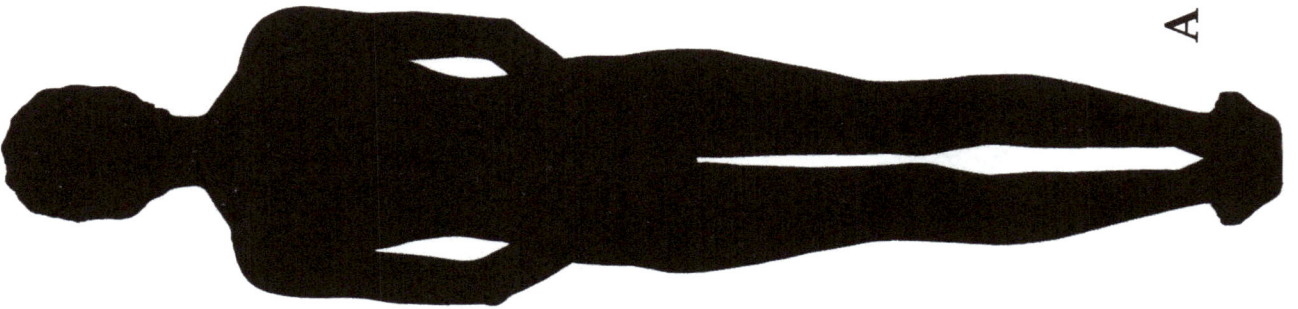

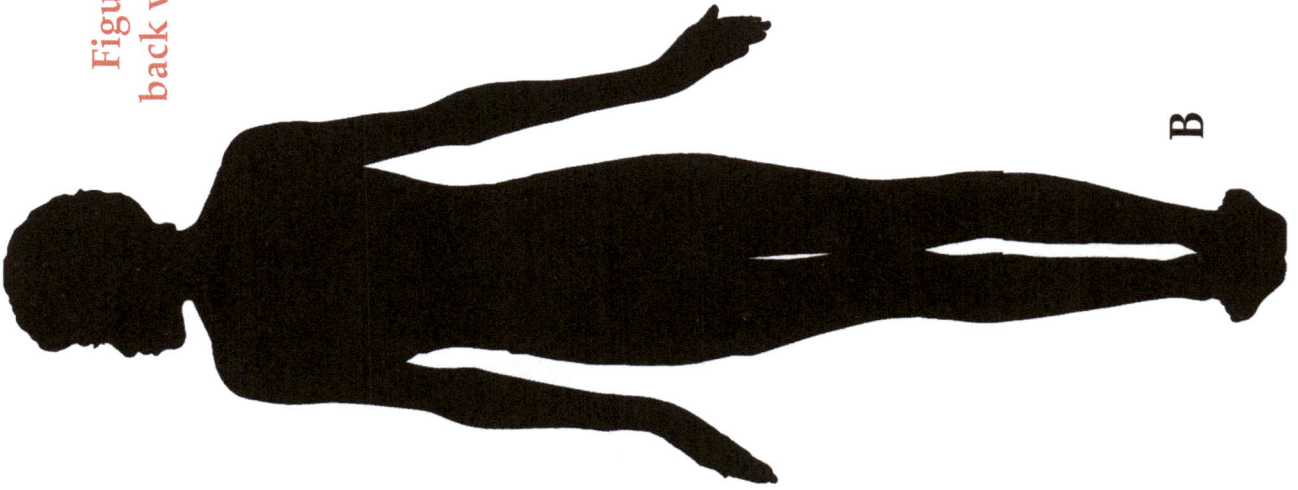

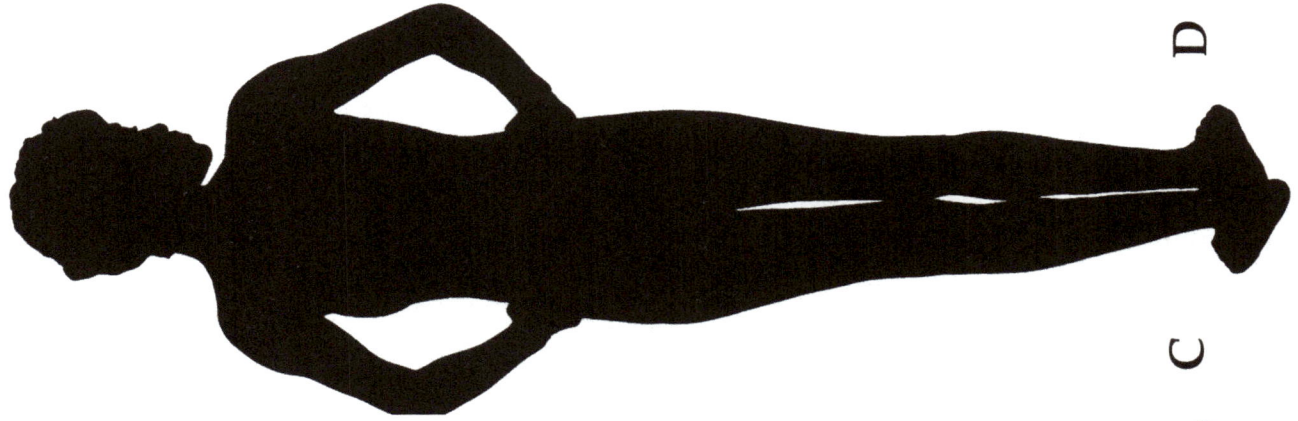

A

B

C

D

**Figures
back views**

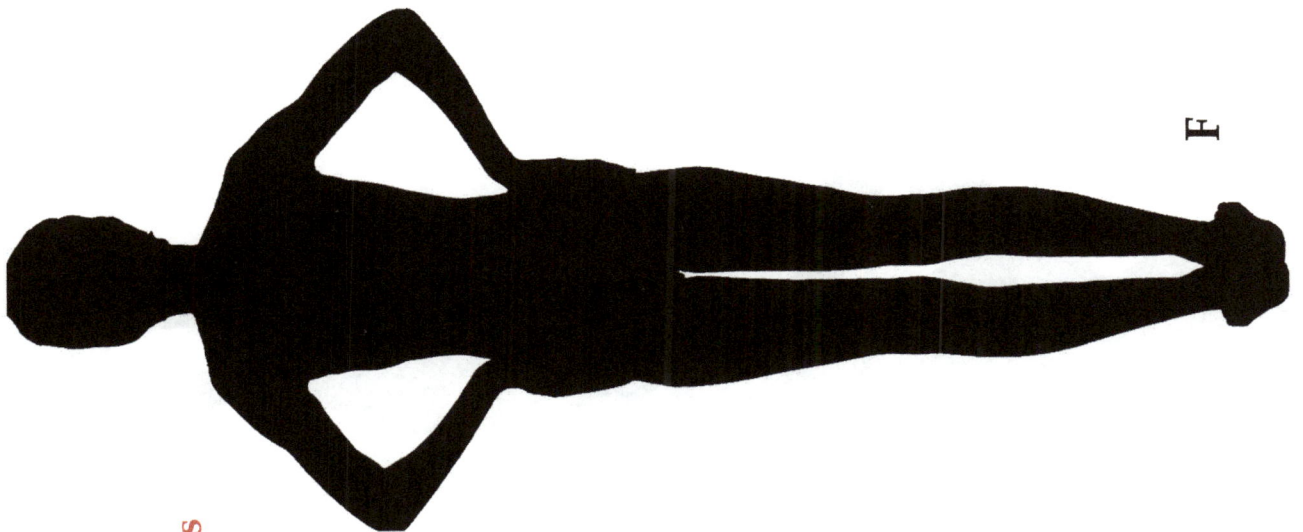

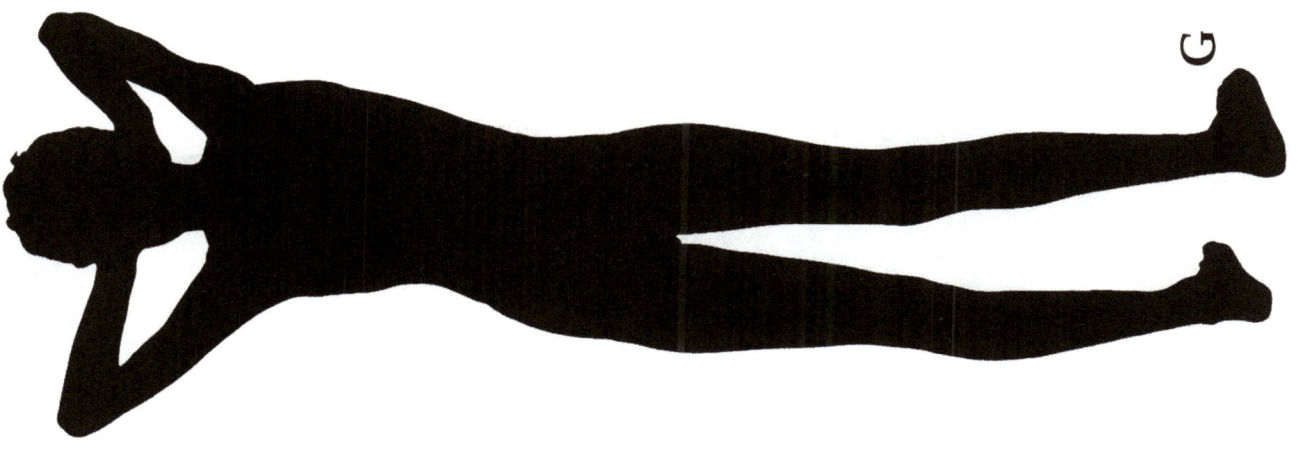

E

F

G

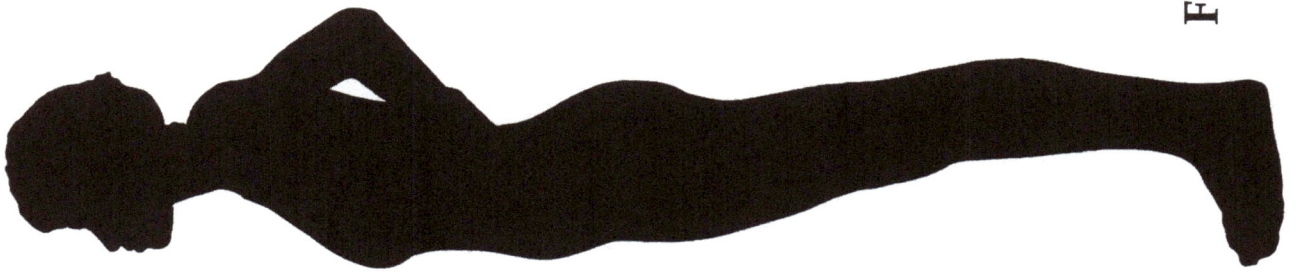

Figures
side views

A

E

F

Figures
extra front views

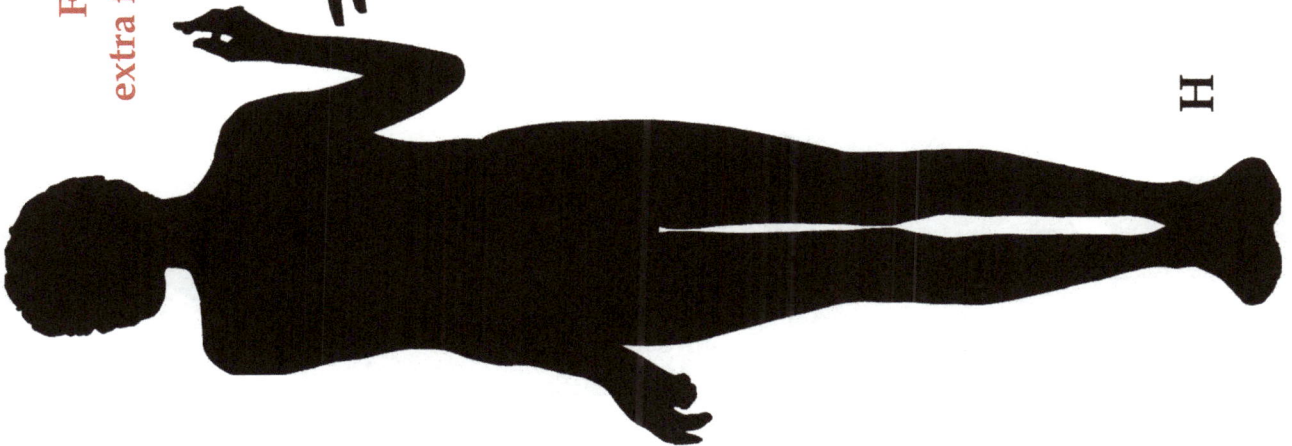

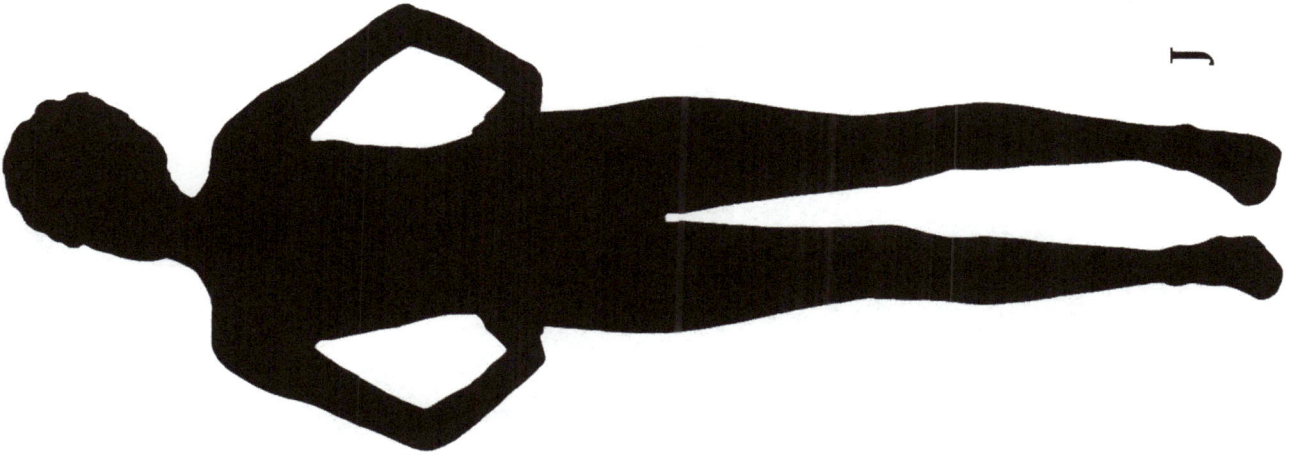

H

I

J

Figures
extra front views

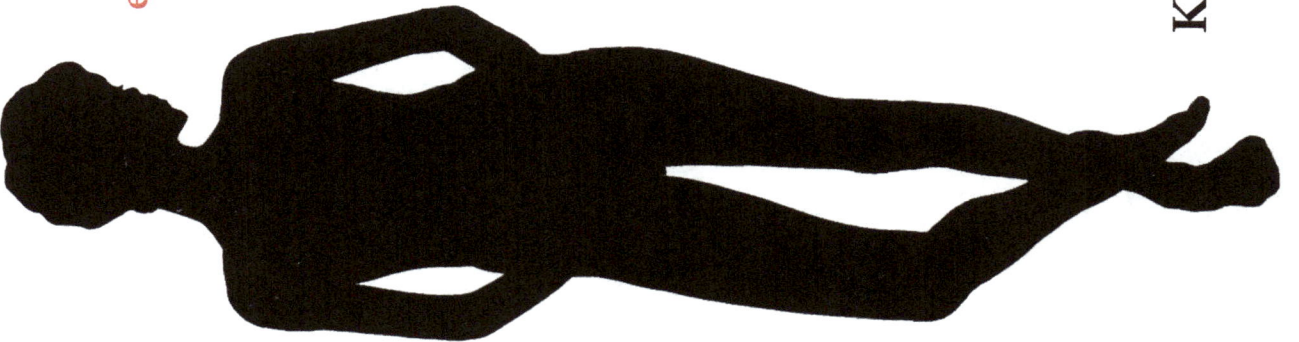

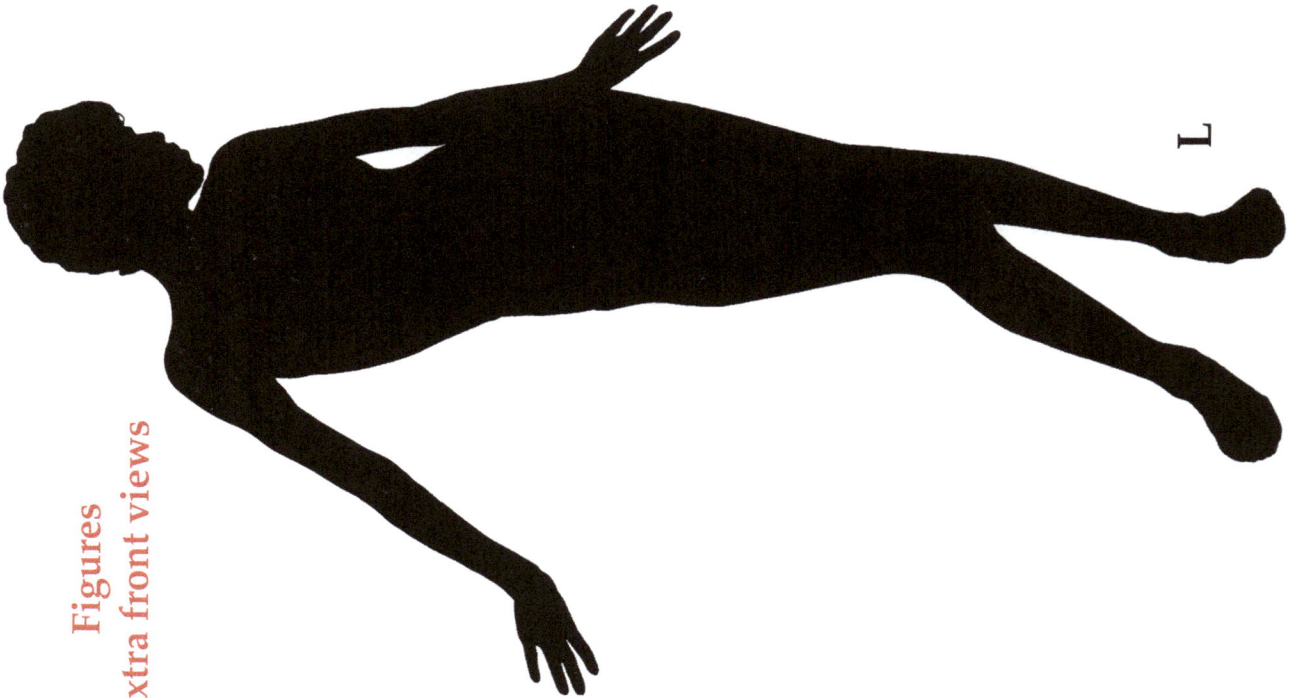

K

L

M

PART SIX: MODEL FIGURES AND GARMENT BLOCKS

Chapter 14 Creating the one-fifth and full-scale blocks (methods – manual, CAD or Internet access)

The basic blocks

Block patterns are foundation patterns constructed to fit the body measurements of an average figure of one of the size groups (10, 12, 14, etc.), see the chart below. The blocks include the basic amount of ease (or reduction for stretch jersey fabric blocks) for the function of the garment. Underwear requires less ease than over-garments.

The designer completes a pattern in a sample size, usually size 10 or 12. The design is made up into a sample garment. When the design is accepted, the garment is graded into the remaining sizes required by the buyer.

Body measurement charts used in the clothing industry usually relate to their specific markets, for example, young High Street Fashion or design for mature women. The chart size codes can be in 4 cm, 5 cm or 6 cm increments. The chart below is a chart of 5 cm intervals aimed at High Street Fashion. The two block sizes available on the following pages are based on sizes 10 and 12.

A wider range of size charts and basic blocks with full instructions are available in the books: *Metric Pattern Cutting*, *Metric Pattern Cutting for Menswear*, *Metric Pattern Cutting for Children's Wear and Babywear* and *Pattern Cutting for Ladies Tailored Jackets*.

Size chart (5 cm increments) women's body measurements

women of medium height 160 cm–172 cm (5 ft 3 in–5 ft 7½ in)						
size code	**8**	**10**	**12**	**14**	**16**	**18**
bust	77	82	87	92	97	102
waist	57	62	67	72	77	82
low waist	65	70	75	80	85	90
hips	82	87	92	97	102	107
back width	31.8	33	34.2	35.4	36.6	37.8
chest	29	30.5	32	33.5	35	36.5
shoulder	11.6	11.9	12.2	12.5	12.8	13.1
neck size	34.4	35.6	36.8	38	39.2	40.4
dart	5.8	6.4	7	7.6	8.2	8.8
top arm	25	26.4	27.8	29.2	30.6	32
wrist	15	15.5	16	16.5	17	17.5
ankle	22.8	23.4	24	24.6	25.2	25.8
high ankle	19.8	20.4	21	21.6	22.2	22.8
nape to waist	39	39.5	40	40.5	41	41.5
front shoulder to waist	39	39.5	40	40.5	41.3	42.1
armscye depth	20	20.5	21	21.5	22	22.5
waist to knee	57.5	58	58.5	59	59.5	60
waist to hip	20	20.3	20.6	20.9	21.2	21.5
waist to floor	102	103	104	105	106	107
body rise	26.7	27.3	28	28.7	29.4	30.1
sleeve length	56.7	57.3	58	58.7	59.4	60.1
sleeve length (jersey)	50.7	51.3	52	52.7	53.4	54.1

The blocks and shapes available in this book

Students should see the blocks in this book simply as basic shapes that are starting points from which to explore basic cutting methods and to experiment with fabric qualities. They are offered for projects in a wide range of fashion courses. They could also be useful for printed textile and embroidery students who wish to apply their work to garment shapes. The range of blocks includes shapes based on a simple grid, to blocks that fit closely to the body contours. They provide the opportunity to use shape and fabric quality to generate an infinite variety of new experimental garment forms.

Seam allowances

There are no seam allowances included in the blocks. These should be added after the pattern has been constructed. A standard seam allowance is 1 cm–1.5 cm.

Enclosed seams (i.e. collars and facings) can be reduced to 0.5 cm.

Using and reproducing the blocks

The blocks are one-fifth scale and placed on 1 cm grids. They can be traced and used to create one-fifth scale patterns. They can also be scaled up manually to full size by drawing a 5 cm grid (spot and cross pattern paper can be used). The lines and curves of the block can be drawn on the grid with reference to the diagrams and multiplying any measurement by 5.

Downloading the blocks from the Website
Full size blocks from this book are now available on the Web. They can be downloaded as PDF files at no cost and printed out on A0 or A4 printers. Full details of how to obtain them and print them are given on pages 213 and 214.

The basic grid

Very easy fitting garments can be cut from simple basic shapes; particularly when working with knitted garment shapes, loosely woven fabrics or fabrics with stretch characteristics. The fabric will stretch over complex areas of the body (i.e. the bust), or areas which have extreme movement (i.e. the elbow). The basic grid registers important control points of the body (i.e. shoulder point, armhole depth position) to use as a reference when taking extreme design decisions. It is important to understand that the basic grid is based on body measurements and requires a substantial amount of extra ease on the body measurement points to allow the body to move. Working from a flat

grid only gives you a 2D 'envelope shape'; if a closer fitting shape is required, gusseted pieces have to be inserted for body movement.

The simple kimono

A simple one-piece (back and front from one pattern) kimono shape constructed from the basic grid is very useful for knitted shapes and dramatic overgarments. The sleeve angle can be varied, but if it becomes too acute the underarm movement will become restricted. A more complex kimono shape with some front bust darting can be found on page 197.

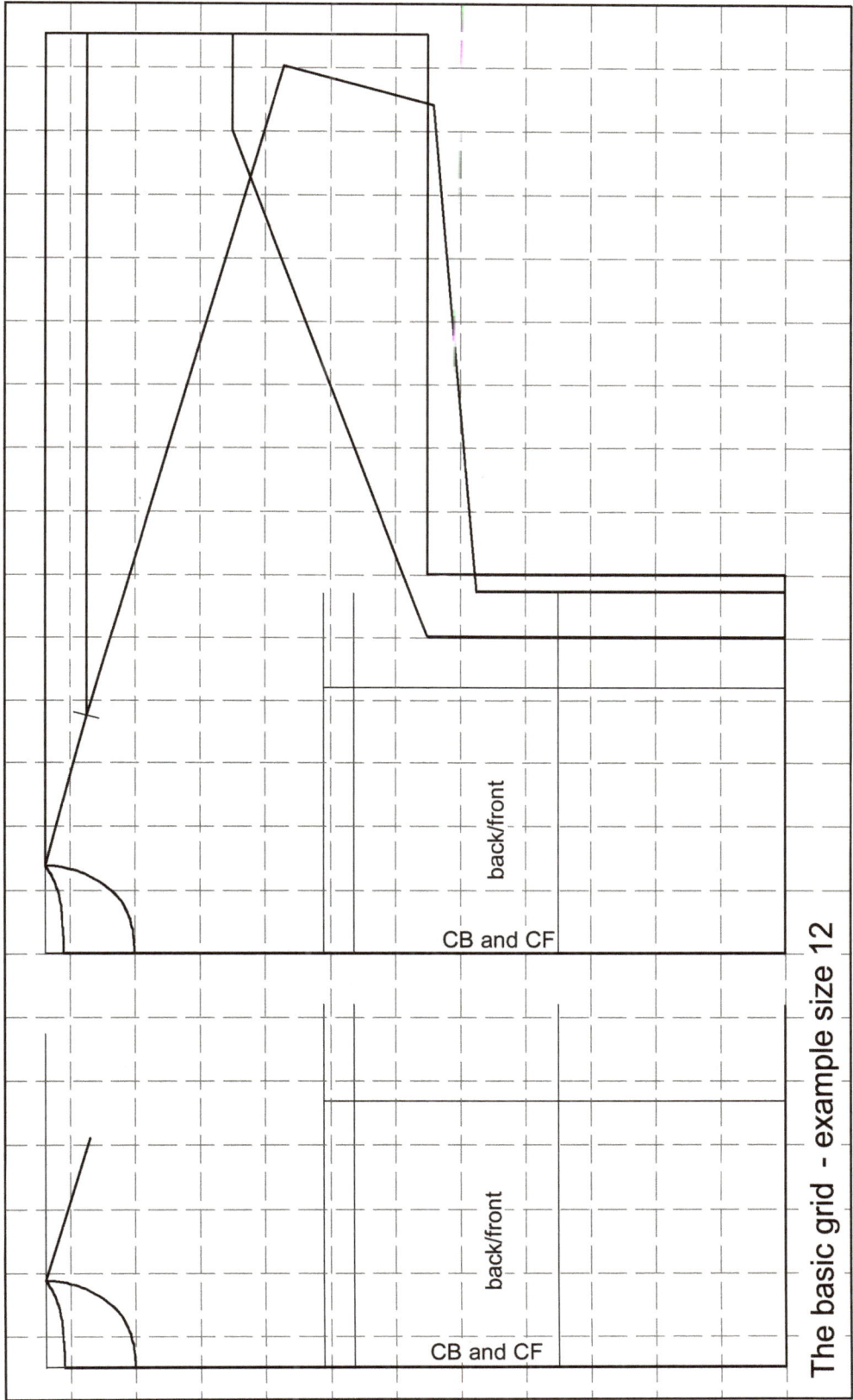

back/front

CB and CF

back/front

CB and CF

The basic grid - example size 12

195

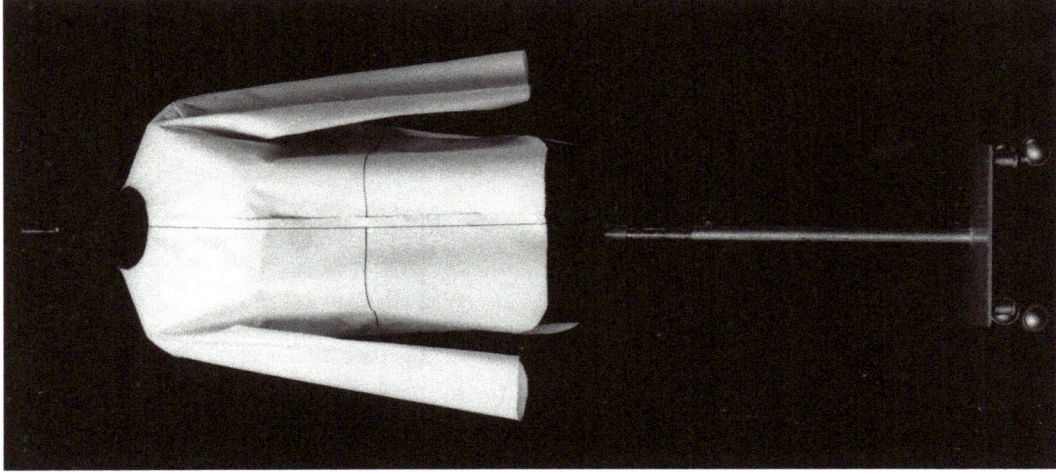

shirt block

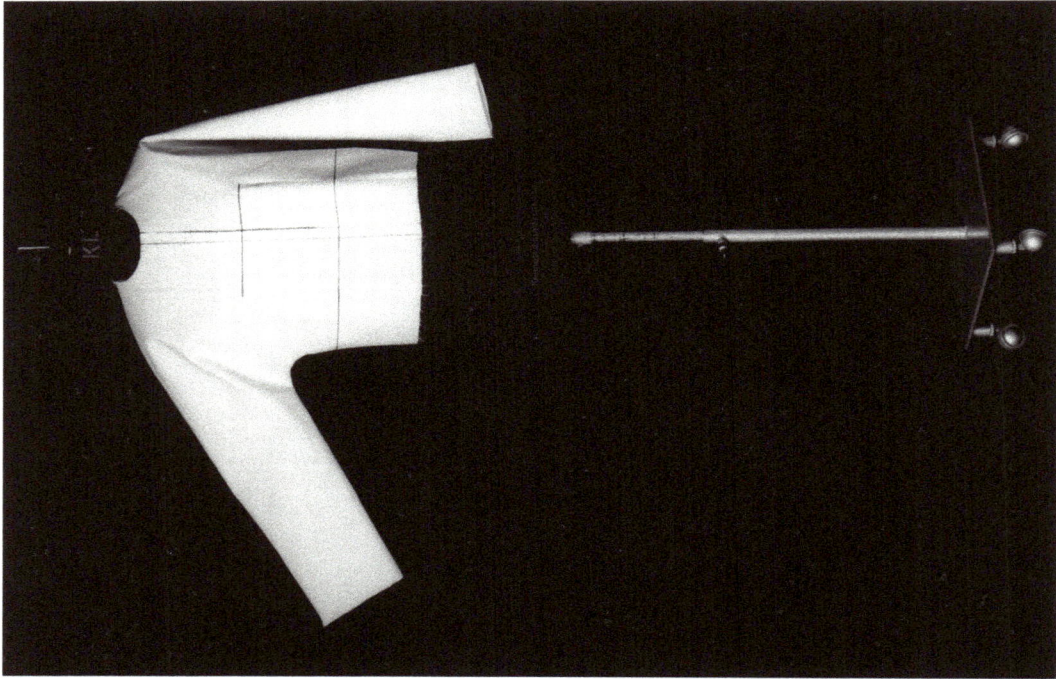

shaped kimono block

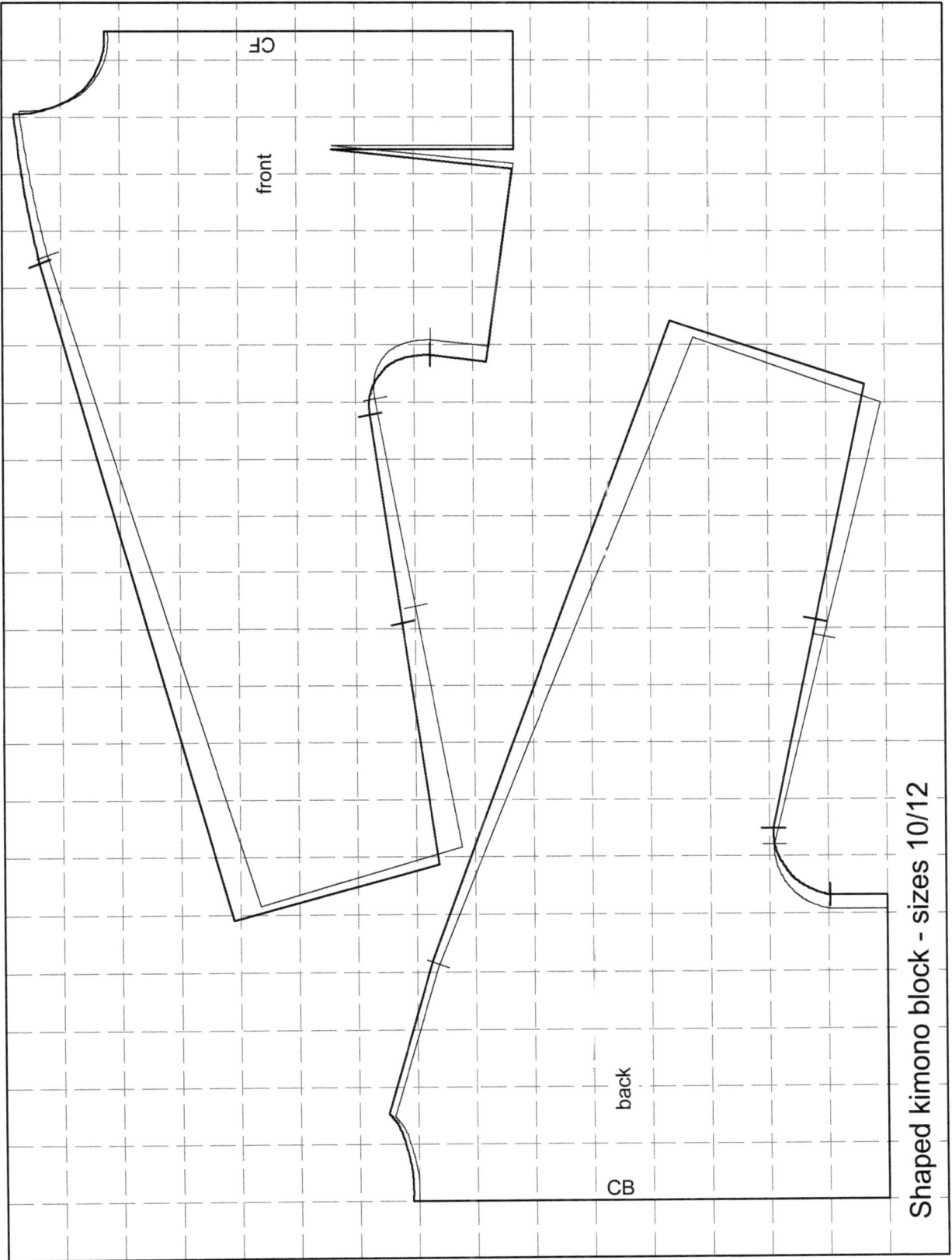

CF

front

CB

back

Shaped kimono block - sizes 10/12

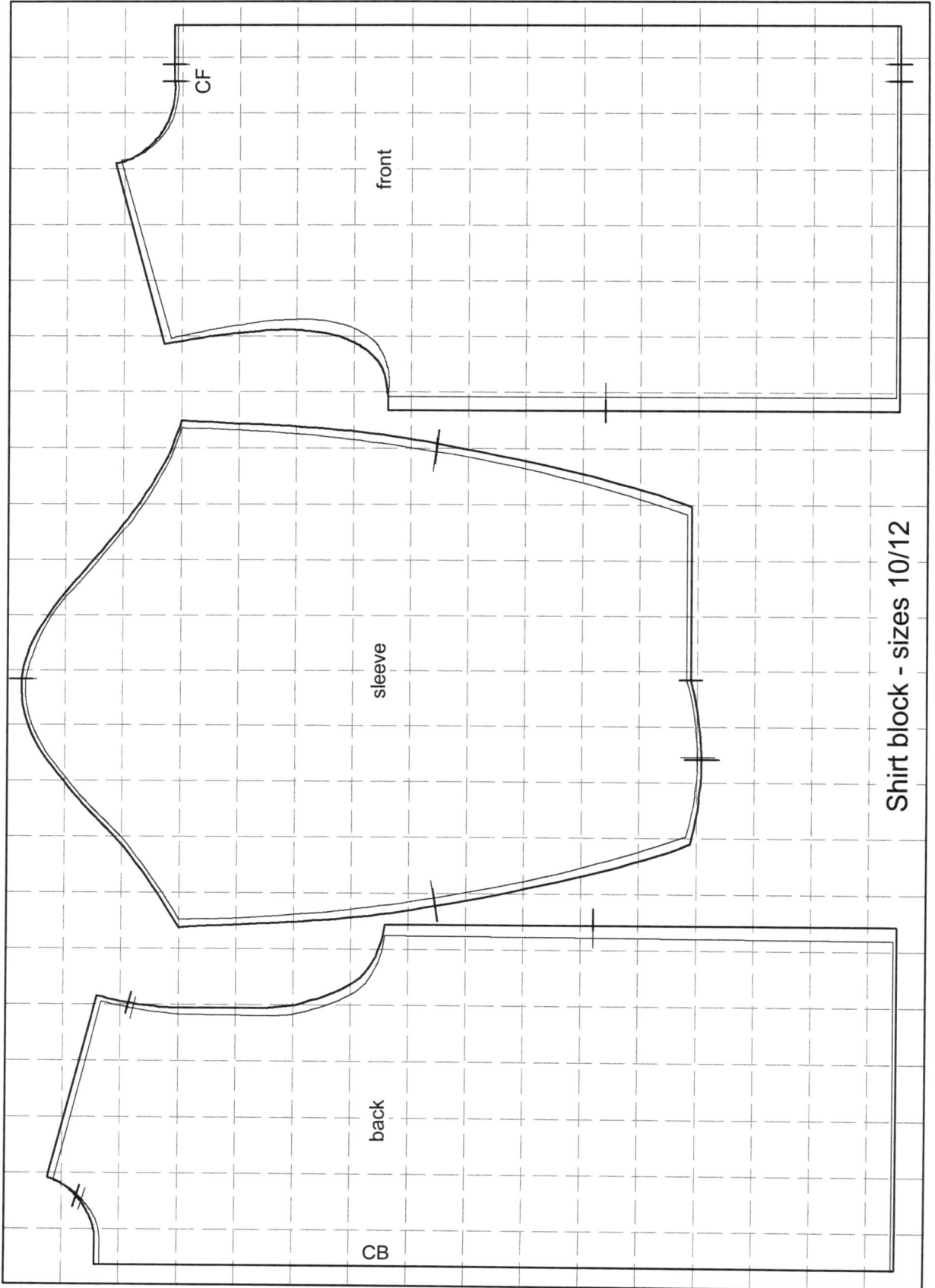

CF

front

sleeve

back

CB

Shirt block - sizes 10/12

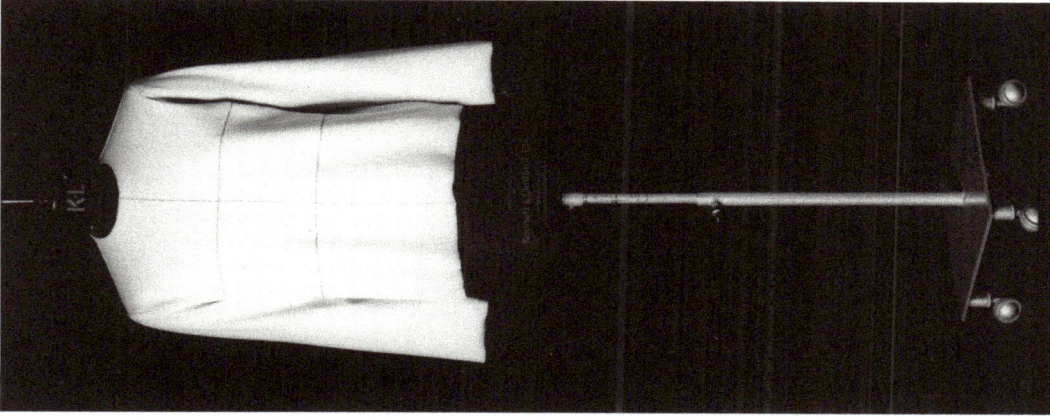

easy fitting

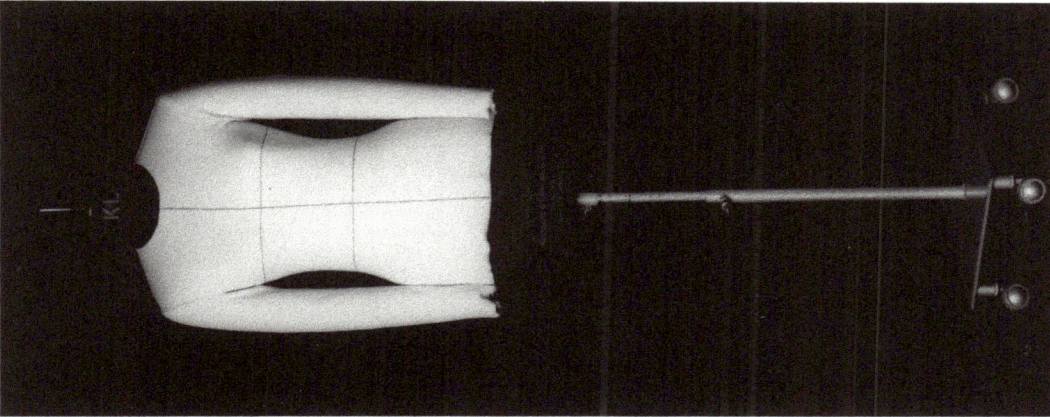

close fitting
Knitted fabric body shapes

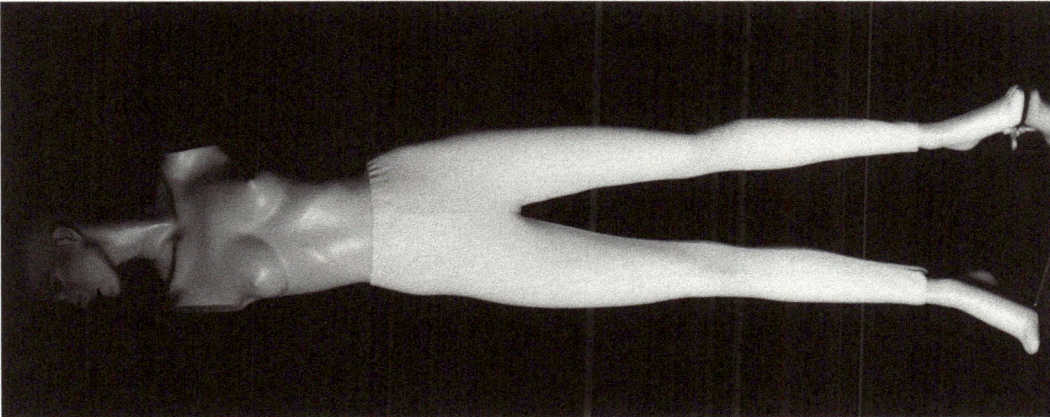

leggings

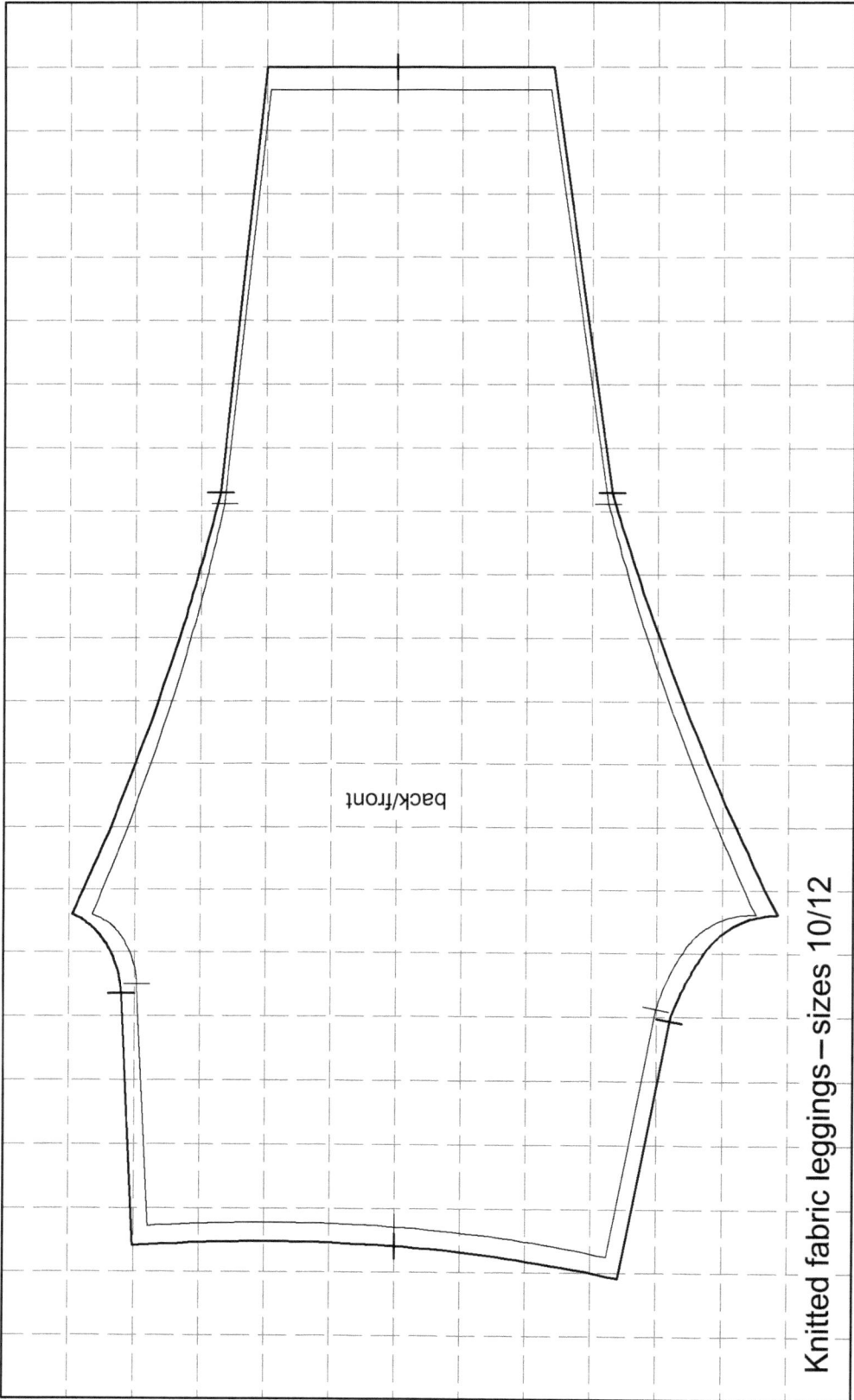

back/front

Knitted fabric leggings – sizes 10/12

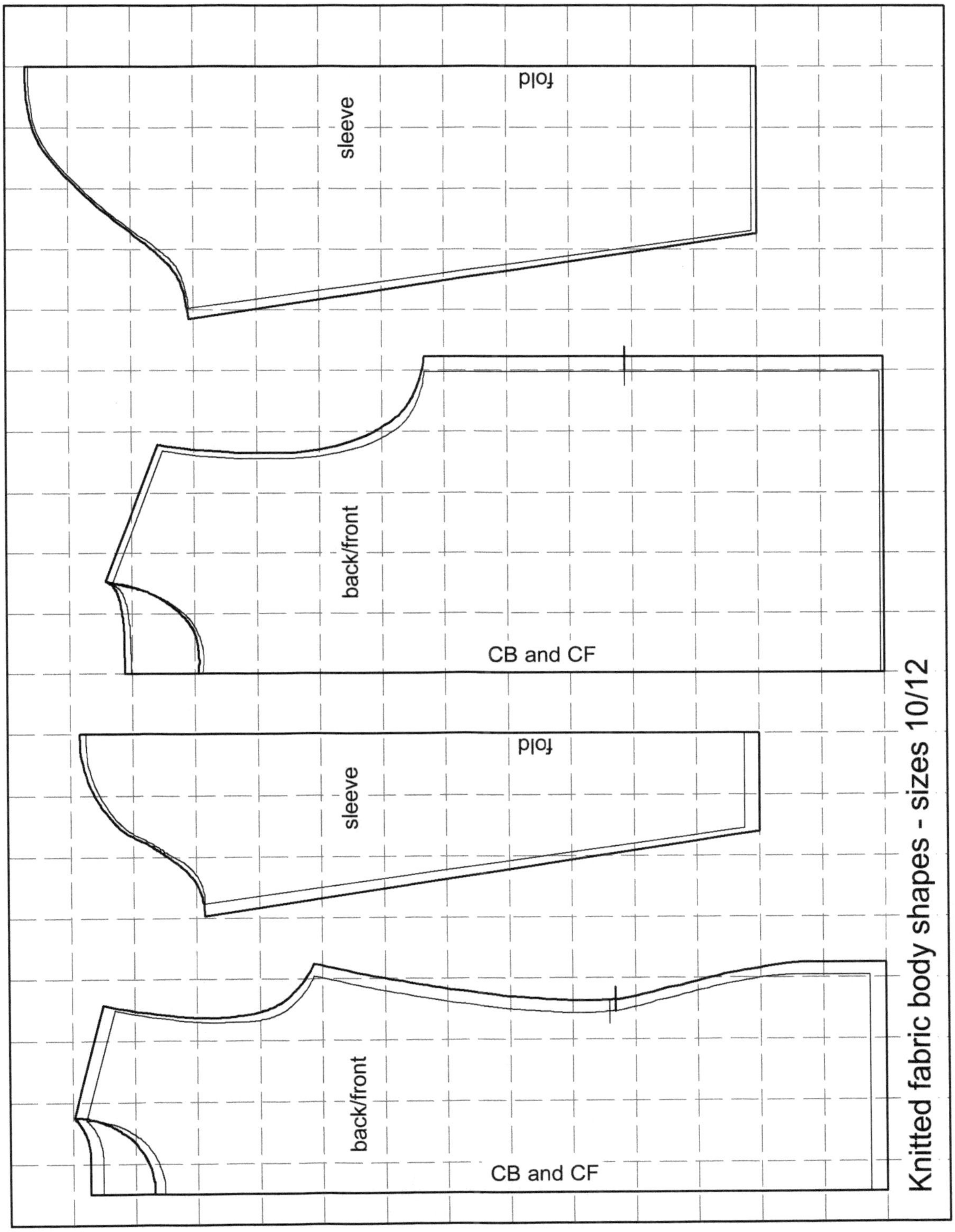

sleeve

fold

back/front

CB and CF

sleeve

fold

back/front

CB and CF

Knitted fabric body shapes - sizes 10/12

easy fitting over shape

easy fitting jacket block

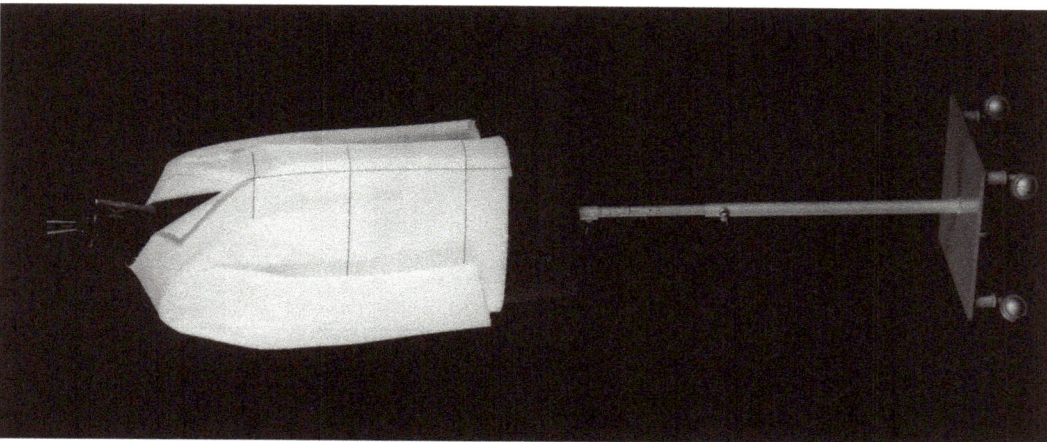

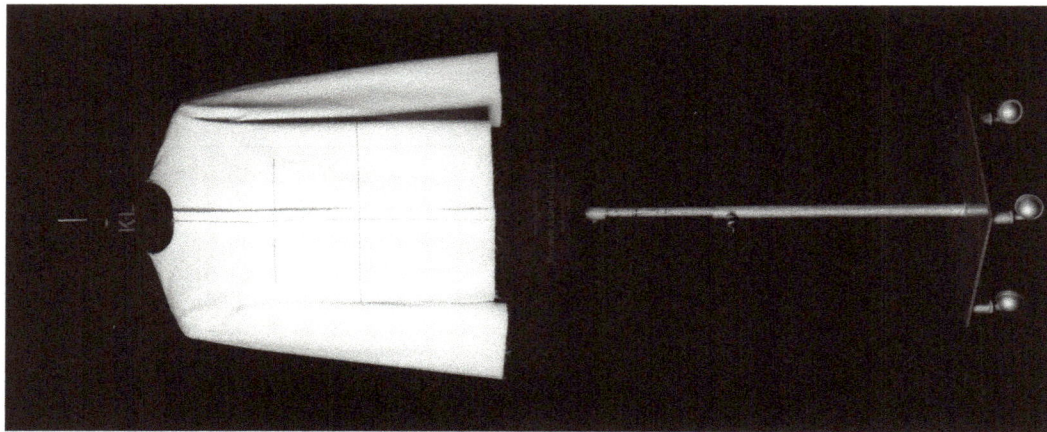

close fitting jacket block

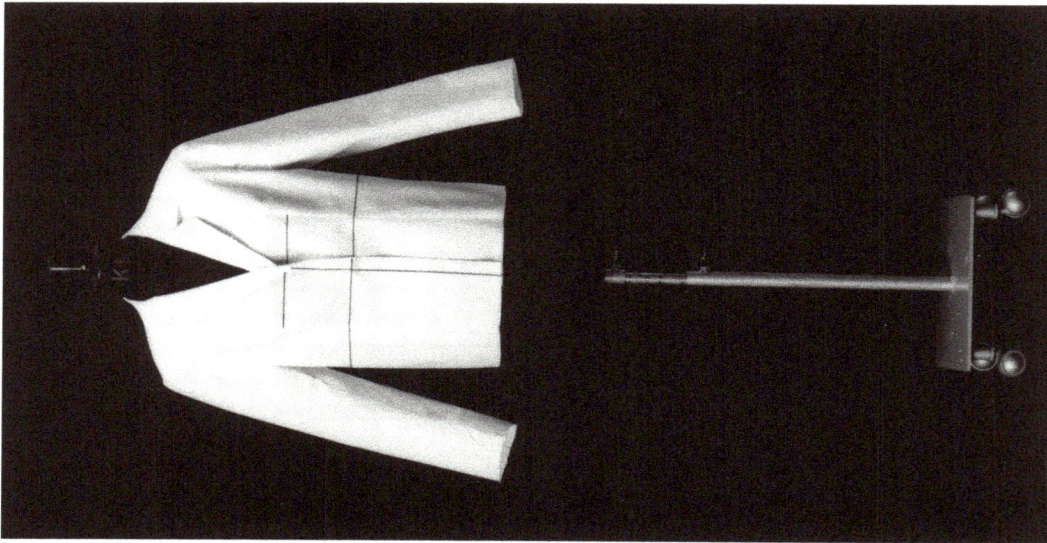

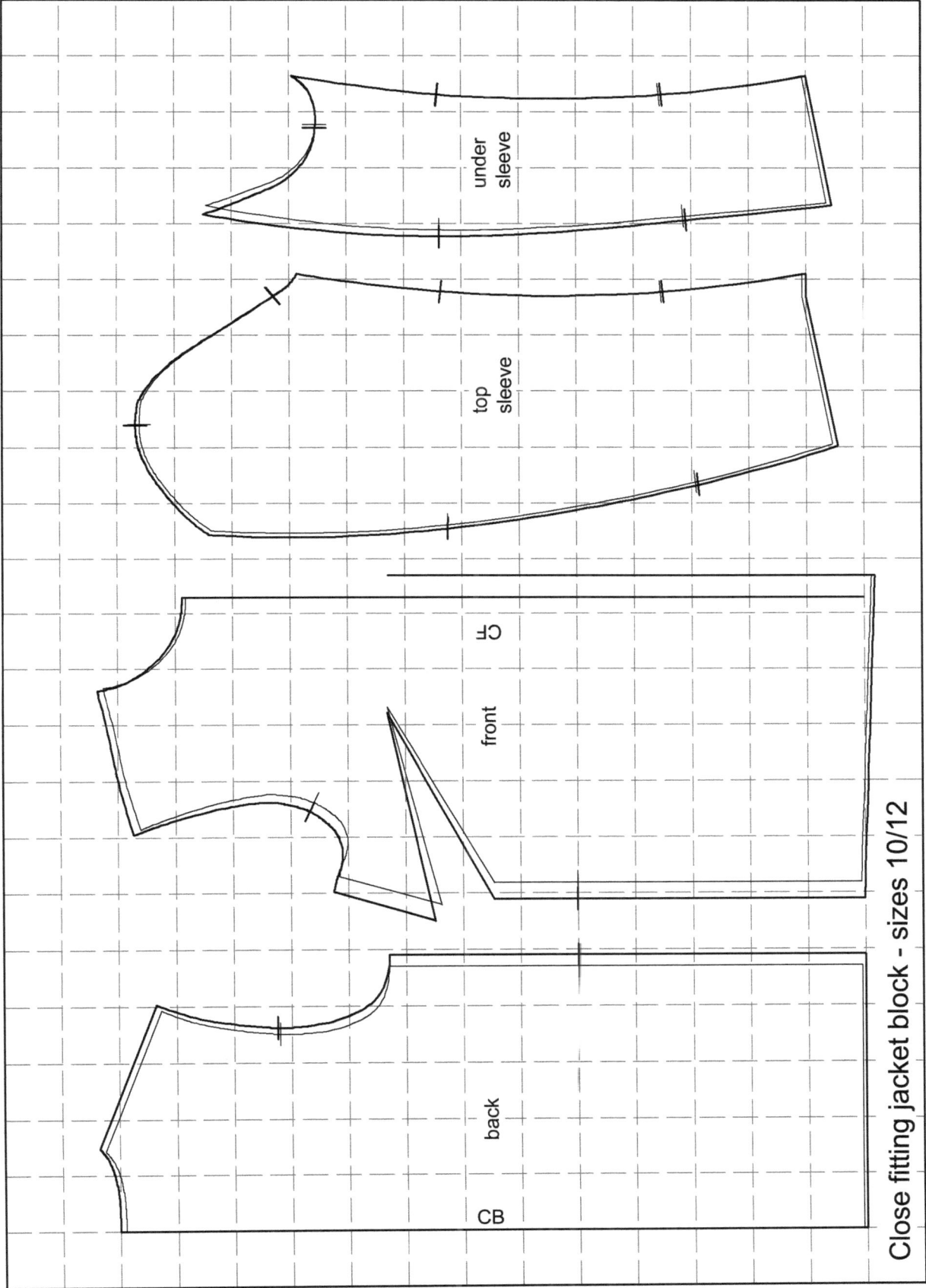

under sleeve

top sleeve

CF

front

back

CB

Close fitting jacket block - sizes 10/12

under sleeve

top sleeve

front

CF

back

CB

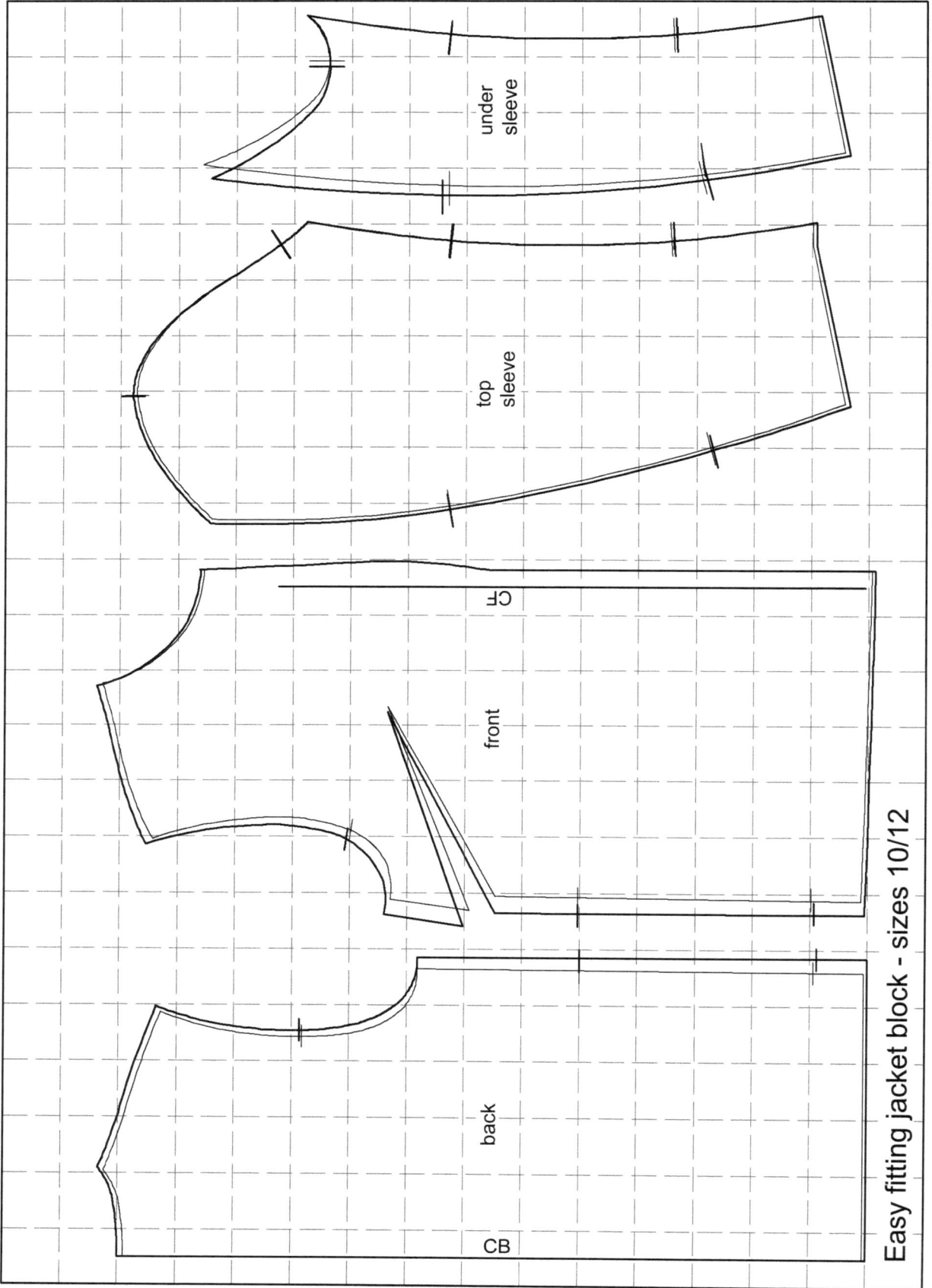

Easy fitting jacket block - sizes 10/12

sleeve

CF

front

back

CB

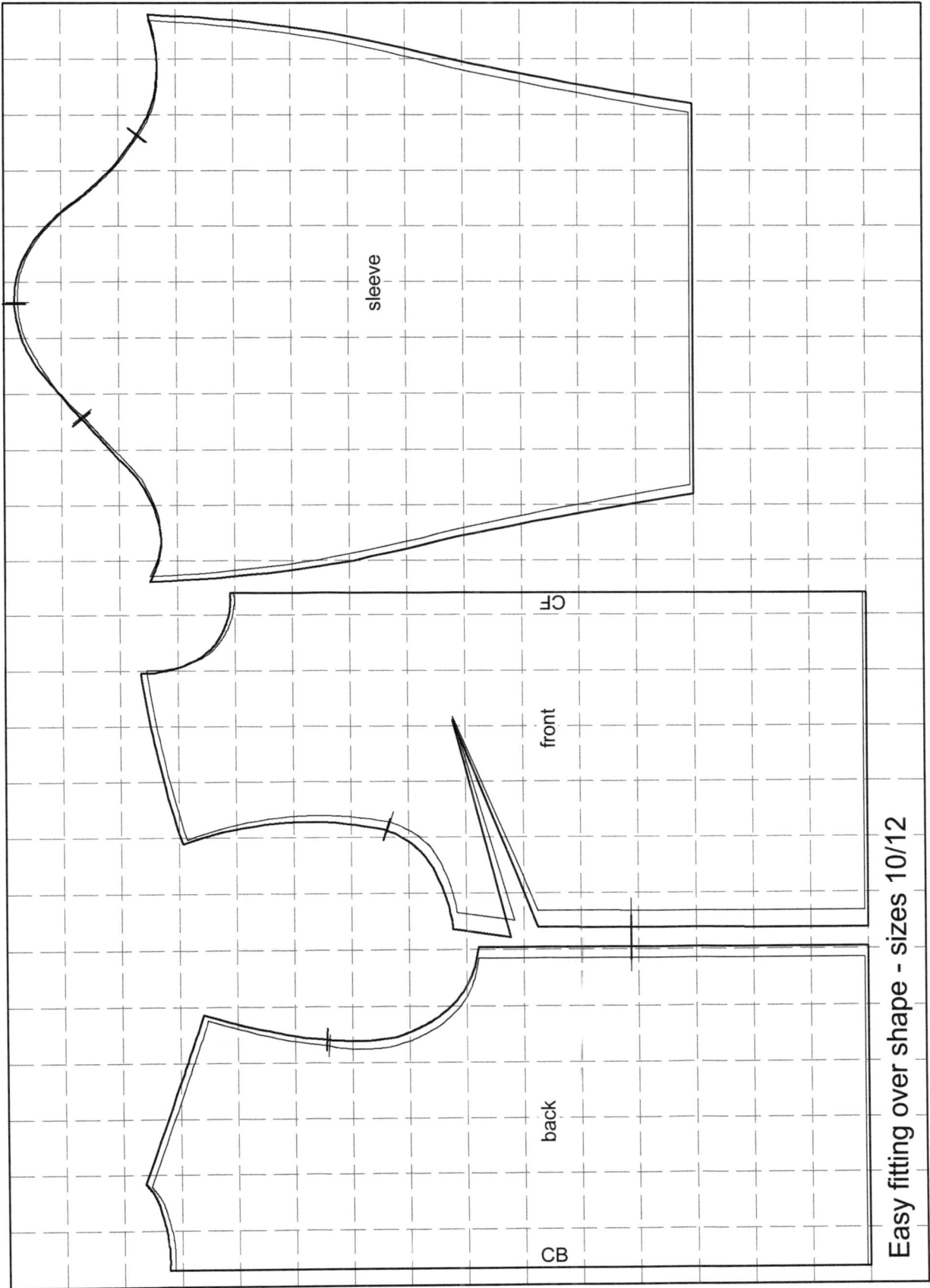

Easy fitting over shape - sizes 10/12

206

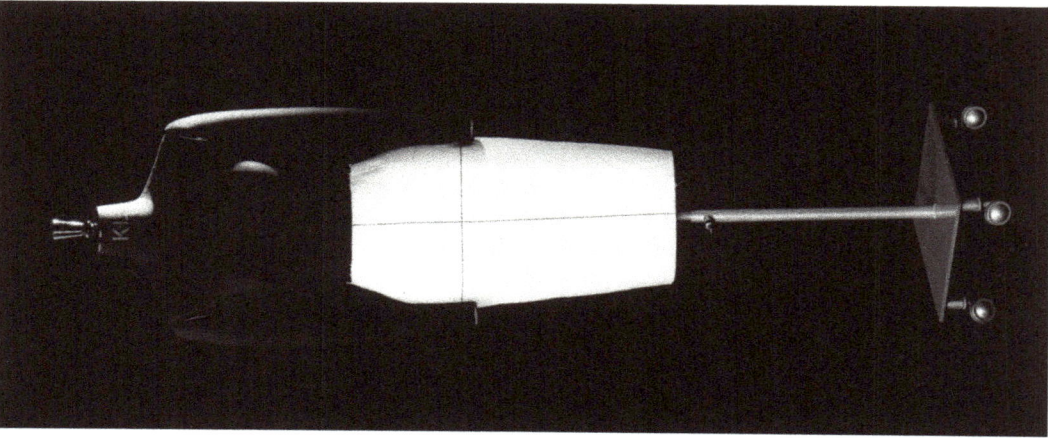

lingerie block

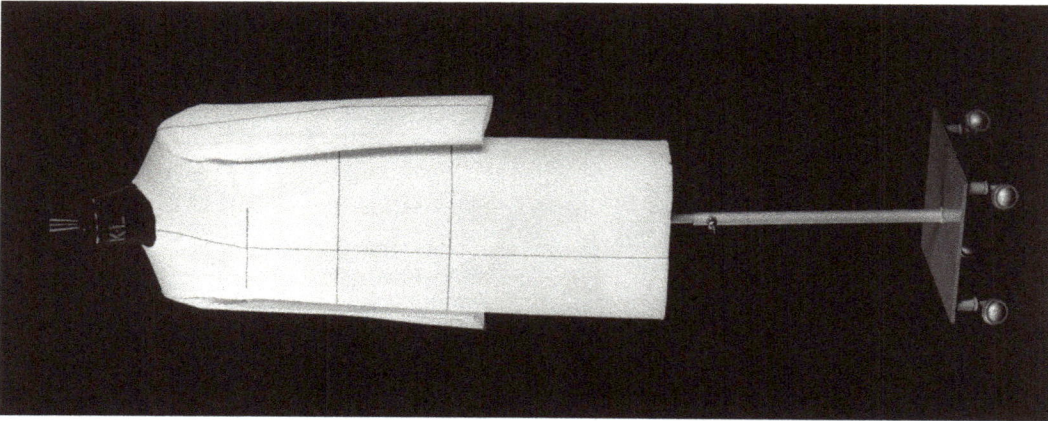

close fitting (dress) block

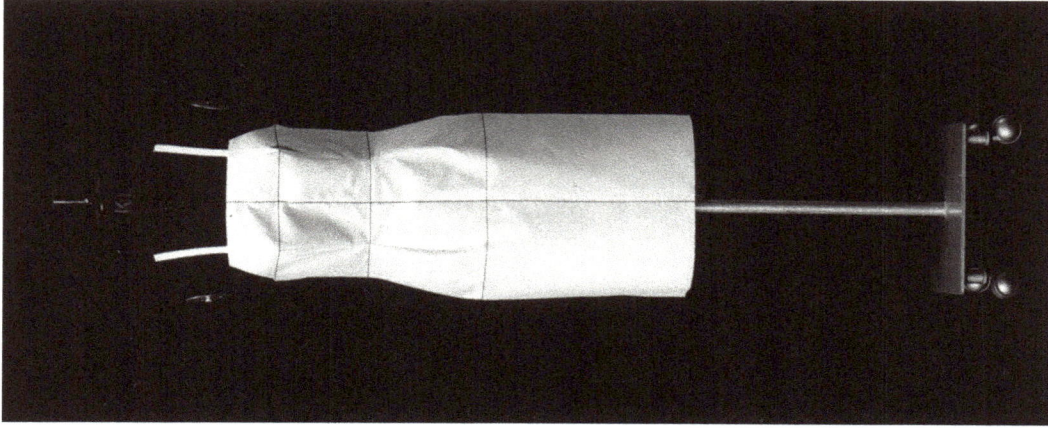

skirt block

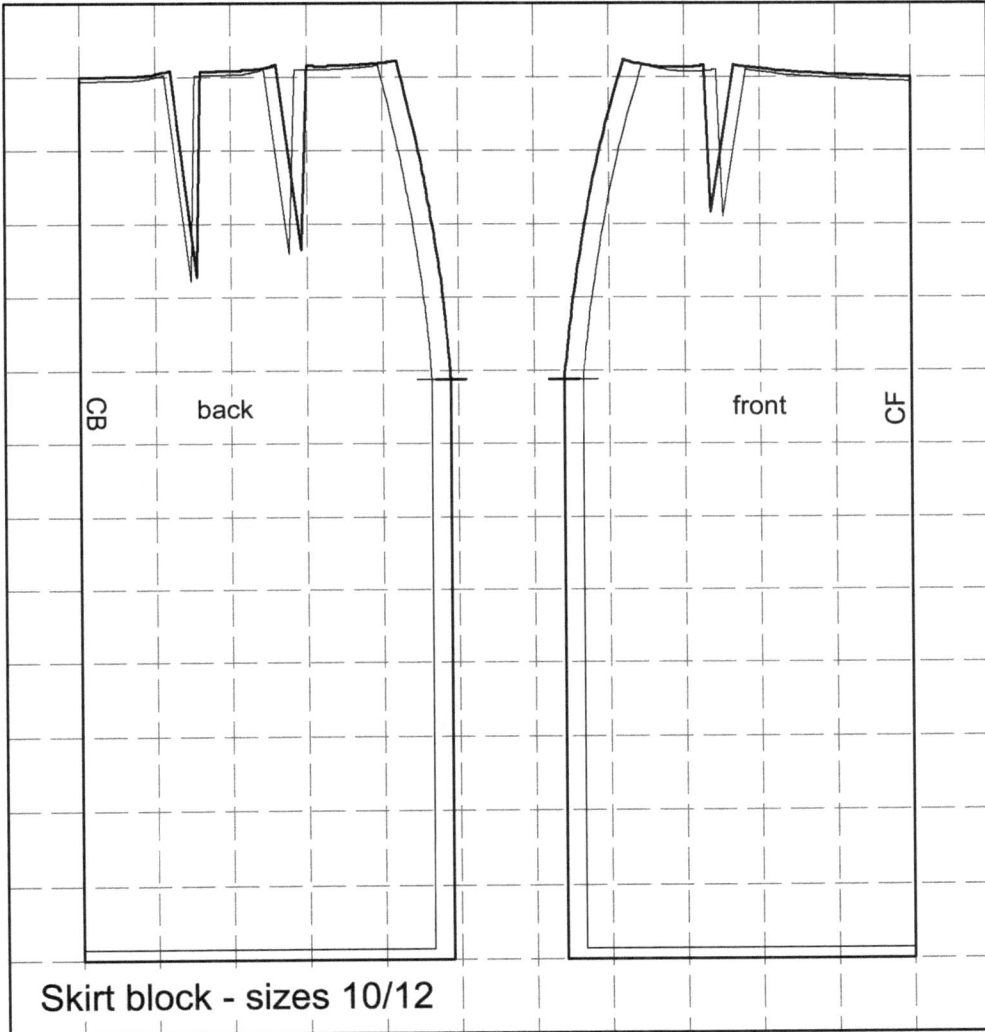

CB back

front CF

Skirt block - sizes 10/12

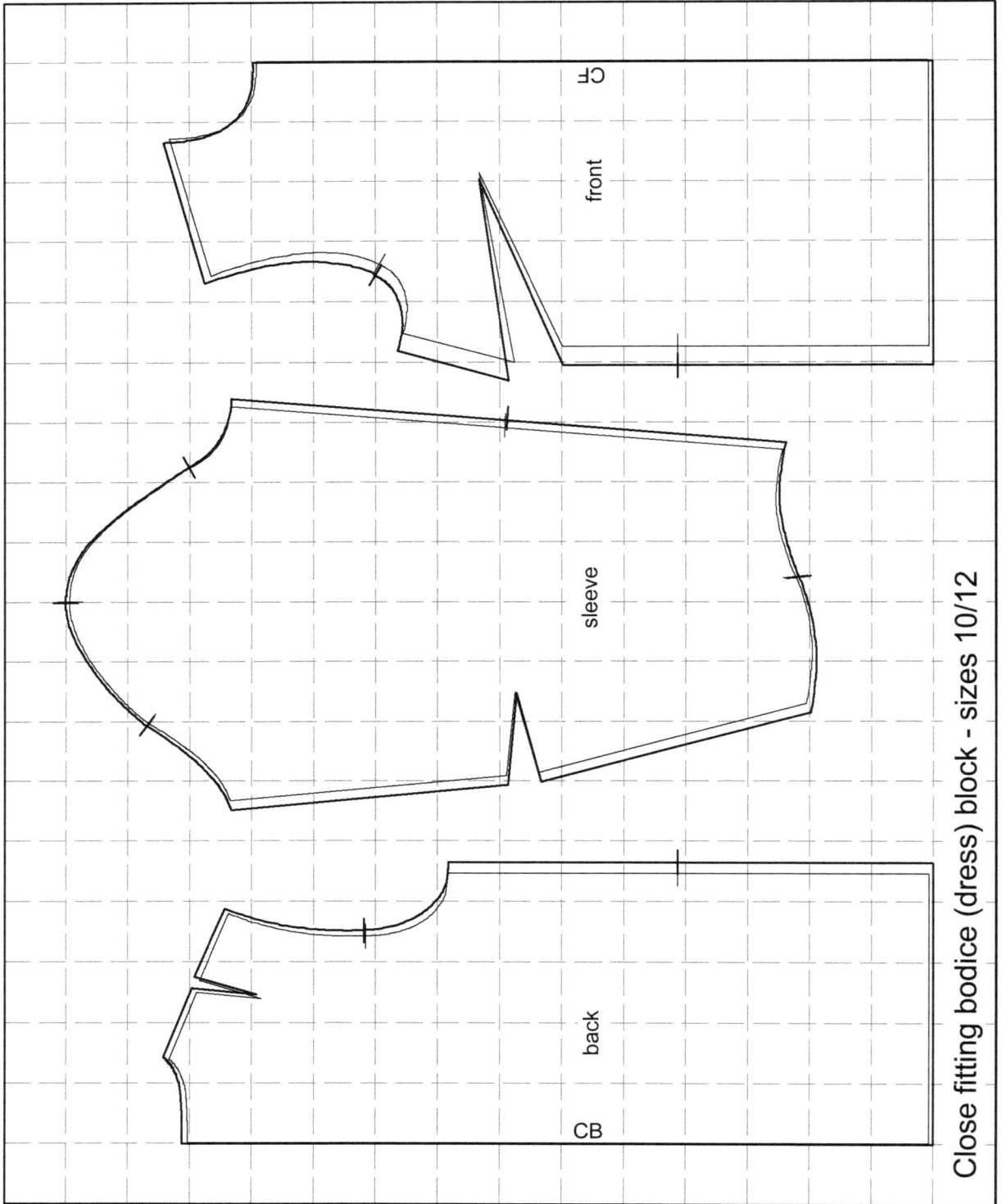

CF

front

sleeve

back

CB

Close fitting bodice (dress) block - sizes 10/12

CB

back

front

CF

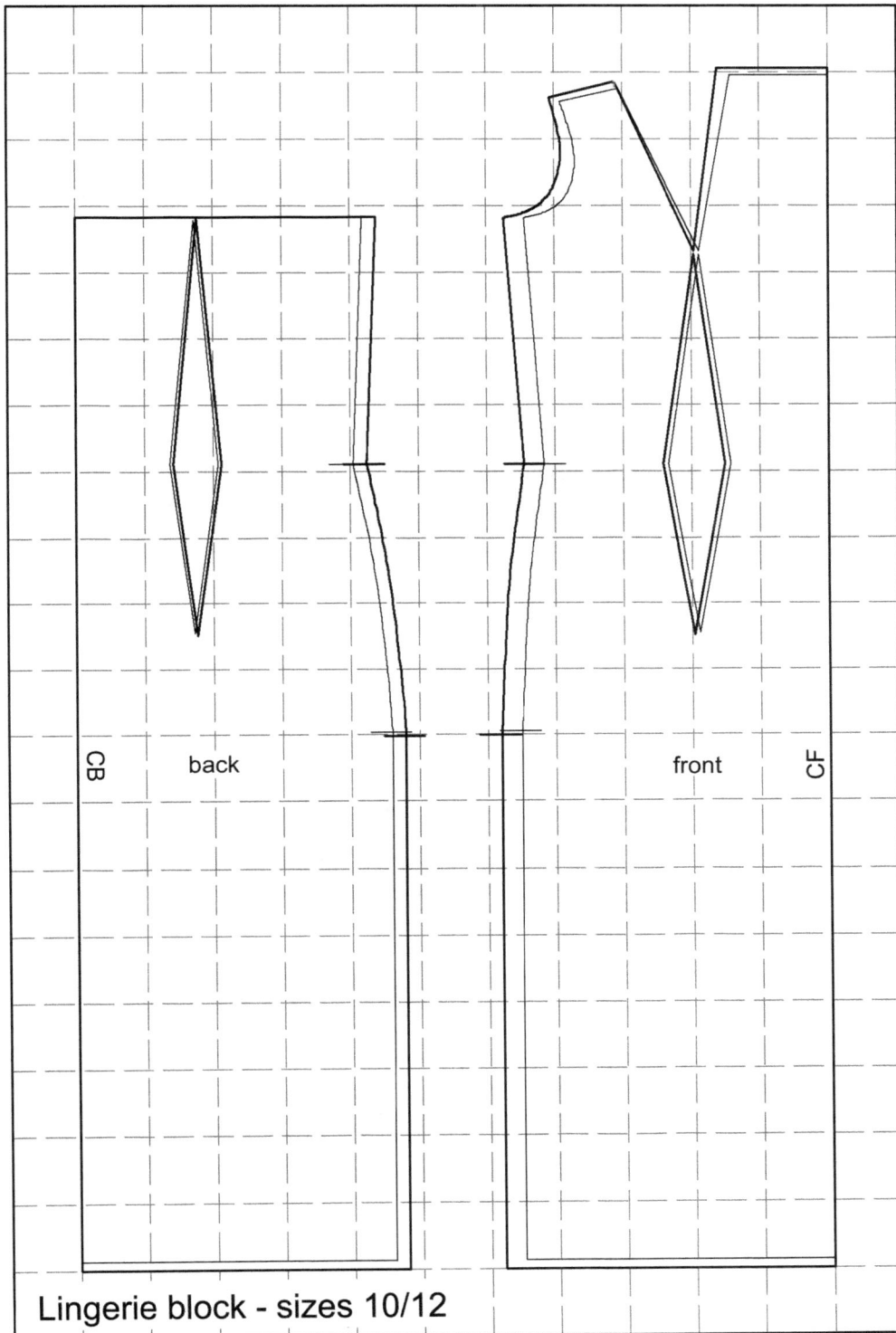

Lingerie block - sizes 10/12

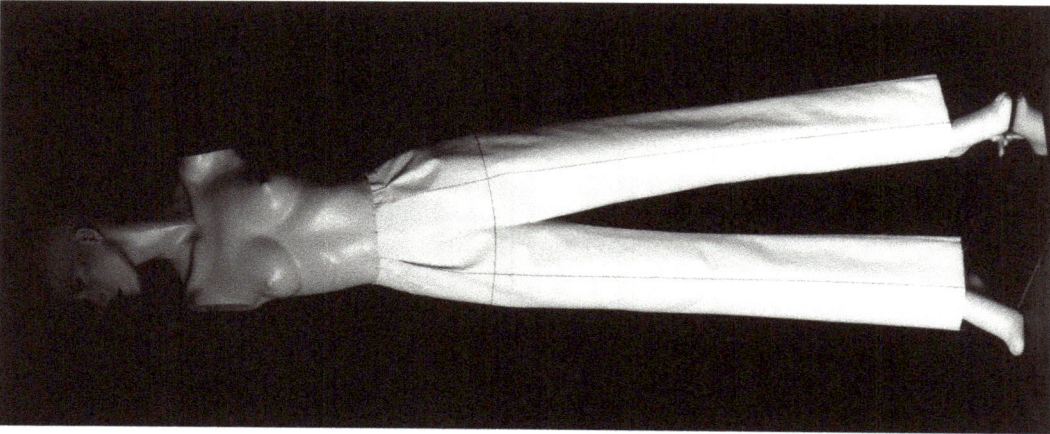

very easy fitting trouser block

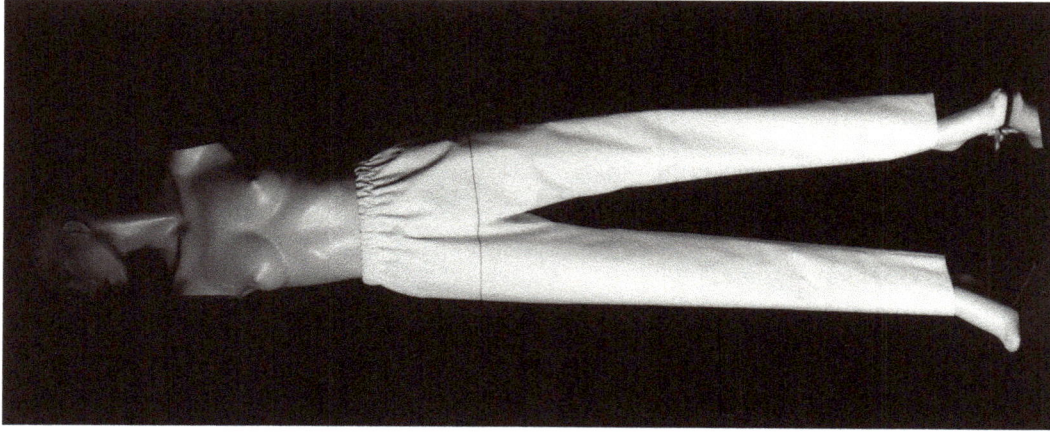

easy fitting trouser block

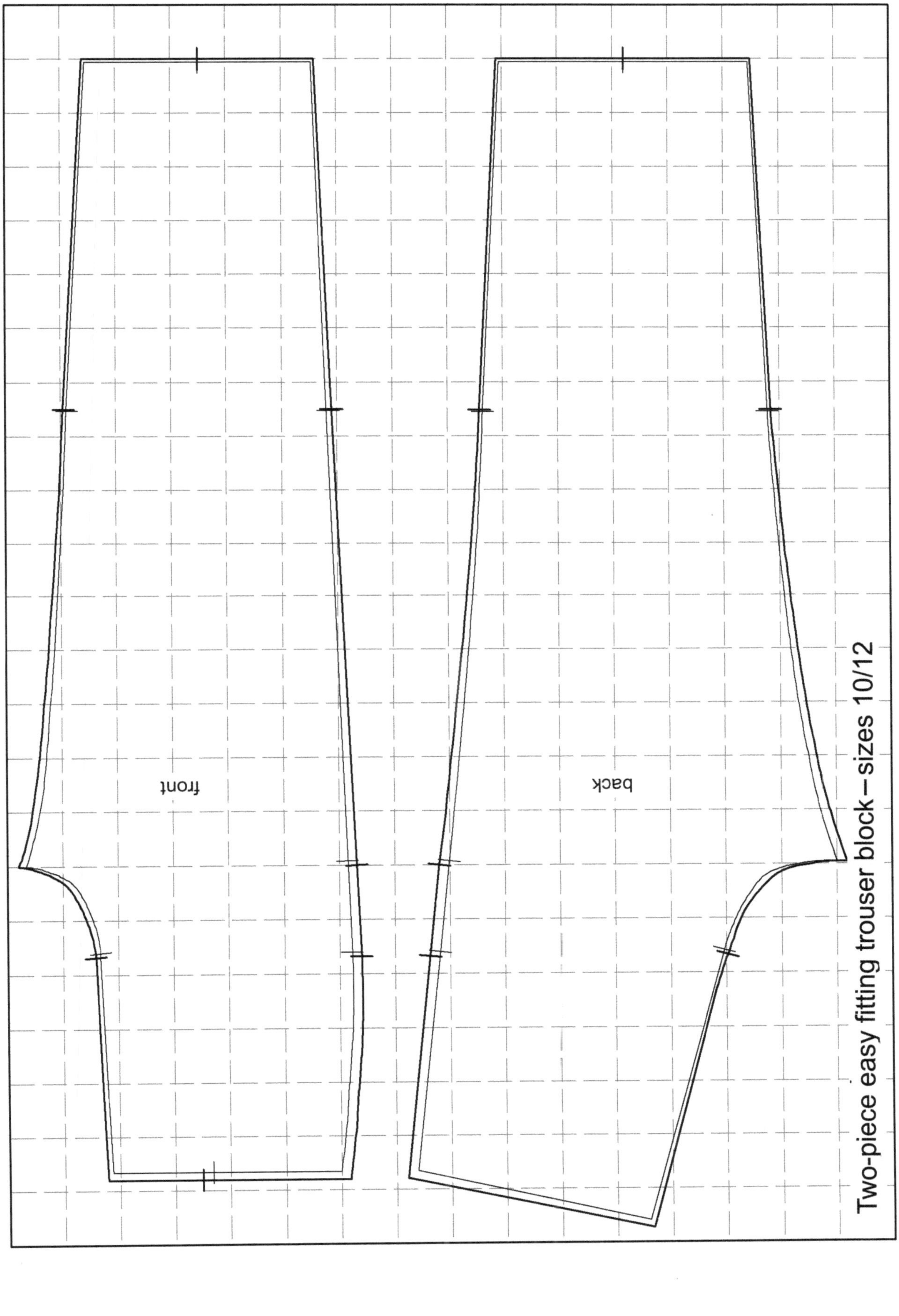

front

back

Two-piece easy fitting trouser block – sizes 10/12

211

back/front

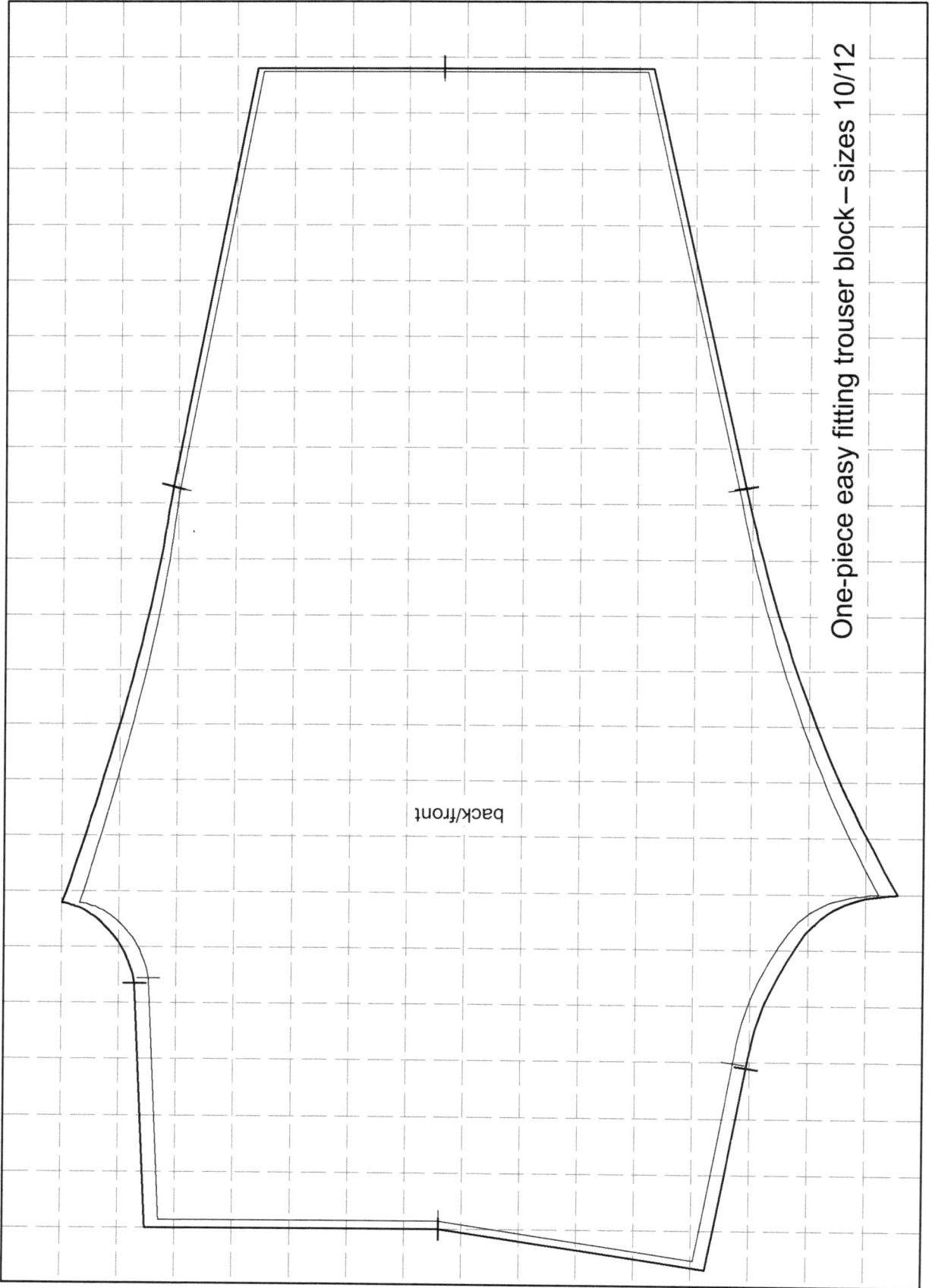

One-piece easy fitting trouser block – sizes 10/12

Full size blocks from the Web site – printing on A0 printers

The online blocks @ wiley.com/go/fabrics

The size 10 and size 12 blocks shown in this book can be downloaded as a zip file from the web site above and saved. There is no charge.
Go to the web site above and follow the on-screen instructions.
The blocks are stored as PDF files that are named by the titles that they have in the book plus their size code.

Example: for the close fitting jacket block, size 12; it will be listed as: – cfjacket12.

A full list of the book reference pages and the web block names to be used are shown below:

P195	basicgrid12	
P197	kimono10	kimono12
P198	shirt10	shirt12
P200	kleggings10	kleggings12
P201	kbody10	kbody12
P203	cfjacket10	cfjacket12
P204	efjacket10	efjacket12
P205	efovershape10	efovershape12
P207	skirt10	skirt12
P208	cfbodice10	cfbodice12
P209	lingerie10	lingerie12
P211	tptrouser10	tptrouser12
P212	optrouser10	optrouser12

Printing from an A0 printer

The block PDF file can be taken to your college or university print shop on a memory stick or CD and printed out on an A0 printer. The cost is usually about £2. Your print shop may be willing to download the files directly from the Internet.
Note: Some retail print shops or large statioery outlets will also print A0 images. They charge approx. £3 and some may also charge for handling the file.

Printing full size blocks from an A4 printer

Printing from an A4 printer from Adobe Photoshop

You should be familiar with the program *Adobe Photoshop* before attempting this method.

This example demonstrates a general method of printing the *close fitting bodice (dress) block* to an A4 printer.
Some options may vary as different versions of the *Adobe Photoshop* software have different screen layouts.

Download the file from the Website:
wiley.com/go/fabrics

In *Adobe Photoshop,* open this file.
The image is very large and you will have to print the block out in sections.

Back pattern piece
In the PAGE SETUP menu, set the paper size to A4 and select the LANDSCAPE option.
Select the RECTANGLE MARQUEE tool and set the FIXED SIZE option to:
WIDTH: 3200 pixels or 27 cm
HEIGHT: 2150 pixels or 18 cm.

Using the RECTANGLE MARQUEE tool, place the fixed sized rectangle over the left section of the back bodice pattern piece as shown in the diagram opposite.

In the PRINT menu, select the SELECTION option. and print out the top section of the back pattern piece.

At this stage, check that the grid squares on your print out are 5cm. If they are not, try another printer.

Deselect the existing rectangle marquee.
Using the RECTANGLE MARQUEE tool, place another fixed size rectangle over the second section of the back pattern piece making sure that you overlap the previous back section.
Print this section as before, and repeat the procedure to print out the third and fourth sections of the back pattern piece.

Use the same procedure to print out the **Front** and the **Sleeve**.

Completing the pattern

The sections can be taped together making sure the squares match exactly.

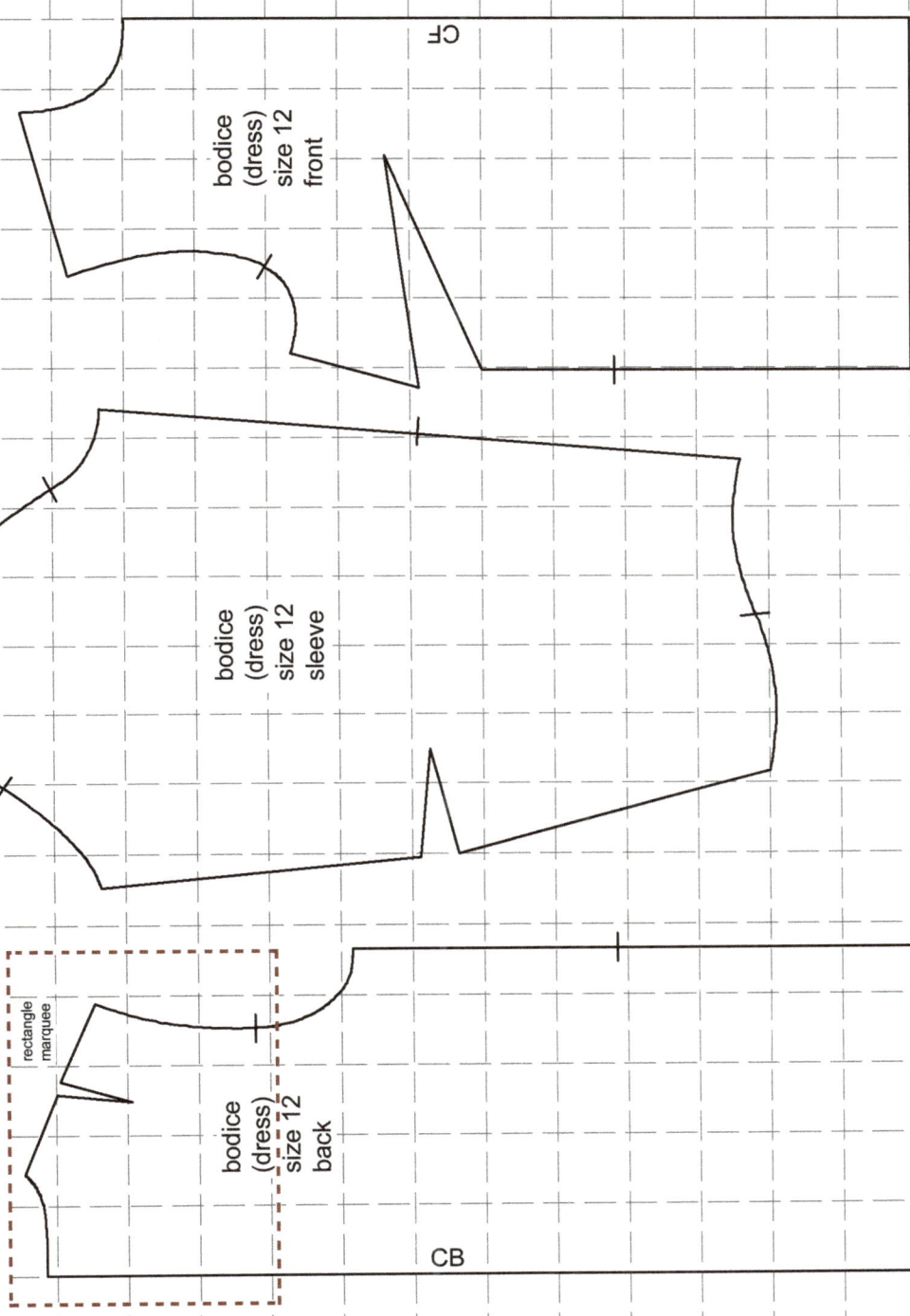

Winifred Aldrich *Understanding Fabric, Form and Flat Pattern Cutting*

CF

bodice
(dress)
size 12
front

bodice
(dress)
size 12
sleeve

rectangle
marquee

bodice
(dress)
size 12
back

CB

Close fitting bodice (dress) block - size 12

Using an A4 printer – printing a block from the Website

APPENDICES

Appendix 1: The original research methods used for obtaining the fabric assessment data

The original research

In the original research 20 cm squares of fabric were measured by the methods illustrated in this Appendix and the data recorded. The codes and divisions that were given in the first two editions appeared to be too mechanistic and to blur the important message that fabrics should be assessed before cutting a pattern. The simpler testing methods, devised for the second edition remain and are given in Chapter 2; however, the divisions were simplified for this book.

The fabrics used for the garments shown on the models in this book have been re-coded in a simpler way and by giving descriptions instead of numbers; but the data were re-calculated from the original research measurements.

Figure 12 Measuring weight In the original research 20 cm squares of fabric were weighed on an accurate TANITA Cal-Q-Scale which calculated to 0.01 gm.

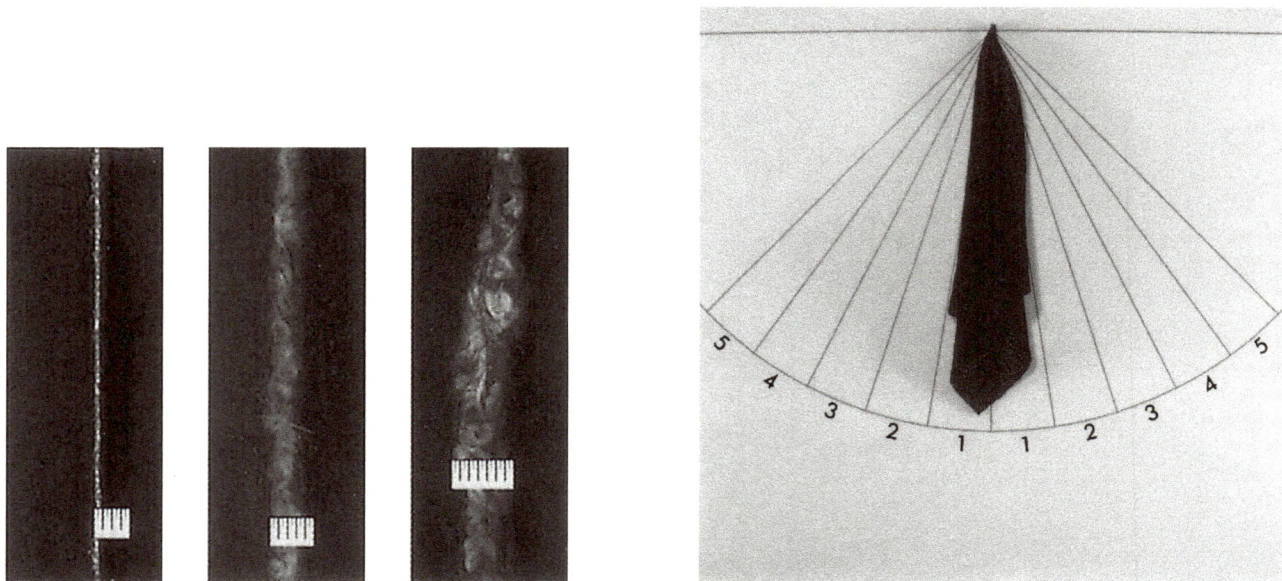

Figure 13 Measuring thickness In the original research 20 cm squares of fabric were hung vertically and scanned on a A4 SHARP flat-bed scanner at 300 dpi. It was then possible to see the thickness of the fabrics and make accurate visual comparisons because the textural density was apparent.

Figure 14 Measuring drape In the original research the corners of 20 cm squares of fabric were hung on the top centre point of a scale marked in five divisions. The drape amount could then be recorded by the position of the fabric square on the board.

Figure 15 Measuring shear In the original research 20 cm squares of fabric were attached to two bars. The first bar was fixed; the second bar could be moved under tension in a shear direction. The shear measurement was the amount that the fabric would shear before ripples began to appear on the surface of the cloth. The amount was recorded by marker peg holes at 0.5 intervals along the slide of the instrument. The amount of recovery could also be measured.

Figure 16 Measuring stretch In the original research 20 cm squares of fabric were attached to two bars. The first bar was fixed; the second bar could be moved to stretch the fabric to the extent at which the fabric was still visually acceptable. The amount could be recorded by pegging holes at 0.5 intervals along the sides of the instrument. The low stretch fabrics would not stretch to the measure 0.5 cm; therefore, in pattern cutting terms, low stretch means virtually no stretch.

Appendix 2: Established fabric tests used in industry

Fabric testing

This book has identified and explained why the fabric characteristics of *weight, thickness, drape, shear and stretch* need to be considered before pattern cutting. However, many practical characteristics, for example, 'fitness for purpose' have to be taken into account when developing a garment style. This is particularly the case in areas such as sportswear or weatherwear. Objective tests exist for many of the following properties that are carried out by large manufacturers and commercial laboratories. Examples of the type of tests are listed below:

Abrasion resistance, absorbency, colour fastness, crease recovery, dimensional stability, durability, dye affinity, exposure resistance, extensibility, flame resistance, fungi resistance, hygral expansion, insect resistance, oil resistance, permeability, reaction to chemicals, shower resistance, shrink resistance, soil resistance, static resistance, strength, thermal conductivity, thermoplasticity, washability, water resistance.

BS, EN and ISO fabric tests

Some textile laboratories work to the British Standard (BS) tests for the objective measurements of fabrics. Their major use is the comparison of the properties of fabrics of a similar type where accurate calculations are required. The European Committee for Standardisation (EN) is recognised in Europe; the International Standard Organisation (ISO) is usually recognised internationally. America sets most of its own standards, which may differ. The BS, EN and ISO tests, which relate to the five characteristics used in this book, are listed below. These tests have a different aim; they are usually comparisons to test against some set norm for quality control purposes.

Weight	BS 2471 (2005) Textiles. Woven fabrics. Determination of mass per unit length and mass per unit area. BS EN 12127 (1997) Textiles. Fabrics. Determination of mass per unit area using small sample.
Thickness	BS EN ISO 5084 (1998) Textiles. Determination of thickness of textiles and textile products.
Drape	BS 5058 (1973) Method of assessment of drape of fabrics. BS EN ISO 9073-9 (2008) Textiles. Test methods for non-wovens. Determination of drapability, including drape coefficient.
Shear	BS 2819 (1990) Methods for determination of bow, skew and lengthy distortion in woven and knitted fabrics.
Stretch	BS EN 29073-3 (1992) Methods of test for non-wovens. BS EN 14704-1 (2005) Determination of the elasticity of fabrics. Strip tests.

Laboratory tests for fabric 'hand'

Equipment is available to cover many tests for a fabric's suitability for its purpose. A main concern of researchers has been to seek a set of measurements that would analyse fabric 'hand' for particular manufacturing processes. Some of the work is contentious. Other researchers have argued that 'hand' can be seen as a human experience of a fabric that is impossible to measure objectively.

The Kawabata Evaluation System for Fabric (KES-F)

The Kawabata system was developed by Sueo Kawabata of Kyoto University and Masaka Niwa of Nara Women's University in Japan. Kawabata claims that the important property of fabric 'hand' can be measured objectively. The system was based on the properties required for men's suits and the method started to spread into industry around 1975. It is now used for many other types of fabric. Fabric 'hand' was judged by 'experts', then summarised and categorised into primary hand values (PHV). Total hand values (THV) are developed for specific types of fabrics used for particular products.

In the KES-F system four instruments are used to measure:

Tensile and shear
Pure bending
Compression
Surface friction

Sixteen fabric measurements are plotted on an HESC data snake chart; comparisons of finishes or weave changes can also be assessed.

Fabric Assurance by Simple Testing (FAST)

Many companies have adopted the FAST test, developed by CSIRO of Australia, as a reliable measurement of the mechanical properties required for the fabrics used in men's suitings. Its aim is to determine the measurements of the qualities required to 'move' fabrics to create moulded shapes; it is claimed by many manufacturers to be a simpler, cheaper system, and a better predictor of tailorability, than the KES-F system. It also comprises four pieces of equipment: compression meter, bending meter, extensibility meter, dimensional stability meter.

FAST-1	Compression	fabric thickness fabric surface thickness relaxed surface thickness
FAST-2	Bending	bending length
FAST-3	Extension	warp extensibility weft extensibility bias extensibility
FAST-4	Dimensional	relaxation shrinkage hygral expansion

Chapter Index

PART SIX: MODEL FIGURES AND GARMENT BLOCKS